D1237407

AMERICAN SOCIOLOGY: *Perspectives, Problems, Methods*

AMERICAN SOCIOLOGY

Perspectives, Problems, Methods

Edited by TALCOTT PARSONS

BASIC BOOKS, INC., PUBLISHERS

New York　　　　　　　　　　　　　*London*

© 1968 by Basic Books, Inc.
Library of Congress Catalog Card Number: 68–19773
Manufactured in the United States of America

LIBRARY
FLORIDA STATE UNIVERSITY
TALLAHASSEE, FLORIDA

The Authors

BERNARD BARBER is Professor of Sociology at Barnard College, Columbia University. He is author of *Science and the Social Order* and *Drugs and Society*. He was a member of the Committee on the Humanistic Aspects of Science of the American Council of Learned Societies.

ROBERT N. BELLAH is Professor of Sociology and Regional Studies at the University of California, Berkeley. He has written *Apache Kinship Systems* and *Tokugawa Religion* and edited *Religion and Progress in Modern Asia*.

REINHARD BENDIX, Professor of Sociology and Chairman of the Department of Sociology and Social Institutions, University of California, Berkeley, has written *Max Weber: An Intellectual Portrait, Social Mobility in Industrial Society* with S. M. Lipset, and *Work and Authority in Industry*.

CHARLES E. BIDWELL, Associate Professor of Education, University of Chicago, is especially interested in the sociology of education, and has been active in the American Sociological Association.

PETER M. BLAU, Professor of Sociology, University of Chicago, held the Pitt Professorship at Cambridge University for 1966–67. He was director of the Comparative Organization Research Program. He has written *Exchange and Power in Social Life*, and with Otis Dudley Duncan, *The American Occupational Structure*.

ALBERT K. COHEN, Professor of Sociology and Anthropology, University of Connecticut, has written *Delinquent Boys, The Culture of the Gang*, and *Deviance and Control*. He is a member of the Executive Committee of the Society for the Study of Social Problems.

JAMES A. DAVIS, Professor of Sociology at Dartmouth College, was Senior Study Director of the National Opinion Research Center and Associate Professor of Sociology at the University of Chicago. He has written widely on small-scale social structures and their effects and on survey methods and he has conducted survey studies of higher education and the professions.

S. N. EISENSTADT is Chairman of the Department of Sociology and Dean of the Kaplan School of Economics and Social Science at the Hebrew University, Jerusalem. He is a member of the International Sociological Association, the International Institute of Differing Civilization, and the Israel Academy of Sciences and Humanities. He has written *Israeli Society, The Protestant Ethic,* and *The Political Systems of Empires.*

EVERETT C. HUGHES is Professor of Sociology at Brandeis University. Among his books are *French Canada in Transition* and *Boys in White: The Culture and Perspectives of Medical Students.* He is a Fellow of the American Anthropological Association, the American Association for the Advancement of Science, the American Academy of Arts and Sciences, and former president of the American Sociological Association.

ALEX INKELES is Professor of Sociology at Harvard University and Director of Studies on Social and Cultural Aspects of Development at Harvard's Center for International Affairs. He has written *Public Opinion in Soviet Russia, The Soviet Citizen,* and *What Is Sociology?*

PAUL F. LAZARSFELD is Quetelet Professor of Social Sciences at Columbia University. He has been a frequent contributor to professional journals and periodicals, and has written, collaborated on, or edited more than twenty books, among them *The Uses of Sociology.*

SEYMOUR MARTIN LIPSET is Professor of Government and Social Relations at Harvard University. He has written *The First New Nation* and *Revolution and Counterrevolution* and is co-editor with Richard Hofstadter of the Sociology of American History series. With M. A. Trow and J. S. Coleman, he has written *Union Democracy.*

LEON MAYHEW is Associate Professor and Associate Chairman of the Department of Sociology, University of Michigan. He has been Associate Editor of *Social Problems,* a member of the Advisory Committee of the Law and Society Association, and is a member of the American Sociological Association.

ROBERT MCGINNIS, Professor of Sociology, Cornell University, is the author of *Mathematics and Statistics for Social Scientists* and has been associate editor of the *American Sociological Review.*

THEODORE M. MILLS, Associate *Professor of Sociology,* Yale University, wrote *Group Structure and the Newcomer, The Sociology of Small Groups,* and articles such as "Equilibrium and Processes of Deviance and Social Control," *American Sociological Review.*

TALCOTT PARSONS, Professor of Sociology, Harvard University, is the author of *The Structure of Social Action, Structure and Process in Modern Societies,* and of several other books, most recently *Sociological Theory and Modern Society.* He is a member of the American Philosophical Society and a Fellow of the American Academy of Arts and Sciences.

THOMAS F. PETTIGREW, an investigator of racial tension, is Associate Professor of Social Psychology at Harvard University. He is a council member of the Society for the Psychological Study of Social Issues and associate editor of the *American Sociological Review.* He is author of *A Profile of the Negro American.*

ALBERT J. REISS, JR., is Professor and Chairman of the Department of Sociology at the University of Michigan. He has served as Director of the Iowa Urban Community Research Center. He has written *Occupations and Social Status* with Otis Dudley Duncan, Paul K. Hatt, and Cecil C. North.

EDWARD SHILS is Professor of Sociology and Social Thought in the Committee on Social Thought at the University of Chicago and a Fellow of King's College, Cambridge University. He is the author of *The Torment of Secrecy* and *The Intellectual between Tradition and Modernity* and the editor of *Minerva.*

NEIL J. SMELSER is Professor of Sociology, University of California, Berkeley. He has served as editor of the *American Sociological Review* and has written *Theory of Collective Behavior* and *Sociology of Economic Life.*

NORMAN W. STORER is Staff Associate of the Social Science Research Council. His special fields of interest are the sociology of science, sociological theory, and deviance and control. He is the author of *The Social System of Science.*

CHARLES TILLY has specialized in French social and economic history. He is Professor of Sociology at the University of Toronto. He is an editor of the *Journal of the American Institute of Planners* and of *French Historical Studies* and a member of the Societé d'Études Robespierristes and of the American Sociological Association.

MARTIN TROW, Associate Professor of Sociology at the University of California, Berkeley, has written widely on the sociology of education. He is editor of the *Sociology of Education* and, with S. M. Lipset and J. S. Coleman, has written *Union Democracy*.

EZRA F. VOGEL is Professor of Sociology in the Department of Social Relations, Harvard University, and a Research Associate at the East Asian Research Center there. A specialist in Asian and Chinese affairs, he has written *Japan's New Middle Class* and was co-editor with N. W. Bell of *Modern Introduction to the Family*.

Introduction

Talcott Parsons

This volume provides a welcome opportunity to piece together at least a partial picture of the state of a rapidly growing and changing discipline in the social science area. The last at all comparable account of the state of sociology in the United States was in the volume *Sociology Today*,[1] which grew out of the 1957 annual meeting of the American Sociological Association.

In addition to the implications of a decade's passage of time, however, the books differ in a variety of respects. First, the present book is in no way officially sponsored by "organized American sociology," that is, the A.S.A. Second, it is much more oriented to a nonprofessional audience, whereas *Sociology Today* was addressed mainly to the sociologist. Third, of course, with different editorial responsibility the organization of the book and the selection of contributors reflect a somewhat different point of view.

There has been an attempt to be representative in two senses, to cover as many as possible of the centrally important subfields of the discipline, and to select contributors who would give a well balanced survey of the special topic of each chapter. It hardly needs to be said, however, that sociology has not reached a stage of development as a discipline where complete objectivity and impartiality can be expected. Though we by no means constitute a randomly variant collection of "schools" of thought, there of course are variant "points of view" which will be reflected in such a book as the present one.

Another editor and list of contributors would have presented a different picture. As "coordinator" and editor, I took primary responsibility for issuing invitations to contribute—by no means all of which were accepted, of course. I have deliberately given each author the fullest possible freedom, within his topical area very broadly defined, to develop his presentation in his own way, and have subjected his manuscript to a minimum of editorial alteration.

As an important part of the much larger set of behavioral-social-cultural disciplines, sociology, as noted, has since World War II been undergoing an unprecedented process of expansion and development in a variety of respects. This has been a world-wide process, but, by a good deal, is most conspicuous in the United States. This expansion has of course included the sheer numerical size of the profession, the expansion and development of instruction and research in the field—part of the general expansion of higher education and research—appreciable expansion of involvements outside the academic setting, expansion of the volume of publication in the field, and of membership in and the activities of the relevant professional associations, not only the central one, the American Sociological Association, but a series of regional societies and a variety of others.

The concern of this volume, however, is not directly with these matters but with the content of the discipline itself, the problems it deals with, the perspectives from which this is done, the methods employed, and some of the empirical and theoretical generalizations at which it has arrived. It is, however, almost in the nature of a situation of expansion and development such as the discipline has been and is undergoing that its substantive structure should also be undergoing rapid and in some respects fundamental change. The present is clearly not a period of consolidation and synthesis but of expansion, experimentation with ideas and techniques, and of many new challenges.

Circumstances such as these greatly complicate the problem of such a presentation as the present one. Not only is there no "official" sociological point of view, but there is no authoritative catalog, to say nothing of logically symmetrical classification, of sectors and subdivisions of the discipline. In part, our policy has been determined by the sheer limitation of the numbers of contributions; if we had two volumes with something close to fifty chapters our organization of materials would be different. In particular a considerable number of perfectly appropriate topics have had to be omitted, both for reasons of space and because of the problem of selection among potential contributors.

It is important, in order to avoid misconceptions, to state the above considerations explicitly at the beginning. They do not, however, constitute a counsel of despair. There is a good deal of inherent order in the subject matter of sociology and I think it is fair to say that, though undergoing continual reorganization, it is in general continually becoming both more explicit and more coherent.

My own personal contribution to this book, the final chapter, attempts an outline of the main theoretical focus of sociology and its subdivision into different theoretical and empirical fields. It seems that after the reader has been through the main body of substantive chapters he should be in a better position to appreciate the rationale of the outline presented in this chapter.

By way of introduction here, I would like to explain briefly the reasons the different contributions are grouped as they are. I conceive the focus of sociology as a theoretical discipline to lie in the problems of the *integration* of social systems—emphatically including obstacles to and failures of integration. Hence, it must be concerned with a wide variety of features, factors, and consequences of the "integrative states" of social systems at many levels, all the way from families and other types of small groups through many intermediate levels such as local communities and formal organizations, to total societies, and indeed systems of societies.

A social system is thereby conceived, not as a concrete entity, but as a certain set of abstractions from concrete interactive behavior and relationships. As such, whatever is defined as a social system is always conceived as an "open" system, standing in relations of interdependence and interpenetration with a number of "environing" systems. The specific modes of articulation with these environing systems must thus be a primary concern of sociology, in one sense its "second order" theoretical concern, but nonetheless vital.

These in turn fall into two categories. The "integrative state" of a social system is first clearly an important function of the states, structures, and processes of other subsystems of a total social system, the primary functions of which are other than integrative. These are most clearly visible at the "macrosocial" levels. In two cases these differences have given rise to clearly defined sister disciplines of sociology; namely, economics and political science. These should be regarded as independent disciplines, but also as crucially interdependent with sociology. The border-line problems then become the objects of study from each side. The subdiscipline of "political sociology" is relatively well defined, and, in a somewhat less defined sense, "economic sociology" may be said to be a going concern.

A third boundary problem presents a greater difficulty. This may best be characterized as the zone in which a social system most fully articulates with the most immediate of the nonsocial factors on its boundaries, which we may for present purposes restrict to the cultural and the psychological. I have called it the "pattern-maintenance system." The aspect of this articulation which is directly relevant here is what we would ordinarily call institutional. The cultural element traditionally comes to a head in the organization of religion with its implications for values. In modern societies secular culture affects society through the arts and the intellectual disciplines of education and research. On the psychological side perhaps the most important context is that of family and kinship, since the two primary functions of the family are what we call the "socialization" of the individual from infancy on and the regulation of motivational balances—in the case of adults, especially through marriage and parenthood.

A subtle distinction must be made between the above boundary problems, which concern relations of the core integrative subsystem to the other primary functional subsystems of a society or other social systems—the economic, political and pattern-maintenance systems—and those concerning the boundaries of the social system generally. These are also in the first instance the cultural and psychological boundaries, but "farther out" in the sense that the cultural and psychological systems, the latter as the "personalities" of individuals, operate autonomously rather than primarily in their capacities as parts of the social system. In the psychological case this latter boundary relation is fairly

xii

well codified in the interstitial discipline of social psychology. Perhaps comparable codifications are taking shape in such fields as the sociology of knowledge and some of the work in cultural and social anthropology, as well as some fields which are classed largely as humanistic, such as linguistics.[2]

Given the complexity of this frame of reference—which I am aware goes beyond the level generally current in the sociological profession—it has seemed best to classify the contributions which are more structural in emphasis than anything else in two groups, namely, Parts I and III, even though there is a certain overlap and hence arbitrariness in placing decisions in a few cases.

The first group, Part I, treats the elements which the sociologist must study as components of the social system, which are universally found, on sufficient levels of differentiation, in not only every system but in every subsystem. These in turn are subclassified into two groups. The first group, Part I-A, lies more at the social-psychological level: namely, the treatment by Alex Inkeles of "Personality and Social Structure"; by James A. Davis of "The Sociology of Attitudes"; and by Everett C. Hughes of "Work and Leisure." These three chapters constitute only a sample of what could appropriately have been included in such a section. Other possible topics include the processes of social learning—often called "socialization"—or the social-psychological aspects of particular motivation complexes of special interest to the sociologist, such as motivation to achievement, or of what some psychologists call "need-affiliation."

There is an important problem of possible overlap here. One of the prime complexes of integrative problems of societies vis-à-vis the personality of the individual concerns motivational "acceptance" of social expectations versus "alienation" from such expectations and, not the same thing, the behavioral outcomes in the form of conforming or deviant behavior. It has seemed better to reserve what we have in this field for Part V dealing with the relation of social behavior to situations of strain, and the balance between tendencies to deviance and mechanisms of social control. Part V contains the chapter by Albert K. Cohen, "Deviant Behavior and Its Control," and two chapters on important concrete fields where such problems loom large: namely,

"Youth in Modern Society" by Charles E. Bidwell, and "Race Relations in the United States" by Thomas F. Pettigrew.

If we had the appropriate essays, a section on cultural boundary problems would be appropriate, parallel to Part I-A. The chapter most likely to fit would be that of Robert N. Bellah on "The Sociology of Religion," but it seemed better to group it in Part IV with that of Norman W. Storer on "The Sociology of Science," as "closer in" toward the social system core in technical terms and in the pattern-maintenance subsystem.

Part I-B, then, deals with collective components of a generic character. It starts on the level of the small group with the chapter by Theodore M. Mills, "On the Sociology of Small Groups," which is especially concerned with the experimental group in the laboratory setting. The next chapter, by Peter M. Blau, "The Study of Formal Organization," deals with the main units of specialized societal function, seen most conspicuously in industry and government, but also in many other fields. The third, by Albert J. Reiss, Jr., "Some Sociological Issues about American Communities," has to do with a cross-cutting basis of organization, the local community as a generic type. Finally, the last essay in the section, by Charles Tilly, "The Forms of Urbanization," discusses the massive phenomenon of urbanization, so central to modern societies, in a comparative perspective.

In the recent development of sociology, along with attempts to deal with substantive problems of the structure, function, and processes of social systems, an immense amount of attention has gone into the development of methods of studying them empirically. It is probably safe to say that all major advances in the states of empirical sciences have resulted from some combination of improved empirical methods and of theoretically oriented problem statements and conceptualization of more or less generalized theory, though the relative importance varies in different cases. Empirical methods, however, cross-cut any classification of substantive problem areas. Though they are differentially applicable to different substantive problems and fields, they are inherently generic in significance for the discipline—and very often for more than one discipline. It hence seemed most appropriate to place our two chapters on empirical method, by

Paul F. Lazarsfeld and Robert McGinnis, in a section immediately following that on substantive components of social systems. They differ somewhat in emphasis on the basis of the older methods particularly prominent in the recent developmental phase of sociology and the newer methods which have come to the fore in very recent years.

Part III then returns to the substantive level, but this time dealing with a different order of differentiation of social systems, namely, what in a broad sense may be called functional. The six chapters which have been classified here fall into three subcategories. The first two, "The Family and Kinship" by Ezra F. Vogel and "The Sociology of Education" by Martin Trow, deal again with the social-psychological boundary area, but differ from those in Part I-A by the specificity of the societal functions involved and the centrality of the structures necessary for their functioning in the social system. Again, to illustrate the difficulty of classification, education might have been put in Part IV with religion and science, but its association with the family is so close that it seemed more appropriate here.

The second pair—"The Sociology of Economic Life" by Neil J. Smelser and "Political Sociology" by Seymour Martin Lipset— fit obviously into the intrasocietal boundary class, namely, the sociological treatment of the phenomena of the economy and of the polity. These two "sociologies" are, as noted, rapidly becoming recognized interstitial disciplines within the social system area in a sense comparable to that of social psychology on its farther boundary vis-à-vis the personality. The last two chapters in this section then deal with aspects of the core field of integrative phenomena of the social system. It is, however, particularly interesting that one of them, "The Sociology of Law," dealt with by Leon Mayhew, looks very much as if it belonged in an interstitial category and indeed in one primary respect it properly does. Obviously law has one of the oldest and greatest intellectual traditions of all of modern culture as well as of many other cultures. With the development of sociology, however, which of course is a rather recent phenomenon, a new mode of integration has in fact been rather slowly developing, especially in the United States. Its focus, of course, is the fact that in highly differentiated societies, law is the most explicit and formalized aspect of the normative component which is central to societal integration. It is at the basis of social "order" not mainly in the sense of suppression of "disorders" but in the regulating or definiteness of expectations in social interaction.

Sociologists are exceedingly fortunate in having available the rich materials which legal thought and legal process have developed over a very long period. As in many such cases, however, there are considerable difficulties in articulating the two interests. It may be said that the legal interest—in the professional sense— has two main though not exclusive foci: first, in the conditions and procedures for the settlement of cases through adjudication, and second, in the structure and content of the "body" of the law, its problems of consistency and inconsistency, levels of generalization, statement of principles, appropriateness of application in different situations, and the like. The sociologist, on the other hand, is primarily concerned with the operation of a social system as a whole, hence with the relations of the normative content of the law and of adjudicative and other legal procedures, to a whole series of other determinants of social structure and process.

The last chapter in this section, on "Social Stratification Structure and Trends of Social Mobility in Western Society" by Bernard Barber, deals with a traditional core problem area of sociology as such, one which no other discipline has seriously attempted to pre-empt, and which, probably all sociologists would agree, is of central importance to the discipline. Like other living systems, such as organisms and species, social systems become differentiated, and one major axis of differentiation is always the "vertical" one. This raises acute problems of articulation between the normative components of social structure, as in values and legal norms, and the integration of "interests" at the level both of groups and collectivities and of the motives of individuals in the social system. One primary focus of the problem of course is that of "distributive justice" as defined in the normative perspective, but also as dependent on many complex conditions.

From one point of view, "social change" is a generalized aspect of the phenomena of social systems which is coordinate with that of "social structure." Perhaps a major difference of the organization of the present book from those which some others would put together lies in the fact that change has not been singled out for salient treatment as an independent focus. I would not, however, think that many readers would gain the impression from the various chapters that their authors were writing mainly in terms of a "static" point of view. As noted, Part V in particular deals with topics of special relevance to change, and the same is true of the last substantive section, Part VI. The two differ in that Part V looks to certain problems with some emphasis on the microscopic level and especially the particular society at a particular stage of its development. Part VI, however, explicitly turns to the macroscopic point of view, and with it inevitably a comparative emphasis. Here Reinhard Bendix deals with the general rubric of modern societies, Edward Shils with the general problem of the plural occurrence of societies, varying in character over a wide range, and finally S. N. Eisenstadt—the only "foreign" sociologist among the contributors—who, however, knows American sociology exceedingly well—deals with another area on the boundary of society and culture, namely, "Ideology and Social Change," which, in the comparative-macroscopic framework, is very much involved in social change in the contemporary world.

I think I can speak for most if not all of my fellow contributors in saying that we welcome the opportunity to present this survey of American sociology, fragmentary and incomplete as it is, on two principal counts. The one, more in common with the significance of *Sociology Today*—to which several of us also contributed—lies in the significance of a kind of stock-taking of the state of the various topical subdivisions of sociology with which we have dealt, and of the discipline as a whole, which benefits ourselves and, we hope, our professional colleagues. The other is the opportunity to reach a wider public, in other social science disciplines and in other professions and occupations, to give them some idea of the state of sociology as a whole, or of particular parts of it.

Most educated men have been made increasingly aware of the vast importance of the growth of the intellectual disciplines in our time, of the burgeoning of the volume of research and scholarship, and of the whole network of higher education associated with them. Within this larger framework, in which of course the natural sciences occupy the largest place, the relative role of the social sciences has been rapidly increasing. Indeed, on any but a very small scale they scarcely existed before the present century, and the increase since World War II has been immense. To use a term favored by analysts of economic growth, they clearly have reached the "take-off" stage. Since they deal not with the physical conditions underlying social life, but with the latter as their own direct object of study, if they produce scientifically sound and important results, as they already have done on a considerable scale, their long-run importance for the shaping of man's social world can scarcely be underestimated. It seems to us that communication between those who, as social science professionals, are in the midst of this development, and intelligent citizens who, though not direct participants, are going to be immensely affected by it, and in turn have an immense influence on the course it takes, is one of the most urgent needs of our complicated society.

The chapters of this book stem from material prepared for the *Forum* Series of the Voice of America.

January, 1968

NOTES

1. Robert K. Merton, Leonard Broom, and Leonard S. Cottrell, Jr., eds., *Sociology Today: Problems and Prospects* (New York: Basic Books, Inc., 1959).
2. On a more technical level than seems appropriate here, I should also stress the independence of the social system–organism boundary, which is clearly involved in such areas as many aspects of health problems, and in the forces operating on growth of population and restraints on it. Other relations are the special relation of the economy to the physical environment through technology, and of religion as both social and cultural, to the "ultimate reality," orientation to which is involved in the answers men have arrived at to the "problems of meaning." My own most recent

relatively full discussions of the frame of reference underlying this very schematic discussion are in the article, "Social Systems and Subsystems," forthcoming in the *New International Encyclopedia of the Social Sciences,* and the theoretical chapters in my two contributions to the *Foundations of Modern Sociology* series (Alex Inkeles, ed., Prentice-Hall): *Societies: Evolutionary and Comparative Perspectives* (1966), Chapter 2; and *The System of Modern Societies* (forthcoming, 1968), Chapter 2.

Contents

Introduction **Talcott Parsons**   ix

PART I. *Components of Social Systems*

A. SOCIAL ATTITUDES
  1 Personality and Social Structure **Alex Inkeles**   3
  2 The Sociology of Attitudes **James A. Davis**   19
  3 Work and Leisure **Everett C. Hughes**   32

B. COLLECTIVE TYPES
  4 On the Sociology of Small Groups **Theodore M. Mills**   45
  5 The Study of Formal Organization **Peter M. Blau**   54
  6 Some Sociological Issues About American Communities
        Albert J. Reiss, Jr.   66
  7 The Forms of Urbanization **Charles Tilly**   75

PART II. *Methods of Investigation*

  8 Measurement **Paul F. Lazarsfeld**   93
  9 Methods of Research: The New Developments
        Robert McGinnis   107

PART III. *Functional Subsystems*

 10 The Family and Kinship **Ezra F. Vogel**   121
 11 The Sociology of Education **Martin Trow**   131
 12 The Sociology of Economic Life **Neil J. Smelser**   143
 13 Political Sociology **Seymour Martin Lipset**   156
 14 The Sociology of Law **Leon Mayhew**   171
 15 Social Stratification Structure and Trends of Social
        Mobility in Western Society **Bernard Barber**   184

PART IV. *Sociology of Culture*

16   The Sociology of Science **Norman W. Storer**   199
17   The Sociology of Religion **Robert N. Bellah**   214

PART V. *Strain, Deviance, and Social Control*

18   Deviant Behavior and Its Control **Albert K. Cohen**   231
19   Youth in Modern Society **Charles E. Bidwell**   244
20   Race Relations in the United States: A Sociological
       Perspective **Thomas F. Pettigrew**   258

PART VI. *Total Societies and Their Change*

21   Modern Society **Reinhard Bendix**   275
22   Society and Societies: The Macro-Sociological View
       Edward Shils   287
23   Ideology and Social Change **S. N. Eisenstadt**   304

CONCLUSION

24   An Overview **Talcott Parsons**   319

     Index   337

PART I

Components of
Social Systems

1 PERSONALITY AND SOCIAL STRUCTURE

Alex Inkeles

The central thesis of this essay is that adequate sociological analysis of many problems is either impossible or severely limited unless we make explicit use of psychological theory and data in conjunction with sociological theory and data. Indeed, I would assert that very little sociological analysis is ever done without using at least an implicit psychological theory. It seems evident that in making this theory explicit and bringing psychological data to bear systematically on sociological problems we cannot fail to improve the scope and adequacy of sociological analysis.

THE ROLE OF A GENERAL THEORY OF PERSONALITY

The student of a social structure seeks to explain the action consequences of a particular set of institutional arrangements. In order to do this, he must correctly estimate the meaning of those arrangements or their effect on the human personality. All institutional arrangements are ultimately mediated through individual human action. The consequences of any institutional arrangement, therefore, depend, at least in part, upon its effect on the human personality, broadly conceived. The human personality system thus becomes one of the main intervening variables in any estimate of the effects of one aspect of social structure on another. The need for a theory of personality is perhaps most evident in the study of those "rates" which represent the summary or end product of thousands or millions of individual de-

3

cisions and acts, yet which are of distinctive size for different societies or cultures. To illustrate the role which personality theory can and should play in such analysis, I must limit myself to the briefest consideration of two—suicide and delinquency rates. The same type of analysis is, however, equally relevant to other "rate" problems, such as that presented by the frequency and pattern of residential and occupational mobility.

In his strictly sociological analysis, Durkheim found that the rate of suicide—particularly egoistic suicide—was determined by the degree of integration of particular social structures, whether church, family, political party, or national state. Even those who are most skeptical of Durkheim's analysis cannot deny the fact that he has exposed the main pattern of correlation. But one is left in serious doubt as to the causal nexus which converts a state of integration of social structure into a rate of suicide. Indeed, despite his intention to go "directly" to the causes of suicide, "disregarding the individual as such, his motives and his ideas," Durkheim was in the end forced to introduce a general theory of personality as the intervening variable between, on the one hand, the state of integration of social structures and, on the other hand, the varying rates of suicide he sought to explain. To the question of how the origin of suicide could lie in the degree of integration of a social structure, he replied by referring to man's "psychological constitution," which, he said, "needs an object transcending it." This object is lacking in the weakly integrated society, and consequently "the individual, having too keen a feeling for himself and his own value . . . wishes to be his own only goal, and as such an objective cannot satisfy him, drags out languidly and indifferently an existence which henceforth seems meaningless to him."[1]

This is not the place for an evaluation of the adequacy of the psychological theory that Durkheim finally used or of the consequences of his failure to introduce this theory explicitly and systematically into the analysis. I wish, rather, to stress the uneven development in the study of suicide. Durkheim's brilliant analysis provided so definitive an argument and so strong a model that for nearly sixty years there was virtually no advance in our understanding of the phenomenon. Generations of stu-

4

dents, taught to take *Le Suicide* as the model of sociological analysis, went through their training and out into the world to do battle for "pure"—i.e., nonpsychological—sociological analysis, whatever the cost.

It has been only recently, in the work of Henry and Short on *Suicide and Homicide*,[2] that a major advance has been made in research on this important area. It behooves us, therefore, to ask what made this advance possible. Not the discovery of mountains of new data, although some new data are introduced. Nor does the advance stem from the application of new methods, statistical or otherwise, that were not available in Durkheim's time. The achievement of Henry and Short has, rather, been made possible largely by their systematic use of an explicit psychodynamic theory in conjunction with Durkheim's theory of the role of social integration and social restraint. Henry and Short treat suicide as an act of aggression following from restraint and consequent frustration. They assume that both suicide and homicide have this characteristic,[3] although the two responses differ in the direction in which the aggression is expressed—in the former case inward; in the latter, outward. By combining in their analysis the situational factor stressed by Durkheim—namely, the degree of external restraint—and the personality factor of propensity to express aggression inwardly or outwardly, Henry and Short are able to suggest important connections between suicide and homicide rates, to resolve certain contradictions in Durkheim's analysis, to explain some new data in a manner consistent with the rest of the analysis, and to suggest important lines of further research. All this is accomplished without any "reduction" in the importance of the sociological factors, and certainly without reduction of the social reality to personality. This small work is a landmark which surely points the road along which we will or should be traveling in the next decades.

Durkheim and the study of suicide provide the model case, but the importance of my point depends on the existence of other cases. Time permits only the briefest allusion to a parallel development at a much later date, this time in the study of juvenile delinquency. In his classic study of *Delinquency Areas*,

Shaw[4] developed an explanation strikingly parallel to Durkheim's theory of suicide. Differential rates of delinquency, he found, are determined by the degree of community disorganization and the consequent weakening of social control. (Shaw also added a new element, the conception of the delinquency area of having a special subculture and of delinquency as learned cultural behavior. Although significant, this conception is not of great importance for our present purposes.) Like Durkheim, however, Shaw failed to specify the mechanism by means of which a quality of the community could be translated into the individual actions which ultimately produce the delinquency rate.

In this area, too, progress has been slow, for it was not until twenty years later, in the Gluecks' *Unraveling Juvenile Delinquency*,[5] that community disorganization was meaningfully linked to delinquency rates through the intervening variable of the personality types typically generated under such conditions of disorganization. In their monumental study the Gluecks have enabled us to see why the previously noticed social conditions in delinquency areas produce the delinquent act, by revealing the creation of response propensities toward delinquent acts in the personalities subjected to those special conditions. They also have enabled us thereby to understand what Shaw could not explain: why only a minority of those exposed to the delinquent subculture actually learn the culture.

This analysis does not, however, minimize the importance of the delinquent subculture or of the objective characteristics of the delinquency area—physical decay in a district in transition to industry, heavy representation of racial or ethnic minorities, high rates of alcoholism and crime, and seriously disrupted family life. But it does vastly increase both our understanding of the phenomenon and our ability to predict and control it through the juxtaposition and integration—but not reduction—of the social and the psychodynamic elements of the situation.

Personality and Social Movements

In addition to its role in explaining the levels of social action which can be expressed as population rates, a general theory of personality is of great importance in the analysis of major social movements or processes.

Max Weber, perhaps the greatest sociological student of large-scale social processes, was not lacking in psychological acuity. Indeed, in many ways his analysis of the influence of protestantism on capitalism[6] is a specification of the personality types which predispose toward and are a necessary condition for the development of capitalism. Nevertheless, the basic formulation of his problem—what elements in the economic ethic of protestantism account for its encouragement of capitalism—does not particularly require the intervention of a general theory of human personality. The personality type is given, at least implicitly, in the religious ethic, and the problem is largely to show the translation of the ethic into action in the economic realm.

Among more recent studies of the social consequences of capitalism, the work of Erich Fromm is an outstanding example of the application of a general theory of personality to explain social movements which follow from a particular form of social organization. In *Escape from Freedom*,[7] Fromm asks no less a question than what is the effect of capitalism as a socioeconomic system on man conceived in terms of a general theory of the human personality.

The framework of Fromm's analysis is the very general problem of "the role which psychological factors play as active forces in the social process." He explores the problem mainly with reference to the effect of two general needs: the need for relatedness to others, and the need for freedom or autonomy. These needs are rooted "not in the bodily processes but in the very essence of the human mode and practice of life." Of the first, "the need to avoid aloneness," he says: "[The] lack of relatedness to values, symbols, patterns, we may call moral aloneness and state that moral aloneness is as intolerable as physical aloneness, or rather that physical aloneness becomes unbearable only if it implies also moral aloneness." It is the state "which man most dreads." The quality of freedom is less precisely defined, but it seems to mean freedom from instinctual and other restraints which prevent individuation, the fulfillment of innate growth potential, or the "growth of self-strength."

7

Having postulated these two general human needs, Fromm asserts that all human history has been characterized by "conflict and strife" because:

> Each step in the direction of growing individuation threatened people with new insecurities. Primary bonds once severed, cannot be mended. . . . However, if the economic, social, and political conditions on which the whole process of human individuation depends do not offer a basis for the realization of individuality . . . while at the same time people have lost those ties which gave them security, this lag makes freedom an unbearable burden. . . . Powerful tendencies arise to escape from this kind of freedom into submission or some kind of relationship to man and the world which promises relief from uncertainty, even if it deprives the individual of his freedom.[8]

Within this framework, Fromm traces the history of modern man, from the Middle Ages through the Reformation to the establishment of modern democracies and their counterpart in modern totalitarianism of the fascist variety. His work is extremely ambitious. Since he is attempting to fit a given theory to the sweep of several centuries of man's history, he has the historian's advantage of being sure in advance that his theory will be consonant with the facts he selects. Nevertheless, Fromm has added something to social history and to our understanding of modern man. Indeed, *Escape from Freedom* is probably one of the most distinguished works of social science of the twentieth century. But my purpose in introducing it here is not to argue in support of its thesis. The importance of Fromm's work for this analysis lies in his explicit use of a general theory of human personality as an independent element in the analysis of a continuing process of social change.

Fromm's general formula, as we have said, specifies that man must have both a high degree of relatedness to others and freedom from restraints which prevent individuation. In social contexts which increase individuation but undercut relatedness, there will be a drive to regain such relatedness by a surrender of freedom to group purposes. Presumably any period could be assessed in terms of its potential for change according to its ability to satisfy these needs.

It is greatly to Fromm's credit that he does not try to derive the character of the economic and political structure from these general human needs. He holds, quite properly, that "psychological forces have a dynamism of their own" and asserts that while "the expression of human needs . . . can be molded, [the needs themselves] cannot be uprooted." Nevertheless, he recognizes that "economic forces must be understood not as psychological motivations but as objective conditions . . . dependent on objective factors, such as the natural productive forces, technique, geographical factors. . . ."[9] In this respect his work is superior to Freud's and to Kardiner's.[10] The latter, although he exempts economic relations, attempts to derive the main outlines of myth, religion, and other projective systems almost exclusively from the specific child-rearing disciplines of the culture.

Since the "psychologizing" of social organization is in bad repute with many social scientists, and perhaps deservedly so, it is important to stress certain crucial differences between the approach developed here and some which have been important in the past. Psychological theories of society and social movements have mainly been of two types. The first derives social behavior and institutions directly from the psychological properties of the human psyche, including, in the case of Freud, the psychological history of the race. A typical if extreme example is the assertion that man has an aggressive instinct and that therefore we have war.[11] The second, which Sorokin has labeled the "psychologistic" school of sociology, simply reduces or translates all social phenomena into psychological terms; in its modern version, it asserts that the only "real" social phenomena or variables are the personalities, the individual psychologies, of those who make up any given group.

Fromm, Erikson, and Cantril cannot be made to fit into either of these patterns. As the quotation given above demonstrates, Fromm recognizes social institutions, particularly systems of economic organization, as relatively independent variables, with their own history and laws of development. He does not treat them as mere projections of personality or need systems. These authors also recognize that many processes in political or economic systems, such as the accumulation of capital, cannot be reduced to or fully described in psychological terms. The essence of this mode of analysis, rather, lies in its insistence that all forms of social organization have personal meaning or psychological implications for the participants, and that different social systems have different psychic meanings. The pattern these authors have followed in their analyses is to state, on the basis of general personality theory, certain general human needs or drives; then to examine a given social setting to assess its effect on those needs. Where the needs are not satisfied or are met in a peculiar way, they again draw on personality theory to suggest the typical modes of human response to such frustration. They then assess the effects of the personal reaction on the social system, with especial attention to the prospects for equilibrium or further frustrations which may set in motion a different social movement. In this model, the action propensities in the individual are derived, not from society, but from a general theory of the human personality. In turn, culture and social structure are perceived historically, not as derived from or reduced to personality factors. But they act on personality and, according to their mode of influence, produce reactions from personality which may generate movements of social change in the original sociocultural system.

THE ROLE OF MODAL PERSONALITY PATTERNS

Not only does the student of social structure need an adequate general theory of personality; it may also be important for him to measure the particular qualities of personality which characterize the "population" of any given social structure. Such information is of great importance in the study of at least two major sociological problems: (1) the recruitment of persons into, and the adequacy of their performance in, the major social roles; and (2) the integration and change of the diverse institutions that make up a society.

Sociologists have traditionally explained regular role performance as a logical consequence of the system of sanctions imposed on those who fail to meet, and rewards granted to those who do meet, the expectations of society. Performance is thus seen as largely dependent on factors "outside" the person. The only thing that need be posited as "inside" in this view is the general desire to avoid punishment and to gain rewards. Important as such drives may be, they do not seem sufficient to explain the complex phenomenon of differential role performance. Without in any way challenging the crucial importance of the objective factors which determine role behavior, I wish to stress that recruitment into roles and the quality of role performance may to an important degree be influenced by personal qualities in individuals which predispose them to move toward one or another role, and which have a marked effect on the quality of their role performance once they have been placed. It must be assumed, further, that this happens on a sufficiently large scale to be a crucial factor in determining the functioning of a particular institution, of a small- or large-scale social system. To the degree that this is true, to predict the functioning of a particular institution, or a small- or large-scale social system, we need to know not only the system of statuses but also the distribution of personality characteristics in the population at large and among the incumbents of particular roles.

Whether they are based on recruitment or on development on the job, such modal personality differences are relevant to the sociologist only if they can be shown to affect individual role performance and consequently institutional functioning. Studies in which data on personality and on role performance are simultaneously reported are rare, and little has been done systematically to exploit the promising lead which Merton[12] gave us years ago. The few available studies do indicate marked effects of personality on role performance. In a study of the performance of nurses' aides in a mental hospital as judged by their supervisors, Gilbert and Levinson[13] rated them as "custodial" or "humanistic" in their treatment of patients. Aides rated as "custodial" made more threats to patients and placed prime emphasis on keeping the wards quiet. The "humanistic" aides were more friendly and respectful to the patients and assumed the role of "social" therapist for their wards. For the female aides in three Boston hospitals, the rank-order correlation between custodialism in the treatment of patients and score on authoritarianism in personality as measured by the F scale was .75.

Several outstanding studies relate personality to school performance. Rosen[14] drew a sample of students stratified by social class from public high schools in New Haven and obtained measures of achievement motivation and school performance. Those who scored high on need achievement tended to make good grades, 69 per cent having "B" or better as against 35 per cent of those with low need achievement. A test of value orientations, incidentally, failed to discriminate significantly the low- and high-grade performers. Need achievement was also very highly associated with social class, but a separate control run on class showed that it had virtually no independent effect on grade performance when achievement motivation was controlled.

Stern, Stein, and Bloom[15] obtained a series of performance measures for two groups of sixty-one students who were rated, respectively, high and low on stereopathy, a trait broadly similar to authoritarianism (F scale). Intelligence accounted for only a modest part of the variance in the stereopathy score, but any possible effect of differences in intelligence between the two groups was controlled by matching on this dimension. On entrance and placement examinations there were marked differences in the performance of the two groups in tests on the humanities, social sciences, and English. By contrast, there was only random variation in their performance in biological sciences, physical sciences, and mathematics. The emphasis at the college concerned (presumably the University of Chicago) was on "capacity for detachment, for delaying resolution or closure, and for tolerating ambiguous relatives rather than demanding structural absolutes." This placed a premium on qualities which were characteristic of non-stereopaths and relatively lacking in those high in stereopathy. Such qualities were, however, obviously less important in the natural-sciences and mathematics examinations, for which fields the requirements and tests are also more standardized.

Striking differences also emerged in the later school performance of the two groups. At the end of the first year, 20 per cent of the stereopathic students had withdrawn from the college, whereas none of the nonstereopaths had done so—a difference significant at the .001 level. Intelligence made virtually no difference in this performance. The complaints of the withdrawing stereopathic students strongly suggested that their action resulted from a lack of congruence between their personalities and their consequent ambitions and hopes, on the one hand, and on the other the special requirements of the particular college they had entered. They complained most about the seeming lack of discipline, the refusal of instructors to give the "right" answers, and the separation between course content and their immediate and practical vocational interests. This outcome was largely what had been predicted from an examination of the distinctive qualities of education at the particular college and the distinctive personality attributes of the stereopathic students.

It is clear from these studies that role recruitment and particularly role performance cannot safely be predicted solely on the basis of the extrinsic features of the status and its place in the larger social structure. The personalities of those occupying the statuses will strongly influence the quality of their role performance. And since it seems likely that personalities are not randomly recruited to statuses, the effects of the modal personality patterns in any given group of status incumbents may be a strong influence on the quality of role performance in the group. The impact on other parts of the social structure may therefore be substantial. We see again, as in our earlier observations on social rates, that both social structure and personality must be treated as important independent but interacting variables influencing the flow of the social process.

Personality and the Social System

If the study of personality as it influences role recruitment and performance seems to pose major methodological problems, they are as naught compared to the problems posed for him who seeks to discover the role that personality patterns play in the integration and change of social systems. The concept of "national character" not only is old but has long been under attack for its presumed kinship with discredited theories about racial psychology. However eager we may be to avoid seeming prejudiced—or worse still, "racist"—as scientists we cannot avoid dealing systematically with the question: Is there a significant difference among various national or subnational populations in the distribution of discrete traits or personality types, and, if so, how does this affect the functioning of the social system? Can we assume that a given social structure will operate in much the same way regardless of the set of personalities placed in that context? What stimulus to social change follows from the lack of congruence between personality needs and system requirements, and what limitations on such change follow from the lack of certain motivations in the participants?

To answer questions such as those above, we must be able to measure in an adequate sample of a national population the distribution of personality traits and personality syndromes or types, much as we now chart the distribution of attitudes and voting intentions. Before we attempt this difficult task of measurement, we need to know what elements of personality should be measured for purposes of sociological analysis. Having measured important personality dimensions in such populations, we need to learn how to interpret the results, and then to integrate our findings with data on the structural aspects of the system, to develop predictive propositions, and to test the adequacy of our theory in new populations and situations.

Although this may sound exceedingly ambitious, we are much closer to the attainment of this objective than many realize. Recent theoretical efforts have moved us far toward the delineation of some of the components of personality which we assume to be of greatest relevance for social-system analysis. In the last two decades, substantial progress has been made in devising apparently valid and reliable personality tests which can be easily and simply administered to large samples—notably, modifications of the sentence-completion test, the TAT, and other paper-and-pencil tests. Indeed, very limited and simple personality tests on a single dimension have already been included in national opinion surveys. Many dilemmas, particularly those involving the cross-cultural validity of psychological tests, still are unresolved, but the path ahead seems fairly clear and the prognosis good.

Another major point of articulation between psychological and sociological studies is the study of child rearing. The particular child-rearing disciplines which produce one or another consequence in the adult personality present what is clearly a predominantly psychological problem. It seems to me, however, that the sociologist has an important contribution to make to the question why the parent does what he does. If child-rearing practices are variable, we can hardly assume the variation to be unrelated to the life situation of the parents and the pressures to which they are subjected. The work of Miller and Swanson[16] on these issues represents a substantial step forward by showing the intimate connection between the occupational setting of the parent, the child-rearing practices he adopts or adapts, and the consequences in the personality of the child. I think it no exaggeration to say that one of the most important clues, and an extraordinarily neglected one, to the means whereby social stress in one generation leads to social change in the next lies in the various ways in which parents raise their children.[17] Unfortunately, I have only enough space to note in passing that here again are major opportunities for the independent but coordinate action of personality modes and social structure in fostering social stability or generating social change.

SUMMARY AND CONCLUSIONS

I have argued that sociological analysis—the attempt to understand the structure and functioning of social systems—will often require the use of a general theory of personality and knowledge of the distinctive personality characteristics of participants in the system as a whole or in major subsystems and in particular roles. To many, this may at once suggest that I am proposing a "reduction" of sociological analysis to the presumably more basic level of psychological analysis. I am by no means implying or suggesting this course of action. What is at issue here is not the reduction of one discipline to another but the articulation of the two for certain specific purposes under specific conditions. I have already emphasized that I conceive of the two disciplines as having quite different analytic foci. Let me add that there are many areas of traditional sociological research for which personality theory or knowledge of modal personality patterns would seem to have little or no relevance—for example, most demographic research, a substantial part of urban sociology, and a great many problems in measurement or social mapping, including the mapping of class structures. But if we go beyond the mapping of a class structure to deal with the behavior of members of different classes and the rates, say, of stability in or mobility out of the particular classes, then psychological data may assume great importance in the general model of analysis. This is not to say, however, that the problem reduces itself to personal psychology. Obviously, in an occupational pyramid with relatively few jobs defined as very desirable and many defined as less desirable, the amount of mobility out of the lower classes is objectively given by the nature of the pyramid. If education of a given level or quality is a prerequisite to attaining certain occupational levels, and such education is generally not available in rural areas, the rate of mobility for those of rural residence will be primarily determined by these facts.

Within the framework of such structurally set limits, however, there is a broad area in which other forces have considerable room to operate. For lack of appropriate motivation, those who are otherwise eligible may not use the opportunities for mobility to maximum advantage. Among those who are eligible, some will make the effort, others will not. Of those who strive, some will have the capacity, some will not. Even a cursory glance at the many recent studies stimulated by our national need to discover and train inborn talent will reveal the serious miscalculations we have made by assuming that only objective factors of "opportunity" are important in determining mobility drives. If we are to go beyond the mere statistical charting of mobility rates for different strata to more complex explanatory schemes with predictive power in new situations, we must be able to deal with the personal component—the motivated actor in the situation of social action. The mobility rate for the society is not thus reduced to a matter of mere personal psychology. It remains a social, not a personal, datum.

The same is true of the other aspects of the individual's social context of action. But the actions of individuals in any situation are personal, however much they reflect the determining influence of the social environment. And that environment, in turn, can be reflected in individual action only to the extent that it is mediated through the personal system or personality. A full understanding of any social situation and its probable consequences, therefore, assumes a knowledge not only of the main facts about the social structure—the gathering of which is presumably the special province of sociological study—but also of the main facts about the personalities operating in that structure. What is required, therefore, is an integration or coordination of two basic sets of data in a larger explanatory scheme, not a reduction of either mode of analysis to the allegedly more fundamental level of the other.

NOTES

1. Emile Durkheim, *Suicide,* translated by J. A. Spaulding and George Simpson (Glencoe, Ill.: The Free Press, 1951), pp. 151, 208–261, 356.
2. A. F. Henry and J. F. Short, *Suicide and Homicide* (Glencoe, Ill.: The Free Press, 1954).
3. It is not sufficiently realized, even by Henry and Short, how clearly Durkheim saw this connection. He said: "Anomy, in fact, begets a state of exasperation and irritated weariness which may turn against the person himself or another according to the circumstances; in the first case, we have suicide, in the second, homicide" (*op. cit.,* p. 357).
4. C. R. Shaw, *Delinquency Areas* (Chicago: University of Chicago Press, 1931).
5. S. Glueck and E. Glueck, *Unraveling Juvenile Delinquency* (Cambridge, Mass.: Harvard University Press, 1950).
6. Max Weber, *The Protestant Ethic and the Spirit of Capitalism,* translated by Talcott Parsons (New York: Scribner's, 1930).
7. Erich Fromm, *Escape from Freedom* (New York: Farrar and Rinehart, 1941), p. 19.
8. *Ibid.,* pp. 36–37.
9. *Ibid.,* p. 298.
10. Abram Kardiner, *The Psychological Frontiers of Society* (New York: Columbia University Press, 1945).

11. See T. H. Pear, ed., *Psychological Factors of Peace and War* (New York: Philosophical Library, 1950).

12. Robert K. Merton, "Bureaucratic Structure and Personality." *Social Forces*, XVIII (1946), 560–568.

13. D. Gilbert and D. J. Levinson, "Role Performance, Ideology, and Personality in Mental Hospital Aides," in M. Greenblatt *et al.*, eds., *The Patient and the Mental Hospital* (Glencoe, Ill.: The Free Press, 1957).

14. B. C. Rosen, "The Achievement Syndrome: A Psycho-Cultural Dimension of Social Stratification." *American Sociology Review*, XXI (1956), 203–211.

15. G. G. Stern, M. I. Stein, and B. S. Bloom, *Methods in Personality Assessment* (Glencoe, Ill.: The Free Press, 1956).

16. D. Miller and G. E. Swanson, *Inner Conflict and Defense* (New York: Henry Holt, 1957).

17. For a pilot study of these processes, see Alex Inkeles, "Social Change and Social Character: The Role of Parental Mediation," *Journal of Social Issues*, XI (1955).

2 THE SOCIOLOGY OF ATTITUDES

James A. Davis

Attitudes are among the most studied and least clearly defined variables in social science. Indeed, there may be a connection between the two generalizations, for the feeling of liking or disliking, choosing or rejecting, being favorable or unfavorable toward, approving or disapproving; whatever the words, such positive and negative sentiments are so universal that the definitions one finds in textbooks serve rather to identify the author's theoretical camp than to identify the object of analysis.

The purpose of this chapter is to sketch some recent trends in American sociological theories about liking and disliking. In particular, I want to sketch the development of what can be called the *structural* approach toward attitudes, that is, a set of theories which treat attitudes as a function of the structure of interpersonal relations.

Let me add quickly that sociology has no monopoly on attitude studies. Much of this chapter falls technically within that hybrid discipline called social psychology, and many of the most important contributions come from those political scientists who have studied voters and their attitudes. Furthermore, if attitudes are defined so loosely as to include preferences and choices in general, then it is economists who have provided the most highly developed theories; and economic theories are beginning to loom large in sociology, but that is another trend which I shall not discuss. As a final qualification, let me quickly note that my stress is on American research—that is, research conducted in the United States—although research workers all over the world are contributing to the development of the ideas I shall outline.

see where we are, we must know something about
me from, if only to find out whether we have been
circles. Where to begin is a matter of taste, and no
stotle had much to say about attitudes. For those of
historical horizons are narrower, Gordon Allport offers
ert Spencer as the founding father of attitude studies,
since the word turns up in Spencer's 1862 volume, *First Principles.*

The real history of academic ideas, however, is that which can
be traced from teachers to graduate students who then become
teachers of graduate students, and so on. In this sense, attitude
studies in American sociology began in 1918 with the publication of *The Polish Peasant in Europe and America* by W. I.
Thomas and Florian Znaniecki. Few of the hypotheses of this
monumental study of the adjustment of immigrants have survived intact, but many a sociologist remembers that Thomas
and Znaniecki *defined* social psychology as the scientific study
of attitudes. *The Polish Peasant* was followed by a remarkable
flowering of sociological work at the University of Chicago during the 1920's. The "Chicago school" ran the gamut from statistical studies of urban ecology to the biographies of thieves, and
many famous names are associated with it. Its contribution to
attitude studies, though, reached a high point in the writings
of George Herbert Mead, a social philosopher. Mead's writings
are abstract, intricate, and conceptual, which is to say that he
was a philosopher, not an attitude researcher. When we add to
this the melancholy fact that Mead's published books are not
his own text but transcriptions of his classroom lectures, we see
why his writings are challenging in more ways than one. Yet
despite the obscurity and complexity of Mead's doctrines, his
main theme is clear, and it is this theme which dominated American sociology in its approaches to attitudes during the 1920's
and 1930's.

The theme is this: that our attitudes toward objects, toward
others, and especially our attitudes toward that favorite object
of thought, ourselves, are socially forged and socially maintained.
What we like and what we dislike, and whether we like or dislike ourselves, emerge from our experiences with others, especially from our ability to see the world, and ourselves, as seen

by others and as defined by social symbols. The key hypothesis of Mead is that we develop our attitudes by taking over—his word is "internalizing"—the attitudes of others.

To most of us now such ideas sound neither bold nor original, but this is the triumph of Mead's thought, not its failure, for his interpersonal, cultural, and phenomenological stance has become axiomatic. In the intellectual climate of the United States between the world wars, though, characterized by a popular ideology of "rugged individualism" and psychological doctrines of Watsonian behaviorism, such ideas were far from axiomatic.

Granted the subtlety and scope of Mead's social psychology, its very scope provided its greatest limitation, for as the slogan runs, "something which explains everything doesn't explain anything in particular." While his social psychology gives us a framework in which attitude studies may be placed, neither Mead nor his many disciples have provided us with many concrete hypotheses of the sort which are amenable to scientific research. Mead assures us that "others" are crucial in shaping our attitudes, but except for the special case of the infant, he doesn't tell us which others. In this sense, the development of sociological theories of attitudes may perhaps be seen as a series of answers to the question, "Which others?"

Before we turn to that question, however, we must mention another trend, perhaps a detour; and it is interesting to note that radio had much to do with it, along with the rise of totalitarianism. Both the astounding popularity of radio and the systematic use of mass-media techniques by totalitarian regimes in the 1930's led to the proliferation of empirical mass-media research, one of the leading traditions in American attitude studies. It is thus no coincidence that one of this country's leading sociological research institutes, Columbia University's Bureau of Applied Social Research, began its life as The Office of Radio Research.

Studies of radio and the mass media produced an extraordinary volume of findings on attitudes simply because the broadcaster is frequently attempting to create or change attitudes, whether he is a statesman attempting to shape support for momentous policies or an advertiser seeking converts to his brand of tooth paste.

I hinted that the media research of the 1930's and 1940's may have represented a detour. It came about as follows. By and large, those concerned with radio were awed by its potentialities. The notion that a single man talking into a bulbous stick could reach millions of ears is a striking one, and the raw facts on listenership, readership, and now we must add viewership, in the modern world are astounding.

It was thus natural to assume that the mass media represented an enormous power to affect attitudes. Whether one was a literary intellectual who believed that this power would corrupt the culture of the nation or an educator who looked forward to a vast extension of learning, there was agreement that radio, newspapers, and magazines had a tremendous capacity to mold attitudes. When we also remember the apparent successes of the propaganda ministries of the totalitarian nations, there seemed to be a good case for viewing the mass media as a sort of physical force which could leap through the air with invincible power to support or reverse attitudes.

Consequently, a good deal of attention during this time was given to unmasking the hidden powers of the mass communicator. Content analysis attempted to find the subtle themes which swayed men and women, while intensive studies were made of particular communications. The most famous of these, undoubtedly, is Hadley Cantril's study, *The Invasion from Mars*. In 1938 a particularly realistic radio version of H. G. Wells's novel, *The War of the Worlds*, precipitated panic among some listeners. Cantril attempted to find out why some were fooled by the broadcast and some were not. It is characteristic of the time that his major variable was a personality characteristic, "critical ability."

As might be expected, not all the research supported the idea that mass media have a strong effect on attitudes. First of all, there was the plain fact that the majority of United States newspapers had routinely opposed the candidacy of Franklin D. Roosevelt, who nevertheless was swept into presidential office repeatedly. Furthermore, carefully executed studies of American presidential elections beginning in 1940 showed surprisingly few changes in voting intentions—that is, in attitudes—during the heat of an American presidential campaign. Studies of particular events, such as the National Opinion Research Center's postwar study of a campaign to increase interest in the United Nations in an American city, also tended to show small effects.

I should not allege that mass media have no effects. There is voluminous research evidence that they are extremely important in spreading information, in drawing attention to issues, and so on, but the burden of the research findings so far is that mass media in themselves are relatively weak factors in changing or creating strong attitudes.

Nothing daunted, sociologists merely reversed the problem. Instead of asking, as Cantril did, why the media are so effective, they began to ask why the media have so little effect on attitudes. Oddly enough, this reversal of the question has led to considerable theoretical progress and a return to the themes first raised by Mead.

One of the major themes in this second generation of attitude research comes from numerous studies of "source credibility" or "prestige suggestion." Lewis' 1941 study is typical. She distributed political slogans to groups of students, indicating to some that the slogan was written by this political leader and indicating to others that another political leader was the author. As you might expect, the students' reactions varied with the purported source. Slogans attributed to popular political figures were received more favorably.

This study and many others support the following generalization: If we like the source of a communication we will tend to accept the content, while if we dislike the source we will tend to reject the content. The principle goes a long way toward explaining the limited power of mass media to change attitudes because it means, in effect, that most preachers reach the converted and repel the sinners.

The principle is well accepted and intuitively obvious, yet it provides the best single answer so far to Mead's question—Which others? It seems to be the others we like or dislike strongly. Furthermore, the principle has an interesting logical status in that it doesn't add a new variable to our thinking; it adds another person, the communicator. What I mean is this. We began with a lone person and asked which other people influenced his attitudes. Source credibility or prestige suggestion, however, can be viewed simply as another attitude, a favorable or unfavorable attitude toward the communicator. Thus the smallest social unit in attitude formation seems to consist of a structure involving two people, a listener and a communicator, the attitude which the communicator is urging, and the listener's attitudes toward the communicator.

Out of these primitive elements: two persons, the "something" which is being discussed, and three attitudes, emerges one of the most influential theories of contemporary social psychology, Fritz Heider's theory of structural balance. Heider, a psychologist, first proposed his theory in a 1946 article and has presented it in further detail in a 1958 book. His theory is very simple but, like many simple theories, it has an elegance which makes it an extremely useful tool for thought and research.

The theory of structural balance is a simple mathematical model involving three elements, a person (designated by the letter P), some other person (designated by the letter O), and the object of an attitude (designated by the letter X). The three elements make up what is called a P-O-X triangle. The various attitudes involved among the three are thought of as lines connecting the three elements to form a triangle. Thus, for example, Person might be a voter, Other might be a political columnist, and X, the object, might be a political candidate. There are a number of possible combinations of attitudes. For example, Person admires the columnist, the columnist criticizes the candidate, and Person dislikes the candidate. The model is straightforward and Heider makes a number of specific predictions. That is, he says that some possible combinations of attitudes in a P-O-X triangle are stable (he uses the word "balanced"), while others are unstable ("unbalanced"). He predicts that we tend to prefer situations which are balanced, and his predictions have been supported by a number of research studies.

Heider's theory—the theory of structural balance—is an extremely important tool in modern attitude studies, and it can be used to make sense out of a wide variety of research findings. Yet if we return again to the question which Mead left for us, "Which others?," balance theory alone is not sufficient. It tells us to look for the others to whom we have strong attitudes, but it does not tell us where they are.

Some persuasive answers to this problem are presented in *Personal Influence*, a 1955 book by Elihu Katz and Paul F. Lazarsfeld of the Bureau of Applied Social Research. Their thesis is known as "the two-step flow of communication" and they put it this way: "Ideas often seem to flow from radio and print to opinion leaders and from them to the less active sections of the population." In other words, granted the importance of source credibility, there are other concrete individuals who play an important part in the communication process. *Personal Influence* has given us a familiar term, "opinion leadership," and has sparked a considerable amount of research on interpersonal factors in the communication process, ranging from studies of farmers' decisions to plant a new kind of corn to studies of physicians' decisions to prescribe a new drug.

Important as this line of research is in media studies, it is equally important for general theories of attitude formation because it suggests this generalization: personal influence on attitudes seems to be inverse to social distance. It is those who are close to us, the people we run into every day, who have the powerful pull on our attitudes, not the glamorous figures of the larger world. Thus, for example, voting research repeatedly finds that we tend to get our political attitudes from our friends, not from newspaper pundits or party spokesmen. Studies of the military indicate that a soldier's attitudes are much influenced by his buddies and little influenced by the exhortations of headquarters. The generalizations should, perhaps, be amended to allow for the effect of prestige, but if so, the qualified proposition would be this: those who have the greatest impact on our attitudes are those who are socially closest to us but a little higher in prestige.

We now have two propositions: first, that it is sentimental ties which are most important in the sociology of attitude formation; second, that it is those who are close to us who are the most

25

effective influences on our attitudes. When we put these two ideas together we have the framework for what may be called the structural approach to the sociology of attitudes.

From this structural point of view a group or even a total society may be seen as a complex network or fabric of inter-personal sentiments in which all but a few individuals are linked to some others by attitudes of liking, disliking, respect, hatred, and so on. While each person has strong attitudes toward only a small number of persons, they are involved with others and these others have links to still others. Thus, ultimately an entire society may be thought of as a loosely woven web of interpersonal sentiments or attitudes. Any given person may be seen as sitting in the center of his own web, tied directly to a few others and indirectly to the larger society.

Now if we return to Heider's theory of structural balance, we see that any two persons who are directly connected in the web constitute two points of a P-O-X triangle. Heider predicts, in effect, that if their sentimental tie is positive—if they like each other—their attitudes will tend to become similar, while if the tie is negative they will tend to develop opposite attitudes. The total web, then, consists of thousands or even millions of these Heider triangles, just as physical matter consists of an astro-nomical number of elementary particles.

Our capsule history has brought us to this point. We began by noting a continuity, that in the forty-eight years since Thomas and Znaniecki, sociologists have accepted the proposition that attitudes are heavily influenced by particular others; we then noted the burgeoning media and voting research of the 1930's and 1940's which began to give this frame of reference some concrete propositions. Specifically, we noted a number of studies of prestige influence and source credibility which culminated in Heider's leading hypothesis: that it is the sentimental relation between Person and Other which affects their attitudes toward X. Finally, we noted the influence researches which have led us to think not of pairs of persons but of a gigantic network of inter-personal sentiments.

Clearly our task now is to specify the properties of this net-work and to state the principles which will allow us to predict how it operates. The work is just beginning, but enough has been accomplished that I can conclude by outlining some recent developments in theory and research methods.

The theoretical analysis of networks (more properly, "linear graphs") is a well-developed specialty in mathematics and many of the advances in understanding sentimental networks come from applications of graph theory to social relationships. Let me review briefly two important papers, both published in 1956 and both authored by research workers associated with the Research Center for Group Dynamics at the University of Michigan.

We begin with a well-known paper by Dorwin Cartwright and Frank Harary. It is a mathematical elaboration of Heider's theory, and while I must skip the details, I can note two features. The first is that Cartwright and Harary managed to generalize Heider's principles to systems involving any number of people rather than the two in the original model. The utility of this extension for thinking about networks is obvious.

Second, Cartwright and Harary deduced a rather remarkable mathematical theorem. It says that if Heider's propositions are true and if a system of interpersonal relations contains negative sentiments as well as positive ones, then the system must consist of two cliques such that within each clique all attitudes are positive while between cliques all are negative. This theorem has recently been extended to allow for multiple cliques as well as the two-clique situation.

Now, if this theorem should hold empirically—and the evidence, while promising, is just beginning to come in—it leads us to modify our notions about the web of sentiments. It is better perhaps to think of it as consisting of clusters, small groups connected internally by positive attitudes toward one another, and separated from one another by enmity or indifference. The notion reminds us of George Homans' hypothesis in his book *The Human Group,* "the liking of friends within a group carries with it some dislike of outsiders."

From this perspective, we may think of one of the major processes of attitude formation as a process in which we bring our likes and dislikes into line with those of our friends within our cluster and simultaneously move away from the positions associated with various outgroups. James Coleman in his monograph *Community Conflict* has outlined a model of the typical development of a community controversy which is quite close to these notions.

The second theoretical development is J. R. P. French, Jr.'s paper, "A Formal Theory of Social Power." French reasons that if we tend to take on the attitudes of those we admire, then if we map the flow of sentiments in a group, we merely reverse this to see the channels of influence. To the extent that sentiments within a cluster, though positive, are not equally positive, a structure of interpersonal influence will exist. Thus, for example, if A and B are friends, but A respects B much more than vice versa, then over the long haul B will influence A's attitudes more than A will influence B's. The notion is an old one. It appeared in E. A. Ross's 1920 volume, *The Principles of Sociology*, and in Willard Waller's "principle of least interest." What French does, though, is to show that if one is willing to make a few plausible assumptions about the influence process, it is possible to predict from the structure of the network of sentiments whether a group will arrive at a unanimous attitude once a process of mutual influence much like that envisioned by Heider has begun. For example, French shows that a group in which everyone likes everyone else equally will arrive at a unanimous attitude very quickly.

French shows that if sentiments are not perfectly mutual and if they take the form of a hierarchy (technically, a partial order), then the group will tend to reach as a unanimous attitude the attitude originally held by the leader. If there is no single leader, but a group of leaders, then the final common opinion will be some sort of average of their initial attitudes. To my knowledge we have no concrete data giving a specific test of French's hypotheses, but so many studies of small groups have suggested that there is a hierarchy of popularity within positive clusters that French's models seem quite plausible.

Taken together the two theoretical papers provide the following broad hypothesis about sentimental structures and attitudes: the dynamics of attitude formation involve a twofold process in which opinions within a cluster or clique move toward unanimity as followers adjust their attitudes toward those endorsed by the more popular members, while the opinions in different clusters tend to diverge from one another to the extent that intergroup sentiments are negative.

Needless to say, such models grossly oversimplify the real world, where sentiments seem often to resemble the proverbial "can of worms" rather than the neat patterns of structural models. In particular, one may hazard the guess that clustering is far from perfect in that many positive clusters contain some negative feelings and a number of people have friends in otherwise antagonistic cliques. The latter is a most interesting situation, for such persons undoubtedly serve as bridge or liaison persons who prevent the structure from breaking down into feuding subgroups.

Let me now turn from theory to research. As you might imagine, this trend toward structural theory has provided a challenge to the research worker. Studies of attitudes are usually based on sample surveys in which a large number of individuals are sampled. While we thus routinely collect information on representative persons scattered all over the web of sentiments, traditional methods give us little information about the structure itself. Obviously, description of the total web is a phenomenal challenge, and it is quite a job to cover even a small subsystem. James Coleman has treated such subsystems in his book *The Adolescent Society,* which presents findings on networks of friendship in ten high schools. Similarly, Walter Wallace has studied interpersonal influence in an entire liberal-arts college by means of a very large sociometric questionnaire.

There is, however, a research technique which promises to be of some aid. It is called "contextual analysis," and like so many advances in sociological research it is associated with Paul F. Lazarsfeld of Columbia University, although many others, especially Peter Blau of the University of Chicago, have contributed to its development. An example may give the flavor of contextual analysis.

As we all know, the decision to go to college after graduation from high school is a crucial one. Furthermore, we know from many studies in this country and others that young people from lower-socioeconomic-status levels are less likely to go on to college. What is less obvious is the finding, now repeated in several studies, that young people from lower-status origins are more likely to plan to go to college if they attend a high school where a high proportion of the students are from high-status homes. This is a contextual relationship, a correlation between group context (the social composition of the high school) and an individual's behavior. Furthermore, the finding cannot be explained by such obvious controls as intelligence-test scores.

Why should this contextual relationship turn up? Those of us who are interested in structural theories of attitudes would argue this way: a high-school student's attitude toward higher education will be strongly influenced by the attitudes of his friends and those he admires. Assuming that students from higher-status homes are initially more favorable toward a college education, then the greater the proportion of high-status students in a school the more likely it is that a low-status youngster has a high-status friend who influences him to go to college.

The example is not chosen at random, for a recent paper by Ernest Campbell and C. Norman Alexander demonstrates each of these points in a sample of students in thirty high schools. Their data show that it is friendship which explains the contextual relationship, for when friendship is held constant, the original contextual relationship no longer holds.

The Campbell and Alexander paper is the only one I know where it has been possible to document sentimental structures as the intervening variable in a contextual relationship, but if further research supports the proposition, it raises the hope that we can study the impacts of gross sentimental networks without tracing out each possible relationship, just as the statistical models of population genetics enable the geneticist to study heredity without examining individual genealogies.

We are now at the moment where ideas and hypotheses far outrun the data. For the theoretician and research worker this is a period of excitement, but for those who want well-established facts it must be a period of waiting.

Whether or not future work will support the social structural models of attitude formation and whether or not it will be possible to analyze opinion formation in the aggregate in the fashion of population genetics are open questions. Certainly the demise of the models which viewed mass media as omnipotent must give us pause. Yet the failure of a theory gives us evidence, too.

Thus, whether the final result will be to confirm the ideas I have outlined here or to reveal much better ones, we are slowly moving toward more definite answers to the problem which George Herbert Mead left us—"Which others?"

3 WORK AND LEISURE

Everett C. Hughes

The Life and Labour of the People of London was the name
Charles Booth gave to his report of a great survey of the poor
people of London undertaken in the 1890's. The several volumes
were devoted to people of the various trades—their wages, their
conditions of work; their spendings for food, clothing, drink, and
housing; and the general conditions of their life. In the title
there is no mention of leisure. But when Booth and his associates
undertook in a final set of volumes to describe *Religious Influences,* they had to admit that religion had little influence on the
laboring poor; and that Sunday had, in fact, become a day of
recreation. Facts of this same order led the American sociologist
Robert E. Park to comment in a seminar some years later that
religion was a leisure-time activity, in competition with motion
pictures and the golf courses. The survey movement, in England
and America precursor to much that was later called sociology,
was concerned with the poor, how they earned their money, and
how they spent their time and their money when not at work.
It was not a new problem, for Daniel Defoe had long before
written that

> The lab'ring poor, in spight of double pay,
> Are sawcy, mutinous and beggarly
> So lavish of their money and their time
> That want of forecast is the nation's crime
> Good drunken company is their delight
> And what they get by day, they spend by night.

In the industrial age, the urban laboring poor with money and time to spend became more numerous. In all industrial countries both their work and their leisure came to be considered social problems demanding both study and action. More and more frequently work and leisure became the two terms in titles. This came to be true of North American as much as, and perhaps even more than, of European industrial countries. Here, as in England, the early social surveys were concerned, not as today with opinions and tastes, but with the work and the spending of time and money by the working classes. The old surveys and the new are, however, not unrelated, for the present surveys are devoted very largely to the choices people say they make in spending their time and their money. The differences are in technique and also in the fact that the present-day surveys do not seek out the poor, but rather—by taking "random" samples of the population—tend to emphasize the great and growing middle level, the people who have the bulk of the buying power.

A difference between the early English social surveys and the American ones came from the fact that a very large proportion of the working people in American cities—as in Pittsburgh, where the first great American survey was done—were recent immigrants from Europe. The surveys turned out to be studies of the customs of immigrants as well as of poverty. The American Protestants who made the surveys were intrigued by the songs and dances of the immigrants, but on the whole appeared to believe that it would be good for them to be assimilated to American ways of spending their time and money. The settlement house became in America an institution where older immigrants were encouraged to practice their old-country ways of spending their leisure, and their children were schooled in American ways.

At this period—before, during, and after World War I—there arose a great movement for improving the facilities available to the masses of the people for recreation. The playground movement, efforts to plan and beautify cities, the settlement-house movement, all these were directed toward providing for the increasing hours of leisure of working people. Even the temperance and prohibition movements emphasized the importance of better facilities for recreation. They sought substitutes for that "workingman's club," the saloon, where beer and whisky as well as time were consumed. The various reform movements sought both to increase leisure and to see to it that leisure would be spent in better ways. The leisure was to be increased by getting rid of child labor and shortening the working day and week. But since free time is potentially dangerous, the same reformers sought to provide evening schools, parks, and playgrounds, and to get rid of the institutions where drink and gambling prevailed, and to promote temperance.

It is not quite exact to attribute these movements to sociologists, but the people who were coming to be called sociologists were part of these movements and a good deal of their teaching and research had to do with them. In the earlier American sociology there was not a great deal of concern with the experience of work itself; interest lay rather with the life of the workers outside their places of work.

In the meantime in France at the turn of the century, Gabriel Tarde gave his lectures on *Psychologie Economique*. In a prophetic mood he proclaimed the epoch of leisure thus:

> The economic life of man consists not only of work, but of leisure as well; and leisure, which economics almost entirely neglects, is indeed the more important to consider, in a sense, than work; for leisure does not exist for work, but work for leisure.[1]

He elaborates the point:

> In the measure that the working day is shorter for the peasant and the worker, new wants, born of new leisure, arise in these classes and open up an ever larger outlet for production. For the less men work, the more they have need to consume.

He speaks further of a past time in which increases of production merely increased the number of people of the leisure class, in contrast to the nineteenth century in which increase of production per man-hour had led to the distribution of leisure among all of the working population. Whether Tarde was right about the past, he was certainly right about his own time and the period to follow. For there has been an enormous increase of the amount of goods a man produces in an hour and a corresponding decrease in the number of hours per day, days per week and per year, which the masses of working people have to spend at wage work. If one may speak of time free from work for wages as leisure time, there has of course been a vast increase of leisure. At the same time there is no longer, in North America at least, a leisure class. Whatever inequalities of income there may be, American men are equal under the pressure and the expectation that they will work from the day they leave school until the day when they formally retire. On the whole, the working day of men with the higher incomes is longer than that of men with ordinary income. Some go to school longer, and interesting studies have been made of how much is added to their life income by each year of formal schooling.

The expectation that *she* should work has also been internalized by a large proportion of American women. A woman enters the labor market after or during her years of formal schooling, leaves it when her children are young, and is very likely to return in her thirties and to work for wages or salary for some part of her time from then on. Her work is spoken of as "part-time" work if she works fewer hours per day or fewer days per week than do men in the same place and kind of work. But since men work fewer hours than before, and since the hours of work vary in various kinds of work, the woman who is said to work part-time may be working longer than many men who are said to be working full-time. Yesterday's part-time is today's full-time, or even overtime.

One may thus speak of a colossal redistribution of work and leisure. Nearly all people expect and are expected to work. But the amount of time they put in at work varies greatly, whether measured by hours of the day, days of the week, weeks of the year, or years of a lifetime. Leisure, or time free of work, varies inversely as the time of work. But, of course, people are subject to other obligations than that of wage work, and these, too, vary according to one's age, sex, position in a family, place in society, and other circumstances.

Perhaps we should speak of a new economy of time and of its

uses, rather than simply of an increase in the proportion of the population who sometimes work for wages and a reduction of the time required to produce as many goods as people can use, given their supply of money and free time. The journey to and from work, chores about one's dwelling, the care of children, participation in various activities as well as recreation and amusement and the care of the instruments of recreation—all these take time. There are differences of opinion about which of these activities are worthy of the name leisure. We are not, in this chapter, concerned with a philosophy of leisure, but rather with the actual uses of time by the people of an industrial civilization.

Certain it is that the American economy depends very largely on the consuming power of its own working population. It is an economy in which production has reached a new high level, so that it requires great per capita consumption. Consumption requires leisure. Kenneth Boulding, an economist, calls our economy post-industrial. He means that distribution of goods and services has become more of a problem than production itself. This is reflected in the character of our labor force, which requires relatively fewer production workers and relatively more and more workers who distribute goods, produce, and services (for a service is in effect an operation in which production and distribution are one and the same). This further affects the distribution of time. In industry one speaks of work flow, meaning the manner in which all aspects of supply and preparation of materials and of working operations are so coordinated that no part of the process is delayed by another part. The ideal is continuous operation of the machinery, with workers coming and going according to the needs of the machines. Production is meant to be kept constant while the working force may vary from hour to hour, day by day, and so on, but in a predictable and manageable manner. The resulting goods can be stored, to be distributed as wanted.

In the institutions which distribute goods, produce, and services, the problem is more complicated. People demand and consume goods and services on varying schedules and calendars. For instance, just before Christmas and the New Year, as well as at other times of festival, shops and department stores require many more salespeople to serve the buyers of gifts, new clothing, and festive food. There are busy days, hours, and seasons in hospitals. Many middle-aged women are employed to help out in schools, shops, hospitals, clinics, and government agencies at the seasons of special demand on the part of the public. The work flow, however, is predictable by the use of computers, and the number of people employed can be adjusted to it; the length of the work day, and even of the careers of people at work, has thus become more and more varied and adjustable. The result is an intricate interaction of workers and consumers, each person taking his turn at both roles; one man's work is another's consumption. The more our economy depends upon distribution—that is, upon an ever-increasing consumption of goods and services—the more complicated the distribution of working time becomes, and correlatively, the more complicated the distribution of free time— that is, of leisure.

Thus far I have said little about American sociology. I have rather attempted to give an impression of the ever-changing social setting in which American sociologists work. It is a setting in which merely to keep up with the currents of change in work and leisure is itself a task requiring almost feverish investigation. And it has been characteristic of American sociology that it tries to tell the news of social change in certain areas of life; critics are divided between those who complain that we devote too much time to telling the news instead of developing general theories, and those who complain that we are always a little behind in telling the news of the main trends of our society.

What aspects of work and leisure have attracted the attention of sociologists?

One aspect is what one might call the racial and ethnic division of labor. Black Africans were early imported to North America (as also to the West Indies and South America) to work on the cotton, tobacco, and sugar plantations. Later on, great numbers of European artisans and peasants came both as settlers on the land and as industrial workers. Chinese and Japanese came across the Pacific as construction and general laborers, farmers, and small traders. We conquered and partially settled territory previously settled by French, Spanish, and Mexican people. These

37

migrations and expansions of our territory have given us an extraordinarily varied labor force. It is not merely varied but also, as in most parts of the world, patterned. Many ethnic groups have become concentrated in certain kinds and levels of occupations, industries, and businesses, but by no means always in lines of work which they had performed in their home countries. Migration has generally meant a revolution in kind and style of work. A group may have found itself discriminated against when it entered the American labor market, and again when its members tried to escape from their first kind of American work to new levels and occupations. Having achieved a place, they themselves become discriminators against newcomers; but ambivalent discriminators who espouse the social doctrine of equal opportunity and who, in considerable measure, actually practice it.

During the period of the settling of the country and the development of industry there was always demand, except in times of economic crisis, for great numbers of unskilled workers. Thus each ethnic wave of immigrants could find a place from which to rise in the labor force, slowly or rapidly. But that demand for unskilled labor has disappeared. To survive at all in the American economy, prospective workers must have experience of urban, bureaucratic work habits and must have schooling far beyond that previously required for entering the labor force. It is the fate of Negro Americans to have lost their place—miserable though it may have been—in the agriculture of the Southern states after the changes which have made it difficult for them to enter the urban, post-industrial labor force. The newcomers from Puerto Rico and Latin America are in the same situation, all of them finding it more difficult to find places because other groups are entrenched in the positions which they hoped to compete for.

Ethnic variety of the labor force has been characteristic of all countries where modern industry has flourished. The American case, because of its great diversity, its rapid growth and change, and finally its place as perhaps the first country to pass into the post-industrial phase, is a striking one for sociological analysis. American sociologists have indeed devoted a great deal of attention to the ethnic and racial aspect of the labor force, to the role of ethnic discrimination in it, and to the movements which aim to break it down. The problem still exists, with attention now turned rather more to the advance of groups hitherto concentrated at lower levels of work into white-collar, professional, governmental, and management positions.

In the 1920's a number of American sociologists and other social scientists began to study work itself, rather than the characteristics of the labor force and the social conditions in which workers live. It was a time when in all industrial countries there was much concern over the effects of mass-production techniques on workers, their incentives, and their satisfaction (or lack of it) with their work. The American sociologist Bogardus had written of "industrial fatigue" in 1911; Max Weber had written of "putting on the brakes" by industrial workers in his monograph on "The Psychophysics of Industrial Work" at about the same time. Something called industrial psychology was being developed in England.

The new American observation of industrial workers was directed toward the interaction of workers with each other and with management, the informal systems of communication and mutual control which they developed at work, and the effects on their production and their attitudes of various changes in organization and management. What amounted to a movement in American social science engaged sociologists, social anthropologists, psychologists, and students of labor and industrial management in studies of industry. Research of this kind is perhaps more prevalent than ever, although the techniques of study and some of the objectives have changed. Similar study has been extended to hospitals, social and governmental agencies, and schools; indeed, one of the major activities of American sociologists has become comparative studies of these modern organizations in which enterprise in the achieving of ends is combined in uneasy partnership with bureaucratic standardization of the rules and procedures by which work is done. To the battery of methods used in such studies have been added the experimental research of small groups and the simulating of social situations by use of computers and mathematical models.

These studies have not, as I have said, been confined to people at work in industrial settings. Sociologists have become interested in the older professional occupations, those called *professions libérales* in French and *freie Berufe* in German, but simply *professions* in English; they have also made studies of many of the newer occupations to be found in modern societies. In the nineteenth century the older professions of medicine and law were rather fundamentally reorganized; their relations to the state and the public were redefined by registration and new forms of licensing. The training for them was more thoroughly integrated with the universities than hitherto had been the case in the English-speaking world. Reorganization of those professions continues, especially with reference to the distribution of their services. In addition, there are many occupations, new and old, which claim the title of *profession* and seek the standing and the protection that go with it. It is a sort of collective social mobility, by which a whole category of people seeks to improve its standing. In England, the sociologist Carr-Saunders called attention to this whole series of phenomena, which one might call the professional trend and which corresponds to the need of modern societies for more and more esoteric services. American sociologists have also been concerned with this trend; they have studied professions from a number of angles. One set of problems has had to do with the recruitment and training of candidates for various occupations. This includes initiation into the folkways and rules of conduct of the occupation; the process is generally called "professional socialization."

Another line of study is analysis of the relations of colleagues within an occupation with one another, and the systems of relations among the various professions involved in delivering services to individuals or to organized entities, and of the professions with the public. Various kinds of professional services—medical, educational, social guidance, recreational—are now considered part of the rightful standard of living of the whole population. The distribution of these services is of necessity carried out in ways and in institutions quite different from those of the earlier period, when such services were made available to only a few of the population. The relation between the professional and the persons or organizations who are his clients is seldom simple, direct, and free of involvement with third parties. Study of the complex systems by which professional services are provided and distributed, and of the changing and often conflicting ideologies held concerning them, has become part of the on-going study of society by sociologists.

North Americans have always been self-conscious about the prestige of their occupations. As mentioned earlier, people in many occupations seek to improve the standing of the occupation as a whole, and this is not merely a matter of getting higher fees or wages. People want to be proud of their occupation. It is not surprising that the ranking of occupations according to their prestige in the eyes of the public at large has been a popular activity of American social scientists. Such rankings have sometimes been accompanied by questions as to whether the answering people thought certain occupations to be of the middle class or of the working class. Lately some studies have sought to compare the prestige ranking of occupations by Americans with those made by samples of people in certain other countries. They appear to find only minor differences in the order in which people of industrial societies rank the leading occupations, no matter what the form of government and the political philosophy of the countries. For example, a high place is given to the professions, and especially to those concerned with science and technology.

There is a paradox in these findings, for although the professions are ranked high in prestige and desirability, there is much unrest in some of them; as in Western Europe, there is, in America, talk of strikes by physicians, teachers, engineers, social workers, nurses, and civil servants. Some American sociologists have given attention to the attitudes of the professions, and especially of the lesser professions and of the whole white-collar sector of the labor force. While the people in these kinds of work, for which more and more years of schooling are required, have nominally high prestige, they are found to be uncertain of their place in society and to be rather ambivalent toward the institutions in which they work and toward the public they are expected to serve. The truth of the matter appears to be not merely that the conditions of work of the older professions have so changed that their autonomy is somewhat questioned, but that the line between professional and nonprofessional has become blurred, as has that between the lesser professions, white-collar work, and manual work.

Large numbers of people in various occupations and ranks are engaged, with less than burning enthusiasm, in courses of study pursued either in their free time or in working hours and at their places of work. These courses are designed to train those who pursue them for advancement, or to give them new skills in place of those which are becoming obsolescent. For such people, the demand for additional schooling reduces the amount of leisure time which reduction of working hours would otherwise bring.

In writing of *Leisure* for *The Encyclopaedia of the Social Sciences,* Ida Cravan had this to say:

> It is one of the most striking commentaries on modern civilization that the machine, which offers the possibility of a measure of leisure for all, as slavery made possible leisure for a few, has thus far brought only unemployment on an increasing scale, idleness for many women of the middle class and, on the other hand, extended opportunities for education and leisure to the adolescents of the community.

That diagnosis, made in the time of the great depression of the 1930's, does not fit present-day society. There are some unemployed in the United States today, but a larger proportion of the population is at work than ever before, including those supposedly idle middle-class women. The middle-class woman has an array of small machines to do her household duties for her, but she operates the machines herself. The immigrant and Negro domestic help she formerly counted upon has graduated, or their children have graduated, to other kinds of work.

The industrial worker, while often trying to reduce the number of hours in the official day's or week's work, at the same time often seeks to increase his pay and perhaps even his time away from home by working overtime or by a second job. He still has leisure; the studies of industrial workers show that a great and increasing number of them take vacation trips in their motor cars and own pleasure boats. A study of attitudes toward work on Sunday among a group of North American Catholic industrial workers showed that they wanted to avoid Sunday work, but not because it violated their notions of religious propriety. They wanted to have their days of leisure on the weekend so that they could share them with fellow workers, friends, and kinsmen. Of course, almost all American workers own and regularly use television sets which bring sports and motion pictures into their living rooms.

Most American workers have some combination of a good deal of working time and more leisure than any of their predecessors; they use their nonwork time for family life, community activities, amusements and recreation, and—in greater degree than ever before—for schooling and training. The ratio of work time to leisure time varies. What people do with their free time continues to be a major object of study by social scientists. The reason is not merely that some are concerned lest people—and especially young people—spend their free time in ways harmful to themselves and to society; it is rather that the proportion of the population with free time and with money to spend is so great and that the balance of work, leisure, and the time claimed by other activities is constantly changing. This is an aspect of life of which we Americans are, of necessity, very self-conscious.

Still another related problem engages our attention. The author who said that the machine had brought unprecedented unemployment has been proved wrong so far as the mass of the working force is concerned. But we do have a class of unemployed people. As the demand for cheap, unskilled labor has declined almost to the vanishing point, the people who formerly did such work have become chronically unemployed. Gathered into the slums of great cities or stagnating in the rural slums of certain regions, these unemployed have plenty of free time. It is not leisure, for it takes work to make leisure. Those who used to sing the praises of a leisure class did so because they believed that those who did not have to work for a living would work hard for the common weal. Whether or not they were right is of little practical concern. But it is certainly true that in our time those who cannot find employment cannot do much for the common weal. Some of the people bypassed by the affluent society are of such an age that perhaps little can be done to integrate them into the economy and the society. Others are the unemployed adolescents and youths of rural and urban slums. They are inclined to drop out of school at too early an age to have made proper preparation for employment in the new post-industrial labor force. Many studies are being made and experiments tried to determine whether it is possible, and if so, how, to adapt our educational efforts so as to motivate these culturally deprived young people to continue in school and to learn the skills, attitudes, and habits which will enable them to find the balance between work and leisure that should be the birthright of all.

NOTE

1. G. Tarde, *Psychologie Economique*. Vol. I, pp. 123, 149, *et passim*.

4 ON THE SOCIOLOGY OF SMALL GROUPS

Theodore M. Mills

A tour of universities and research laboratories in America would show social scientists and others directing their attention toward what happens among persons when they meet at close range. They are seeking a new understanding of the dynamics of small groups.

But what, one might ask, *are* small groups? More familiar to us are concepts of the individual, the organization, the institution, and the large society. Yet between the single person and the organization are units composed of two or more persons who come into contact for a purpose and who consider the contact meaningful. Some, like families, are relatively separate, while others, like boards of directors, are parts of larger units. Still others include a construction gang, a hunting party, a town committee, a ceremonial dance team, a bomber crew, and an athletic team. There are many more. In fact, with some 3.2 billion individuals in the world and with each one on the average belonging to five or six groups, and allowing for overlap, an estimate of the total number of small groups existing now would be as high as from four to five billion. When we add past and future groups to the present groups, we see that the universe of small groups runs into the many billions—many more than societies, even more than separate individuals.

Granting their great number, why study them? Four answers illustrate the range of reasons. The first is pragmatic. We need to understand what happens within such groups both because their decisions have a critical effect upon the history of com-

45

munities and because their dynamics affect the way persons lead their daily lives. We know how a handful of leaders can commit their nation to a course of action; and how decisions to continue to have babies made in private by millions of widely distributed married couples can contribute to the population explosion. And we know that the groups which surround the individual in his daily life are not only sources of respect, affection, and protection but are also causes of strain, cross-pressures, conflict, and frustration. Knowledge of group dynamics can help the person manage his group life.

The second answer is socio-psychological. Social pressures and pressures from the individual meet in the small group. It is therefore a convenient context in which to observe and to experiment on the interplay among these pressures. Scientific investigation may lead to general laws about how individuals cope with social realities.

The third answer is sociological. The direct task is to understand small groups in their own right and to create empirically based theories about the dynamics of these many billions of transitory systems, much as the task of physiology is to formulate working theories of the dynamics of transitory living organisms.

The fourth answer is more ambitious. Small groups are a special case of the more general type of system, the social system. Not only are they micro-systems; they are essentially microcosms of larger societies. They present, in miniature, societal features: a division of labor, a code of ethics, a government, media of exchange, prestige rankings, ideologies, myths, and religious practices. Through careful examination of these microsystems, theoretical models can be constructed and then applied to less accessible societies for further test and modification. Small group research is a source of effective ways of thinking about social systems in general.

The scientific study of groups is largely a twentieth-century phenomenon. Nineteenth-century sociologists were understandably preoccupied with major historical trends. Because of the newly emerging capitalist societies and bureaucratic states, the formation of new class structures, and the dissolution of the intimate groupings in the traditional community, attention was drawn more to what was forming than to what was breaking up. And a dichotomy existed between the dislodged individual and the large system. It is true that Le Play described family life, that Durkheim appreciated the importance of primary group ties in counteracting suicide, and that Simmel saw the mutuality in social relations. Yet these were exceptions: small groupings were overlooked and the dichotomy remained. New psychology dealt with the individual; new sociology with the total society.

Partly in response to this gap, Charles H. Cooley, in the United States, emphasized the affinity between the person and the group: the infant savage becomes social through intimate and prolonged interaction in the primary family group. Throughout life, close ties with other persons sustain the individual, stabilize his thought, and give him a sense of direction. Cooley noted the ease with which the boundaries between the individual and the group are magnified and the difficulty in recognizing the connections between them. Such connections were demonstrated in the work of W. I. Thomas, who showed that when groups disintegrate, persons attached to them tend to disintegrate, and in the work of Thrasher, who found that delinquent gangs train their recruits to crime, gain their loyalty, and protect them against society. This type of criminal behavior is as much a group phenomenon as an individual one.

Meanwhile, the group's effect upon individuals was being discovered by experimentalists and by physicians. Moede in Germany found that racing cyclists went faster when they had a pacer; F. H. Allport in the United States found that the presence of others facilitated superior task performance; and Sherif found that persons who lack a secure basis for judging reality tend to adjust their perceptions toward the group's definition of that reality.

The therapeutic effect of groups was discovered, quite by accident, by Pratt in Boston; he noted that his deeply discouraged tuberculosis patients gave each other a kind of aid in discussions about their problems that he could not provide professionally.

47

Important advances were made beyond this point of recognizing that groups make a difference. Industrial output, Mayo found, was materially affected by the network of group relations among workers. Not only did the workers fit their output to the standards of the informal team; their identification with the company, their sense of being part of the larger unit, depended on close primary relations of respect and affiliation between agents of the company and the informal team. Primary ties linked the single individual, the team, and the company. Later field work has affirmed the fruitfulness of Mayo's formulation. For instance, research showed that the fighting man in World War II found his strength and security through loyalty to his immediate comrades. His motivation to fight was local. He did not let his buddies down. More generally, the viability of the larger military machine depended upon an overlapping network of primary ties.

Meanwhile, Moreno, who sought to alter social arrangements in working groups to coincide more closely with the emotional relations among members, invented a technique which has proved enormously useful to sociology. He simply asked members to report to him how they felt about other members, whom they liked, whom they did not, those they wanted to work with, those with whom they did not. The device tapped the important dimension of the emotional relations among members and made it easy to chart and to compare the patterns of these relations. Researchers quickly adopted the method and now use it extensively.

A new direction was given the study of groups by Kurt Lewin, who, coming from Germany in the 1930's, envisioned a more vigorous use of the experimental method in social science. Social behavior, he asserted, is lawful—that is, it follows certain laws. Its laws are to be found through knowledge of the field of psychological and social forces which at any moment serve as causes of behavior. The science of groups depends upon locating and measuring these forces. One technique is to create different groups with known characteristics, then observe their operation. One can, for instance, set up groups under different styles of leaders, observe how the leaders act, how the members respond, compare the results, and then draw empirically based conclusions about the dynamic effects of leadership. Through these and other simple yet scientifically sound procedures, theoretically relevant hypotheses can be tested in the experimental laboratory.

Lewin attracted a generation of able social scientists. Deutsch tested the differential effects of cooperation and competition upon groups; Bavelas artificially controlled who in the group could send information to whom and tested the effects of such communication networks on group efficiency and satisfaction; Festinger, Schachter, and Bach tested the effects of group cohesion upon pressures to conform to group norms. A predominant though not exclusive theme in post-Lewinian experimental research has been the classical socio-psychological question of the group's effect upon the single member.

More distinctly sociological conceptions were presented in the early fifties, particularly in the work of Bales. In close contact with Parsons and Shils and influenced by their conceptual scheme in *Toward a General Theory of Action*, Bales presented a sociological theory of group interaction and an empirical scoring technique to go with it. Groups as miniature social systems confront the standard system problems, such as how to adapt to the realities of the immediate situation, how to accomplish the group's goal, how to hold the group together, and how to satisfy its members' needs. Groups, if at all viable, must address themselves to these problems. Since interaction among members represents attempts to resolve system problems, one may classify each act according to the problem to which it is addressed. While groups vary in their cultures, they all confront a similar set of problems. Consequently, problem-oriented categories may be used universally. By applying a standard method of classifying interaction over a wide range of groups one can discover universal responses to system problems, including trends from the beginning to the end of a meeting, tendencies of members to divide their labor, and how attempts to resolve one problem complicate others.

The importance of Bales's approach is that it shifts attention from the group's effect on people and the situation to the effects of such variables upon the group. Group processes themselves are the phenomena to be accounted for and explained. How do variables such as group size, personalities of members, emotional attachments, and so on affect the interaction process? What laws explain the process we observe? What laws explain the observable interaction throughout all small groups? Do the same laws hold for societies as well?

The simplicity of Bales's technique has led to its wide use as a standard research method. It has also led to the development of supplementary methods to tap additional dimensions of group process, such as the content of what is being said and the emotional orientation of members toward others.

While social-system theory provides an abstract conception of group dynamics, emphasis upon process provides a flexible one. Together they have encouraged both the construction of mathematical models of group interaction and the simulation of decision-making processes in the laboratory and on the high-speed computer.

These trends lead toward the systematic and the abstract. Other trends, however, lead toward closer contact with concrete events. Most important is the invention of the self-analytic group. Its purpose is to understand group dynamics through exploring its own processes. It is studied not by outsiders but by the members themselves. Historically, it is an outgrowth of group therapy and the work of Burrow, who in the 1920's presented a rationale for group therapy: emotional disorders are due to unresolved problems occurring in a network of interpersonal relations; knowledge about them can be gained better when the patient is interacting with a variety of persons than in the traditional, one-to-one doctor-patient relationship; the patient's distorted view of himself is reflected through many eyes, and his confused ways of dealing with others are brought to light and clarified. Burrow's argument was not well received and group therapy lay dormant until World War II. Heavy wartime demand, coupled with shortages of psychiatrists, encouraged group treatment. Several physicians, especially Bion in England and Semrad in the United States, saw the possibility for a new type of therapy.

In practice, however, it soon became apparent that when patients meet together, they do more than simply present their "interpersonal past." Under the protection of the therapist they draw together and create a new primary group with its own code and structure. Members tend to value their group, feel loyal to it, and identify with it. The complication is that if the therapist is to understand the individual patient, he must understand the group and its effect on the patient. In short, he must become a student of group dynamics.

One means of accomplishing this is to set up a special type of group which examines itself. At Harvard University, Semrad conducted seminars where medical students and young social scientists met together, observed their own interaction, and interpreted to each other what the group was doing. Although a simple enough arrangement, it is becoming increasingly apparent that such groups are a revolutionary departure in the sense that they are a new order of social system. The collective purpose of their members is to learn about their collective experience. Goals preoccupying other groups are set aside so that the group is free to develop an awareness of itself, to discover what its "self" is, where "self" means the group. Such groups have a built-in potential for becoming self-aware, self-knowing social systems, and consequently, of becoming a new order among social systems.

Not only do these groups draw attention to the more latent currents in the interpersonal situation and to the need for systematic methods for assessing them, they also provide participants with an immediate, pragmatic experience against which to judge myths and folk beliefs about groups. Such knowledge instills confidence. Reinforced by other research and experimentation, this confidence has led to a remarkable proliferation of attempts to explore groups more deeply and to apply our knowledge about them more freely.

We would find this illustrated concretely were we to make a tour of universities and laboratories. At Bethel, Maine, we find summer training laboratories where business executives, scientists, teachers, and others are gaining firsthand experience in group dynamics. Elsewhere, at a West coast university, we find groups of college students being given one frustrating task after the other in an experiment to determine whether women exclude weak members as readily as men do and to learn how they respond to very strong members. On another campus a group of resident psychiatrists is meeting to try to understand why their own group operates the way it does. At an East coast laboratory we find a mother, father, and their two teen-age children jointly interpreting an ink blot. The investigator tells us that they have done a similar task in their living room at home and that he is now observing how the relations among family members change as they enter the scientific laboratory. At another university an attractive co-ed is pretending to be a rigid racial bigot as part of an experiment testing how groups react to this type of deviance. At a nearby clinic a couple and their son, who is a mental patient, are working together on a series of tasks devised by psychiatrists interested in assessing the role structure of the family and the son's position in it. At another clinic first-born children are being compared with later-born children in their susceptibility to pressures to conform to group norms. At the final stop on our tour we find a large team of researchers perfecting a technique for feeding every statement in a group discussion into the high-speed computer, which reproduces almost instantaneous summaries of what is being said in a group.

What gives these varied activities coherence is the recent rediscovery of small human groups and a growing realization that we can materially advance our knowledge about them.

In its short history the study of small groups has made several important advances. First, the trichotomy among the individual, the group, and society is gradually being resolved. Rather than conceiving of the person as *outside* the group, largely pitted against and contending with it, he is more frequently seen as being *in* the group and *of* society. A case in point is soldiers in battle who are being themselves, being a group, and identifying with their nation when they fight for and seek security in each other. The affinity between person and group is becoming more apparent as data-collecting techniques go beyond classifying elements which are not shared, such as overt behavior, to include elements which are shareable, such as feelings, ideas, beliefs, and values. Extension to sharable elements provides new information about those processes that are both personal and collective.

A second advance is the shift of emphasis from study of the group's effect to analysis of the group itself, from its influence to its process, from its output to its internal dynamics. Operationally, this has meant a shift from depending exclusively upon measures taken *before* and *after* group operation to recording and analyzing processes *during* the group's operation. This advance goes hand in hand with the development of adequate methods for tracing group processes.

The third advance is the successful application of the experimental method. Rather than taking groups as they happen to exist, researchers have created them according to their own purposes, introduced experimental variations, and effectively tested hypotheses.

A fourth advance is the invention of the self-analytic group. Instead of having the observer outside of the group looking in, groups have been composed of persons who simultaneously act as participants and observers, who interact and exchange their observations and interpretations. New information is being gained on what is relevant and important to group members.

Finally, an advance is being made in the application of general social-system theory to the small group.

Though the sociology of small groups is too young for us to be able to say where it will lead, there are immediate frontiers. It needs to devise methods for tracing latent group processes, such as feelings, wishes, and unconscious assumptions; it needs to examine the transformations of long-term groups from their origin to their dissolution; it needs to expand to widely different cultures and to test how culture affects group process; it needs to know how studying and experimenting on groups alters them; and most of all it needs to create new theories to apply to group phenomena even after the groups themselves have become aware of the theories. This is likely to require a major departure from current theory—in any event, a departure from the early theories of Cooley, Durkheim, and Le Play.

5 THE STUDY OF FORMAL ORGANIZATION

Peter M. Blau

If a number of men have a common aim but each simply proceeds to work toward it as he sees fit in disregard of the rest, they are likely to work at cross purposes. Sooner or later, one of them will probably seek to improve the situation by suggesting, "Let's get organized!"

The effective accomplishment of a common task requires that men organize themselves by establishing procedures for working together. Sometimes they do so informally by coming to implicit agreements concerning how to proceed. But often, particularly when large numbers are involved, men establish explicit procedures for coordinating their activities in the interest of achieving specified objectives, which means that they create a formal organization. They establish a club or a firm, they organize a union or a political party, or they set up a police force or a hospital, and they formulate procedures that govern the relations among the members of the organization and the duties each is expected to perform. Once firmly established, an organization tends to assume an identity of its own which makes it independent of the people who have founded it or of those who constitute its membership. Thus organizations can persist for several generations, not without change but without losing their fundamental identity as distinct units, even though all the members at some time come to differ from the original ones. The United States Army today is the same organization as the United States Army in the World War of 1914–1918, even though few if any of its 1918 personnel have remained in it and its structure has undergone basic alterations.

The collective efforts of men may become formally organized either because all of them have some common interests or because a subgroup has furnished inducements to the rest to work in behalf of its interest. Factory workers organize themselves into unions to bargain collectively with management, and management has organized their tasks for the purpose of producing goods marketable for a profit. Unions and factories exemplify formal organizations, as do government bureaus and political parties, armies and hospitals.

THE CONCEPT OF FORMAL ORGANIZATION

Although a wide variety of organizations exists, when we speak of an organization it is generally quite clear what we mean and what we do not mean by this term. We may refer to the American Medical Association as an organization, or to a college fraternity; to the Bureau of Internal Revenue, or to a union; to General Motors, or to a church; to the Daughters of the American Revolution, or to an army. But we would not call a family an organization, nor would we so designate a friendship clique, or a community, or an economic market, or the political institutions of a society. What is the specific and differentiating criterion implicit in our intuitive distinction of organizations from other kinds of social groupings or institutions? It has something to do with how human conduct becomes socially organized, but not—as one might at first suspect—whether or not social controls order and organize the conduct of individuals, since such social controls operate in both types of circumstances.

There are two basic principles that govern social life, and organizations manifest one of these. Social structures may emerge as the aggregate result of the diverse actions of individuals, each pursuing his own ends, or they may reflect the joint endeavors of individuals pursuing commonly accepted ends. Thus, as individuals and groups in a community compete, enter into exchange relations, and use their resources to exercise power over others, an economic system and a class structure develop which reveal organized patterns of social conduct although nobody has explicitly organized the endeavors of individuals. The government of a society or a football team, on the other hand, are social structures deliberately established to achieve certain objectives, and the regularities observable in them reflect the deliberate design. The distinction is essentially the one William Graham Sumner makes between "crescive" and "enacted" institutions. Social systems produced by formally enacted procedures rather than merely emergent forces are organizations. Whereas the distinction is an analytical one, since crescive and enacted forces typically interact in their effects on social systems, it finds expression in concrete entities—the many organizations that can be found in modern societies.

Whenever groups of men associate with one another, social organization develops among them, but not every collectivity has a formal organization. The defining criterion of a formal organization—or an organization, for short—is the existence of procedures for mobilizing and coordinating the efforts of various, usually specialized, subgroups in the pursuit of joint objectives. If all relations among the members of organizations and all their activities were completely predetermined by formal procedures, however, organizations would evidently not pose meaningful problems for scientific inquiry, because everything about them could be ascertained by simply examining the official blueprints and procedure manuals. Actually, the social interaction and activities in organizations never correspond perfectly to official prescriptions, if only because not all prescriptions are compatible, and these departures from the formal blueprint raise problems for empirical study. Paradoxically, therefore, although the defining characteristic of an organization is that a collectivity is formally organized, what makes it of scientific interest is that the developing social structure inevitably does not completely coincide with the pre-established forms.

Organizations generally have an administrative machinery, a specialized administrative staff responsible for maintaining the organization as a going concern and for coordinating the activities of its members. In a large factory, for example, there is not only an industrial work force directly engaged in production, but also an administration composed of executive, supervisory, clerical, and other staff personnel. The term "bureaucracy," which connotes colloquially red tape and inefficiency, is used in sociology neutrally to refer to these administrative aspects of organizations. The common element in the colloquial and the scientific meaning of the term is that both are indicative of the amount of energy devoted to keeping the organization going rather than achieving its basic objectives. Not all soldiers are actually in combat; not all employees of manufacturing concerns are production workers; not all members of police departments are out "on the beat"; many members of every organization have the administrative task to maintain the organization. But wide variations among organizations exist in the degree of bureaucratization, as indicated by the amount of effort devoted to administrative problems, the proportion of administrative personnel, the hierarchical character of the organization, or the strict enforcement of administrative procedures and rigid compliance with them.

WEBER'S THEORY OF BUREAUCRACY

In his classical theory of bureaucracy, the German sociologist Max Weber outlined the distinctive characteristics of formal organizations that are bureaucratically organized. The most important of these characteristics are:[1]

1. Organizational tasks are distributed among the various positions as official duties. Implied is a clear-cut division of labor among positions which makes possible a high degree of specialization. Specialization in turn promotes expertness among the staff, both directly and by enabling the organization to hire employees on the basis of their technical qualifications.

2. The positions or offices are organized into a hierarchical authority structure. In the usual case this hierarchy takes on the shape of a pyramid wherein each official is responsible for his subordinates' decisions and actions as well as his own to the superior above him in the pyramid and wherein each official has authority over the officials under him. The scope of authority of supervisors over subordinates is clearly circumscribed.

3. A formally established system of rules and regulations gov-

57

erns official decisions and actions. In principle, the operations in such administrative organizations involve the application of these general regulations to particular cases. The regulations ensure the uniformity of operations and, together with the authority structure, make possible the coordination of the various activities. They also provide for continuity in operations regardless of changes of personnel, thus promoting a stability lacking in many other types of groups and collectivities, such as social movements.

4. There is a specialized administrative staff whose task it is to maintain the organization and, in particular, the lines of communication in it. The lowest level of this administrative apparatus consists of the clerical staff responsible for keeping the written records and files of the organization, in which all official decisions and actions are embodied. Whereas the "production" staff contributes directly to the achievement of the organization's objectives, whether this involves producing cars, collecting taxes, fighting wars, or curing patients, the administrative staff contributes to goal achievement only indirectly by keeping the organization itself going.

5. Officials are expected to assume an impersonal orientation in their contacts with clients and with other officials. Clients are to be treated as cases, the officials being expected to disregard all personal considerations and to maintain complete emotional detachment, and subordinates are to be treated in a similarly impersonal fashion. The social distance between hierarchical levels and that between officials and their clients is intended to foster such formality. Impersonal detachment is designed to prevent the personal feelings of officials from distorting their rational judgment in carrying out their duties.

6. Employment by the organization constitutes a career for officials. Typically an official is a full-time employee and looks forward to a lifelong career in the agency. Employment is based on the technical qualifications of the candidate rather than on political, family, or other connections. Usually such qualifications are tested by examination or by certificates that demonstrate the candidate's educational attainment—college degrees, for example. Such educational qualifications create a certain

amount of class homogeneity among officials, since relatively few persons of working-class origin have college degrees, although their number is increasing. Officials are appointed to positions, not elected, and thus are dependent on superiors in the organization rather than on a body of constituents. After a trial period officials gain tenure of position and are protected against arbitrary dismissal. Remuneration is in the form of a salary, and pensions are provided after retirement. Career advancements are "according to seniority or to achievement, or both."[2]

Weber presents an implicit functional analysis of the interdependence between the characteristics of bureaucracy, with rational, efficient administration as the criterion of function. Effective accomplishment of complex administrative tasks on a large scale requires that they be subdivided into specialized responsibilities, which can be readily handled by individuals, and that professionally qualified experts be appointed to discharge these responsibilities. This pronounced division of labor creates serious problems of coordination, particularly in a large organization. A special administrative staff is needed to maintain channels of communication and coordination, and a strict hierarchy of authority serves to effect the coordination of diverse tasks in the pursuit of organizational objectives by enabling superiors on successive levels to guide, directly or indirectly, the performance of increasingly wider circles of subordinates. But close supervision of all decisions is inefficient and produces strains. The system of official rules is designed to standardize operations and restrict the need for direct supervisory intervention largely to extraordinary cases. Professional training and official rules notwithstanding, however, strong emotions and personal bias would interfere with the ability to make rational decisions. The emphasis on impersonal detachment has the function of precluding the intrusion of such irrational factors into official decisions. Lest the impersonal discipline in the hierarchical bureaucracy alienate its members, secure careers lessen this burden and promote loyalty to the organization.

In brief, the problems created by one condition in the organization stimulate the development of another to meet them. A number of interdependent processes of this kind give rise to the constellation of features characteristic of the typical bureaucracy, as conceptualized by Weber. He held that these features of an administrative organization and, especially, their combination are "capable of attaining the highest degree of efficiency."[3]

INFORMAL ORGANIZATION

Weber has been criticized for presenting an idealized conception of bureaucracy. His implicit functional scheme addresses itself to the problem of how a given element of the organization contributes to its strength and effective functioning. What is missing is a similar systematic attempt to specify the *dysfunctions* of the various elements[4] and to examine the conflicts that arise between the elements comprising the system. Thus, even if it is true that the hierarchy of authority promotes discipline and makes possible the coordination of activities, does it not also discourage subordinates from accepting responsibility? Or, granted that promotion should be based on objective criteria rather than on personal considerations or family connections, which of the two major criteria is to be selected—seniority or merit? When questions such as these are raised, it is seen that Weber's one-sided concern with the functions of bureaucratic institutions blinds him to some of the most fundamental problems bureaucratization creates.

Another criticism of Weber's analysis that has been advanced is that he is preoccupied with the formally instituted aspects of bureaucracies and ignores the informal relations and unofficial patterns which develop in formal organizations. Selznick has emphasized that the formal structure is only one aspect of the actual social structure and that organizational members interact as whole persons and not merely in terms of the formal roles they occupy.[5] Many empirical studies of work groups in formal organizations have called attention to the importance of the informal organization that emerges in these work groups and that constitutes a dynamic force in the organization.

To be sure, Weber realized that actual practice does not follow in every detail the formal blueprint. The new discovery was, however, that these departures from official procedures are not idiosyncratic but become socially organized. The social patterns that are informally organized by the participants themselves complement those formally organized for them by management. Furthermore, the informal organizations that always arise in formal organizations, as Barnard pointed out, are essential for operations.[6] Simultaneously with Barnard, a research team arrived at the same insight from its study of industrial workers in an electric plant.

Roethlisberger and Dickson[7] found that the informal relations in a work group assumed a distinctive structure, with subgroups and status differences, and that informal norms emerged that regulated the performance of workers. Specifically, workers were expected by their fellows neither to produce too fast nor to produce too slowly, and deviations from these group norms were penalized by ridicule, loss of status, and, eventually, ostracism. In other words, workers informally organized themselves to control output, and an informal status structure complemented this organized social control. The informal organization, therefore, had important implications for production.

Research on human relations in industry proliferated widely after this pioneering study, and a number of case studies of bureaucracies have attempted to apply its insights in order to refine Weber's analysis. Gouldner, for example, shows that managerial succession in an industrial organization promoted bureaucratization, as implied by Weber's theory, because a new manager unfamiliar with informal practices is constrained to rely on official procedures to implement his directives. But such exercise of authority that rests on bureaucratic rules and discipline should be distinguished from professional authority that rests on technical expertness, a distinction Weber failed to make explicit.[8]

The general conclusion that emerges from these case studies of informal organization in bureaucracies is that procedures formally instituted for specific purposes in organizations recurrently create disturbances in other respects and the informal patterns that typically arise to cope with these disruptions often

61

produce a basic reorganization of operations. Whereas the focus on informal practices and relations permitted some refinement of Weber's theory, it also led investigators increasingly away from the study of the fundamental structural features of complex organizations.

RECENT RESEARCH ON ADMINISTRATIVE STRUCTURE

The purpose of a theory of formal organizations is to explain the distinctive features of these complex structures in terms of some general principles; for instance, to explain under what conditions an advanced division of labor develops in organizations, or a separate administrative staff emerges, or an explicit body of rules becomes elaborated. In other words, a theory of organizations cannot take the characteristics of organizations as given but always raises the question of why these characteristics came into existence. The first step in answering this question is to discover which characteristics of organizations tend to occur together, and this requires comparing the characteristics of many different organizations. A basic limitation of the case studies of work groups in organizations is that they have to take the characteristics of the single organization under investigation in each case as given and merely examine how these given characteristics influenced informal relations and practices. These case studies, therefore, necessarily neglected the central problem of organization theory—namely, what produces various bureaucratic characteristics—since this problem can only be studied in a comparative framework in which many organizations are contrasted. Weber's analysis is clearly conceived in such a comparative framework in which the characteristics of the organizations themselves are the center of attention. Case studies of organizations do not have this primary focus, but recent research has again adopted such a comparative approach.

Thus, a number of empirical studies have investigated whether the proportionate size of the administrative staff is bigger in large organizations than it is in small ones. Since Weber held that large organizations are more bureaucratized than small ones and that the elaboration of the administrative machinery is a bureaucratic characteristic, his analysis implies that the relative size of the administrative component should be directly associated with the size of an organization. Actually, however, studies of industrial concerns, hospitals, and some other organizations found that the proportionate size of the administrative component decreases as the size of organizations increases.[9] To be sure, more complex organizations have a larger administrative ratio than simpler ones, and large organizations tend to be complex, but the proportion of staff devoted to administrative tasks declines with increasing size. There is an economy of scale which enables larger organizations to get along with a proportionately smaller administrative staff.

At least one aspect of bureaucratization, the elaboration of the administrative apparatus, is not a function of increasing size, contrary to what Weber implies. Other aspects of bureaucratization, however, appear to be directly related to size, in accordance with Weber's analysis. Thus, one study found a very strong relationship between the size of government agencies and the division of labor in them; the larger an agency, the more specialized are responsibilities.[10] Written rules and procedures also seem to be more prevalent in large organizations than in small ones.[11] Moreover, these recent comparative studies corroborate also some of Weber's propositions about the functional interdependence between organizational characteristics. For example, although task specialization improves operating economy in government agencies, it makes the organizational structure more complex, and the problems of communication produced by such complexity impede economy. A sizable administrative apparatus, apparently serving the function of coping with these problems of communication, restores operating economy in complex organizations.

Comparative research on organizations promises to contribute most to the refinement of organizational theory by indicating the conditions under which various bureaucratic characteristics tend to arise. Finally, one more illustration from an exploratory study of written rules in different types of organizations may be cited. An important and widely discussed issue is that of the relationship between professionalization and bureaucratization. Weber implies that the two tend to occur together, whereas some of his critics have indicated the fundamental differences between these two methods of rationalizing social action. One might assume, for instance, that professionalization lessens the need for explicit written rules. However, the comparative analysis suggests that this is not necessarily the case. If professional organizations are compared with nonprofessional ones, it seems that professionalization has a standardizing effect on the elaboration of written rules. Specifically, professionalization tends to encourage the development of written rules when few exist, as in small organizations, and to discourage their development only when many exist, as in large organizations. The discharge of professional responsibilities appears to be hampered not only by excessive bureaucratic rules that impinge on discretion but also by rules that are insufficient to create an orderly working environment. The tentative conclusion from this exploratory study, which needs to be confirmed in future research, is that professionalization promotes the development of explicit rules in organizations as long as few exist, but that it impedes the fuller elaboration of rules once many exist already.

Comparisons of many organizations are needed to arrive at conclusions of this type, because only such comparisons can specify which characteristics of organizations generally occur together and what conditions give rise to them. Comparative research promises to contribute most to the advancement of organization theory, since the refinement of the theory Weber outlined requires further specification of the conditions under which organizations develop various constellations of attributes.

NOTES

1. Max Weber, *Essays in Sociology* (New York: Oxford University Press, 1946), pp. 196–204, and *The Theory of Social and Economic Organization* (Glencoe, Ill.: The Free Press, 1947), pp. 329–336.
2. *Ibid.*, p. 334.
3. *Ibid.*, p. 337.

4. See Robert K. Merton, *Social Theory and Social Structure* (Glencoe, Ill.: The Free Press, 1957), pp. 50–54, who calls attention to the importance of systematically investigating dysfunctions as well as functions.

5. Philip Selznick, "Foundations of the Theory of Organizations," *American Sociological Review*, XIII (1948), 25–35.

6. Chester I. Barnard, *The Functions of the Executive* (Cambridge: Harvard University Press, 1958), pp. 115–123.

7. Fritz J. Roethlisberger and William J. Dickson, *Management and the Worker* (Cambridge: Harvard University Press, 1939).

8. Alvin W. Gouldner, *Patterns of Industrial Bureaucracy* (Glencoe, Ill.: The Free Press, 1954).

9. For a summary of such studies, see Peter M. Blau and W. Richard Scott, *Formal Organizations* (San Francisco: Chandler, 1962).

10. Peter M. Blau et al., "The Structure of Small Bureaucracies," *American Sociological Review*, XXXI (April 1966).

11. Peter M. Blau and Amy W. Orum, "Conditions of Bureaucratic Formalization" (forthcoming in a book edited by Albert J. Reiss, Jr.).

6 SOME SOCIOLOGICAL ISSUES ABOUT AMERICAN COMMUNITIES

Albert J. Reiss, Jr.

Communities are among the more ubiquitous units of social organization. With few exceptions men organize their daily activities more or less permanently around a common territory. The resulting collectivity is a community.[1] The members of a community interact within an institutional context that derives largely from the great or mass society and is organized on a locality basis. While there is considerable variation among communities in a society, they are essentially microcosms of the society.

Nowhere is this more apparent than in advanced industrial societies such as the United States. While American communities vary in the size and density of their settlement patterns, their economic base, the social composition of their populations, and in the scale of their organization, their institutional and structural arrangements are essentially similar. The class stratification system of American society, for example, is fundamentally the same in all American communities, though the distribution within the class system varies among communities in the United States. Therefore, though one city may be more "middle" class and another more "working" class, the class relationships, the prestige accorded classes, and the behavior of class members are much the same in both communities. For this reason as one moves from one community to another in the United States, he carries his class status with him.

As microcosms of the larger society, American communities, then, show considerable similarity. Yet they show considerable variability as well. However, not all ways that communities in the United States vary are documented equally well. Variability in the composition of their populations, their functional differentiation, the residential segregation of the population along class and ethnic lines, and of the mobility of the population all are well documented. There likewise are studies of differences in the power structures of communities, the optimum size of cities to sustain various cultural activities, and of their economic base and political organization. What perhaps is most lacking is documentation of variation in the ways that the values and organization of the larger society are integrated and function in local communities. Nor is much known about how patterns of innovation and adaptation of local communities to the value structure and organization of the larger society vary among communities.

Within these limitations on our knowledge we shall discuss several issues that the literature of sociology on American communities has generated over the past decades. These may be identified as, first, a decline in community autonomy over organizations and functions located within it. Concomitant with this decline is a growing dependence of the community and its inhabitants upon the culture and organization of the great or mass society, upon organized subsystems that lie beyond the control of the community, and upon other communities.[2] Second, there is a concern with a loss of identity of residents with the local community. A corollary to this is the growth of a mass culture and of the association of members around specialized rather than communal interests.[3] Third, there is a concern with elite control of decision-making and governmental processes in local communities, processes that presumably are organized around democratic forms.[4] Finally, attention is being turned to the community as the arena where many of the value and organizational conflicts in American society actually are played out. In connection with this concern, attention also is being directed to the role that local communities play in stabilizing and changing the social institutions and organization of the great society.

The concern with the autonomy of communities arises from a number of sources: a professional concern with the extent to which the community may effectively plan and control the local environment, a political concern with the operation of democratic processes in the society, and an ideology of localism that is part of the value organization of American society. Considerable evidence is mobilized to document a decline in community autonomy.

A striking feature of communities in advanced industrial societies such as the United States is their interdependence on one another and their dependence on institutional and organizational systems that derive from the larger society. Interdependence among communities in these societies arises in part from the fact that they compete for common, natural, and social resources such as water, land, and tax revenues, resources that usually are scarce and therefore must be allocated. But it arises also from other conditions related to the mobility of both goods and people in a dynamic society, and the problems these exchanges generate for social control.

Clearly a society characterized by dynamic interdependence limits autonomous action. Yet with the growing interdependence of communities in American society, new institutional and organizational means have been developing, as elsewhere in the world, for relating communities and their inhabitants to one another. Some of the major means for relating communities to one another derive from the state and federal polities and their power to create formal organizations for handling problems that arise from the relationship of a community and its inhabitants to others. Indeed, the major formally organized way that American communities exist is as political jurisdictions chartered by the states. Deriving their sovereignty from the state, American communities have always been subject to concurrent jurisdiction with other local units such as the county and legally limited by state and federal jurisdiction.

To a growing extent in the United States these new organizational means for relating communities to one another take the form of functionally specialized authorities, often on a metropolitan or regional basis. These authorities generally assume jurisdiction over a particular function or activity such as transportation, water and sanitation, schools, or law enforcement. The

Metropolitan Boston Transportation Authority, the Chicago Sanitary District, the rural and urban consolidated school districts, and the Los Angeles, California, and Dade County, Florida, law enforcement agencies are examples of such functionally specialized units that serve a large number of political communities in a metropolitan area. But communities are related to one another not only through polities but by organizations in the private sector as well. Community-based activities such as competitive sports organized into leagues and the many voluntary organizations built around public and private functions of communities are examples.

The relation of communities to state and federal polities has been changing toward more state and federal programs related to urban planning and problems. The extent to which federal programs related to urban problems have grown has been recognized in the creation of a cabinet position, Secretary of Urban Affairs. The large number of programs relating to public housing and transportation, urban redevelopment, and the underprivileged in communities undertaken by the federal government undoubtedly change the relationship of the local to federal government. Yet it would be a mistake to assume that such programs serve only to weaken local power and autonomy. Most such programs in the United States are vested in home-based organizations that are accountable to local as well as federal authority. In many ways they have enormously increased the power of local bureaucracies, providing resources that could not be commanded otherwise.

Perhaps the most significant change in communities in the United States (as elsewhere in advanced industrial societies) is a consequence of the ways that communities are integrated with the larger society.

To an ever growing extent, the component organizations within a community become units of organizations whose scope and influence lie beyond the community. One of the important consequences of this fact is that decisions affecting organizations in a community, and therefore often the functional integration of the community itself, are made by individuals or organizations that are not part of the community. The policies and programs of organizations in any locality, then, seem to a growing extent to be made in centralized offices that are more responsive to their organizational demands than they are to those of the community or to the members of the organization who live in it.

In large part these changes come about as a consequence of the economies of large-scale enterprise, the advantages of bureaucratic organization of functions, and the power that develops from large-scale organization. It is as true for the many voluntary organizations that are based in a community as it is for industry and labor. Collective bargaining, for example, becomes less responsive to the requirements of a local community than it does to the requirements of an international union and the industry or craft around which it is organized. And a vertically integrated national corporation is less responsive to what consequences a decision about one of its member units will have upon the community than what effect that unit has upon the corporation.

While many American communities today undoubtedly are subject to external contingencies and decisions that lie beyond local control, the case can be overdrawn. As Thernstrom has pointed out in his historic study of Yankee City,[5] much of the important industry in the early period of many American cities was controlled by capitalists who resided outside the community. Perhaps the change is more one of scale than of kind.

A growing literature on mass culture and organization and on identity with the community strongly suggests that Americans are less tied to local than they are to specialized or extra-local interests. They are characterized as having lost a sense of identity with the local community, as apathetic in local politics, and as mass men.

While these characterizations often are poorly documented several things appear to characterize the relation of contemporary Americans to their local community. Studies of American communities show that their residents identify named areas that have more of a status ascriptive function than a locality function in the sense of a place where residents carry out much of their activity.[6] To the degree that residents utilize local facilities, they are primarily governed by contingencies of convenience rather than by a sense of solidarity with the local organizations.

There is considerable variation among the residents of a local community in the extent to which they are oriented toward it and its problems. Since the studies by Merton of "local" and "cosmopolitan" persons, it is clear that a substantial proportion of persons in any community are "locals" in the sense that their primary interests lie in and their orientations are toward the community where they reside.[7]

Furthermore, a number of studies make clear that while the local neighborhood may have declined as the basis for primary relationships, the urban family typically has extensive contacts with kin who reside in the local community.[8] Other studies show that most urbanites today spend perhaps more, rather than less, time with the nuclear family, largely as a consequence of the decline in hours spent at work and that occupation rather than community size is the major factor in social contact with others on a primary basis.[9]

Finally, it seems clear that with the growth of mass culture there are fewer sharp differences among the residents of American cities. Even the poor have access to television; there are fewer differences in dress and even in life style. Though mass culture may have standardized differences among inhabitants, the distances between the elites and the mass have been reduced in American communities. Indeed, as Edward Shils has pointed out, the mass in modern societies today is perhaps closer to the center than ever before.[10] The same undoubtedly holds for American communities, as is evidenced by the growing pressure they place upon the elites for equality of rights, access to the means of the society, and access to the sources of power.

Studies of American communities stress not only that there is a decline in autonomy to make decisions but that there have been shifts in the power structure of these communities and in their domination by local elites. The main point appears to be that local decisions are made by a local elite that more often today consists of public officials and professionals who are indirectly controlled by economic interests. They suggest that public issues and decisions are controlled by these elites rather than by the members of the local community through processes of referendum and civic control. The facts are complicated, however, by questions of the structure of decision-making in American communities, particularly the role that the electorate in any large community can play in decision-making. Without much comparative study it is difficult to know precisely what elite control means. Decision-making in American communities in the nature of the case represents a balancing of interests. The evidence suggests that whose interests tend to be maximized depend to a great extent upon the issue. Elite control perhaps is less substantial than some studies suggest, particularly since the community is involved in many decisions that lie beyond the control of any local elite. Any local elite in its attempts to control is restricted in part, therefore, to issues that lie primarily within the domain of local autonomy.

Mention has been made of the fact that communities are a microcosm of the larger society. In a most important sense, however, the American community is the arena where the value and organizational conflicts of the larger society are played out. This should be quite apparent in considering the current conflicts that beset American society—conflicts over civil rights, the control of programs to aid the underprivileged, over the quality and quantity of education, over employment and public assistance, even to a degree over international policies.

Such issues clearly come to focus in American communities not only because a community is above all a place where daily activities take place but because, on the one hand, the values of the larger society and their organization impinge on people in their daily lives and, on the other hand, quite often the main agencies for implementing these values and for exercising social control operate in and through the community.

The current conflict surrounding civil rights may serve as a case in point. It is within the confines of the community that some Americans experience differential treatment—in local housing markets controlled by local real estate interests, in local schools where educational means are not equal, in local employing establishments where jobs are not available, or in local cultural facilities where discrimination operates. National pressures to change the situation must operate in part through the mobilization of local groups and organizations operating on these local situations as well as through general system organizations.

It is in the community that violence erupts and where rioting must be dealt with. Under these circumstances it is the local police who first are called upon to enforce the law and it is the local courts that are usually called upon to administer justice—even though in some cases they are under a more general jurisdiction. A local community, too, has considerable power to legislate—legislation that affects people's rights and opportunities. For in the United States much of the law in relation to land use, traffic, housing, health, education, and welfare is developed and enforced at the local level. The community is likewise a major political unit in either stabilizing or changing these conditions. It is not surprising, therefore, that one is most likely to encounter conflict and violent outburst in the context of a governing community in the United States. Indeed, it attests to the fact that communities are perhaps more autonomous and viable as units in the American social system than much of the literature of American sociology suggests.

Geared, as it has been for much of its recent history, to investigating the current structure and functioning of American communities, sociology in the United States has neglected the investigation of the community as the arena within which value conflicts of the society are often engendered, frequently carried on, and usually resolved. The sociology of the next years may well redress these omissions.

NOTES

1. See Amos Hawley, *Human Ecology: A Theory of Community Structure* (New York: Ronald Press Co.) pp. 257–258, and Talcott Parsons, *The Social System* (Glencoe, Ill.: The Free Press, 1951), p. 91.
2. For a summary discussion of this topic see Roland L. Warren, *The Community in America* (Chicago: Rand McNally & Co., 1963), Chapter 3.
3. *Ibid.*, Chapter 3. Also see Maurice R. Stein, *The Eclipse of Community.* (Princeton, N.J.: Princeton University Press, 1960).
4. There is a voluminous literature in American sociology on community

power structures beginning with the work of Robert S. and Helen M. Lynd, *Middletown in Transition* (New York: Harcourt Brace & Co., 1937).

5. Stephen Thernstrom, "Yankee City Revisited: The Perils of Historical Naivete," *American Sociological Review*, XXX (April 1965), 234–242.

6. H. Laurence Ross, "The Local Community: A Survey Approach," *American Sociological Review*, XXVII (February, 1962), 75–84.

7. Robert K. Merton, "Patterns of Influence: A Study of Interpersonal Influence and of Communications Behavior in a Local Community" in Paul F. Lazarsfeld and Frank N. Stanton (eds.), *Communications Research, 1948–1949* (New York: Harper and Brothers, 1949), pp. 189–214.

8. Michael Aiken, "Kinship in an Urban Community." Unpublished Ph.D. dissertation, University of Michigan, 1965.

9. Albert J. Reiss, Jr., "Rural-Urban Status Differences in Interpersonal Contacts," *American Journal of Sociology*, LXV (September, 1959), 182–195.

10. Edward Shils, "The Theory of Mass Society," *Diogenes*, XXXIX, 45–66.

7 THE FORMS OF URBANIZATION

Charles Tilly

For the first ninety-nine hundredths of his time on earth, man lived without cities. In the last ten thousand years he has made up for that long lack with a vengeance. Since the new type of community grew out of the settled agriculture in the lands from the Bosporus to the Persian Gulf between 8000 and 3000 B.C., almost every increase in man's capacity to organize collective efforts and to exploit his physical environment has brought a new spurt of urban growth. Of course, there have been lulls and even reversals of the trend; the period of European history westerners rather parochially call the Dark Ages is only one example of *de*-urbanization. Yet cities have expanded much more often than they have contracted. Their share of all the world's population has grown enormously—practically nil in 3000 B.C., less than 1 per cent in 100 A.D., less than 5 per cent in 1800, perhaps a third in 1965. Their range of influence over the population not actually living in cities, as well as over each other, has increased most of all. How many people are now really outside the range of a big city?

The most sweeping of all the surges of urbanization the world has seen so far is still going on today. We might think of it as beginning around 1700. We might consider it a joint product of large-scale industry and the emergence of nation-states. In reality this is only shorthand for much more complicated processes.

We do not yet understand these complex processes very well. Two very large questions stand in the way. First: Do certain changes in the way men live and organize their activities occur whenever cities grow, regardless of whether their growth depends on industrial production, imperial expansion, international trade, or something else? Is there a single, sweeping process of urbanization? Second: Leaving aside the growth of cities in ancient China, or medieval Europe, or West Africa of four centuries ago, does the industrial urbanization now going on in so many parts of the world follow a common path and lead to a common type of city? Will the countries just moving into industrial production on a large scale repeat the urban histories of the countries which industrialized earlier?

The two questions call for these general answers: To begin with, no one really knows. Next, when it comes to the details of urban organization, there is neither a single, sweeping process nor an unchanging common path. Then, the kind of activity that is producing urban growth—industry, trade, administration, or something else—strongly marks the whole process. Yet, finally, some uniformities do seem to show up in all varieties of urbanization, countries undergoing industrial urbanization do have some experiences in common, and in some respects cities in all sections of the world are moving in the same direction.

Why *don't* we really know how standard the changes occurring in urbanization are? One reason is that theoretical and practical definitions of both "cities" and "urbanization" vary too much. They tend to agree in pointing to cities as communities in which the coordination of the activities of large numbers of people outside their own boundaries takes place, and to urbanization as the concentration of human activities in such communities. But when it comes to specifying, classifying, and indexing, every country and every group of investigators invent their own rules. So even if there were some perfectly standard progressions in the course of urbanization, the welter of conflicting definitions and incompatible statistics could easily hide them from view.

We also lack reliable data. Only a minority of the world's nations have ever taken a reasonably accurate census of all their inhabitants—and it takes at least two good counts to get a clear picture of shifts in the location and composition of the population. Only a tiny number of countries—Sweden, for example—

have anything like continuous registers making it possible to follow population movements from month to month or year to year. No country has a social accounting system allowing the quick, reliable detection of changes in organizational membership, kinship organization, religious allegiance, or even occupational mobility. The valiant recent efforts of the United Nations to assemble international demographic statistics have not eliminated the unhealthy mixture of incomplete information and inconsistent definitions.

Finally, we don't know simply because urbanization is so complicated, because by its nature it occurs only when a great many other confusing things are happening. Many researchers have done one version or another of a study which consists of selecting a number of countries, ordering them in terms of the proportion of population living in cities and in terms of a number of other measures of complexity (such as the flow of mail, income per capita, or proportion of the work force in manufacturing), then examining the relationships among the different measures. They have always found a close connection between the level of urban population and the other variables. The tightness of the statistical connection probably represents the crucial role the growth of cities plays in a society's modernization. But the very combination of crude measurement, short time span, and tight statistical connection makes it almost impossible to sort out the sequence, the causal relations, or even the extent to which the various indicators are really measuring the same thing over and over. As it is, the student of urbanization must coax the regularities from a blotchy historical record, a lumpy mass of inconsistent statistics, a tangle of personal impressions, and a motley, fragmentary array of studies dealing with particular cities, regions, and times.

The first thing that strikes someone who begins to work with this material is the diversity of cities and urbanization. The eminent anthropologist Claude Lévi-Strauss tells us that when he first saw South America after spending his youth in Europe he felt disturbed because the "scale of man and the scale of things had been stretched so far apart that a common standard was no longer possible." The buildings, streets, and cities were just too big. American visitors to Europe regularly have the opposite experience: they find European towns, even the great ones, quaint, crowded, and contained.

Part of this effect comes from the sheer scale of structures and spaces. Another part comes from variations in population density. Even in the United States the density of very large cities ranges from the 900 residents per square kilometer of Dallas to the 9,000 of New York City and the 30,000 of New York's central island, Manhattan. The effective range of densities is even greater, since the intensity of contact among the people using a city also depends upon the volume of daily movements into and out of the center, the extent to which people are stacked up vertically as well as spread out over the city's surface, the amount of activity which goes on in public places rather than indoors, and the sheer pace of movement in the city. The experience of being in one city or another varies accordingly.

North American cities of a given size operate at lower densities than do cities in most other parts of the world. One of the most important reasons is that they have grown up with means of transportation—especially the automobile—encouraging dispersion of the population and consuming a great deal of central city space. Even compared with New York's 9,000 residents per square kilometer, Moscow's 14,000, Paris' 28,000, or Old Delhi's 50,000 give a different texture to daily experience. Since devices like subways and skyscrapers extend New York and Moscow far above and below the surface, while high-density cities such as Delhi, Singapore, or Cairo hug the ground, the statistics greatly understate the variety of density, and therefore of life, at street level.

The statistics also average out complicated variations within each city. Densities normally peak in the center, fall off toward the periphery, cluster along transport lines, pulse with the city's daily rhythm, and fade out in irregular blocks of little-used land or water. Furthermore, the whole pattern varies systematically by type of city—South American cities have higher densities in the new settlements at their perimeters than comparable North American cities do; the decline of density with increasing distance from the center is more drastic in compact Asian cities than in sprawling American ones; industrial cities produce a distinctly nodal pattern of densities and their fluctuations; West African cities break into relatively homogeneous fragments, each one containing a distinctive national or regional population, plus a dense off-center nucleus of commerce and industry. Finally, in western countries recent urbanization has commonly produced a sequence consisting of rapid rises in the densities at the very centers of cities followed by long declines as the cities spread out, while Asian cities, much more often cramped for space, have commonly experienced continuous increases in central density. The difference shows up in the sense of unused space an Asian sometimes feels in the middle of an American city. The urban-density map is like a thumbprint: unmistakably the imprint of a city, varying systematically with the type of city, yet in many particulars representing a single, unique community.

The same blend of uniqueness and uniformity appears in the pattern of land use or in the residential locations of different parts of the population. The geographic site individually shapes land use and dwelling areas. Rio de Janeiro embraces a spectacular harbor. Tokyo expands around a great bay. Princely Buda and mercantile Pest were long divided, then finally united, by the Danube. Because particular societies and special types of cities develop affinities for certain kinds of sites and standard ways of dealing with them, however, even the terrain can help produce uniformity amid the diversity of cities. North American lakeside cities like Toronto, Cleveland, and Chicago, for example, share patterns of rectilinear streets leading to the port, of expansion first along the lake and then at right angles to it, and of remarkably regular, rank-ordered movements of the population toward higher-prestige areas at increasing distances from the center.

What is true of individual cities is even truer of the paths by which they develop. They are enormously various; even cities and urbanizing regions moving in the same general direction retain the stamp of their previous histories. Topography shows these traces of the past most clearly, as boulevards follow the lines of former city walls, capital buildings replace castles, and choked, irregular streets recall neighborhoods established before

79

the automobile. The traces also remain in social organization—the dualism which sometimes reaches the point of producing an "old" and a "new" city in former colonial capitals, the tough persistence of national or tribal divisions, the continuing influence of some traditional elites. Seen from up close, the forms of urbanization display a bewildering diversity.

Seen from a little farther back, the forms of urbanization take on a little more order, an order depending on the major activities encouraging urban growth. In this day of mass production, it is easy to think of *all* urbanization as if it were some version of the concentration produced by large-scale modern industry, the main question being whether the version is timid or bold. There are two things wrong with this assumption: first, several other sorts of activities distinct from manufacturing have in the past reliably spurred urban growth; second, these various activities produce somewhat different forms of cities and patterns of urbanization.

Even in the absence of dramatic changes in manufacturing, the quickening of trade, the forceful building of empires, the rise of new religious organizations, and even the conduct of agriculture on a large and bureaucratic scale have in their own ways regularly encouraged urban concentration. China has only recently begun aggressive industrialization, but China has through most of human history been one of the most urban—and urbane—lands of the world. (This long experience gives an ironic twist to Vice-Premier Lin Piaou's recent call to the "rural areas of the world," led by China, to unite against the "cities of the world," led by Russia and the United States.)

Japan's urban history is not quite so long, but it antedates Japan's industrial growth by centuries. After a lapse of almost two hundred years, Tokyo is again about the largest city in the world. Industrial expansion has played an enormous part in its return to pre-eminence. In the few centuries after the emergence of the city in the 1500's, however, its first sensational expansion depended mainly on its role as capital and central market. The imperial palace was the nucleus from which the great city grew, and even today the life of Tokyo seems to swirl around it rather than any other focal point.

Such dominant structures often record the activities which have prevailed in the building of the city—the fortress and the temple in the traditional Japanese city, the cathedral in the older European town, the office building in the American metropolis. The shapes of cities and their social organizations vary significantly with the activities that build them. Compare the medieval European trading city, with its legal freedom, its governing corporation of merchants, its center pre-empted by a church and a city hall, both strategically near a vast market place and fair ground, fed by tortuous streets blending shops and houses, with the coal-burning nineteenth-century manufacturing city, with its dominant factory area and central business district, its sharp separation of home from work, its geometric lines of transportation, and its incredible ebbs and flows of internal traffic. Then compare both with the traditional Islamic city: fortress, market, and central mosque placed at the intersection of two of the very few streets cutting through the entire city, quarters originating as the settlements of different tribes and nationalities living unto themselves (often walled off from one another) and reproducing in miniature the institutions of the city as a whole, hectic mixtures of land use, an unending encroachment of private uses on public space, an absence of formal arrangements for municipal government, a religious-intellectual elite, the *ulama,* mediating among the quickly shifting factions of the city and speaking to the sultan on behalf of its population. No single activity built any of these cities. But commerce marks the medieval town, mass production the nineteenth-century city, and imperialism plus religion the Islamic metropolis.

The same differences appear in the relations of these cities to their hinterlands. The medieval European city stood among landlord-run villages from which it drew surplus people as migrants and surplus food as subsistence, only slowly and incompletely drawing the villages into dependence, hardly affecting their techniques of daily living. The nineteenth-century industrial center grew in pace with energetic changes in agricultural production, rural landholding, and country life, drew rural people in swarms from short and long distances alike, relied for its vitality both on efficient transportation and on a constant extension of markets into the hinterland. In the old Islamic city the military rulers commonly exacted tribute, food, and a measure of allegiance from the surrounding countryside; nomadic tribes maintained permanent bases in town; people forced off the land by famine, flood, disease, or war straggled to the cities; and the cities themselves grew by adding new, self-contained, homogeneous settlements, very much like the rural communities from which their inhabitants came.

Variations on this last form, of course, appear far outside the Islamic world. One of the fundamental dimensions among the world's cities today goes from those which are organized around a complex, specialized, but partly unified and distinctly urban occupational structure to those which are largely agglomerations of transplanted villages and villagers. All real cities have something of both: there are still Algerian neighborhoods in Paris and Italian neighborhoods in New York, while Nigeria's Yoruba cities have many residents in specialized occupations who claim no tribal ties. Yet the difference in balance between the two forms of social organization produces a large contrast between the social life of Paris and the social life of Ibadan.

The two forms often confront each other with a special sharpness in colonial outposts and cities which used to be colonial outposts. They are divided much more than most settlements into dual dwelling areas, markets, communication systems, and living styles. One pole is the old, indigenous town, the other the compound established by some European power during the eighteenth or nineteenth century for the purposes of trade and military control. Here we have Cairo, the labyrinthine native city to the east, the strangely Parisian colonial city to the west. There is prewar Shanghai, with the international quarter of tall buildings and spacious streets standing out from the low roofs and huddled houses of the Chinese city. Again Delhi, Old and New, splits into high-density and low-density, eastern and western, traditional and modern. Since such major colonial centers often became national capitals with the departure of the European governors, many post-colonial nations are now either struggling to knit together the unwieldy halves of their ruling cities or attempting to move their governments to new, planned, unified, and less clearly colonial settlements elsewhere.

Part of this powerful dualism of colonial outposts comes from the role they have played in the larger territories under their control. The word "parasitic" may be a trifle too strong, but the word "extractive" surely is not. Now, all cities are extractive to some degree, since they always seize their subsistence, security, and population from some hinterland, and since they almost always act to accumulate, convert, and redistribute surpluses of energy, goods, food, power, and capital taken from their dependent territories. Colonial outposts simply emphasize this sort of extraction more than most. They usually do it by concentrating on the exportation of raw materials and plantation-produced foodstuffs. Such a concentration (as compared, say, with the manufacture of textiles) draws a very distinct line between those involved in the trade or its protection and all others in the economy. The line passes through the colonial outpost itself, separating the traders and the administrators from the rest of the population. In East Africa the positions of Dar es Salaam as an exporter of sisal, or of Zanzibar town as an exit first for slaves and then for cloves and coconuts, make the point very well.

When successful, the exporting city concentrates a great deal of a country's resources, population, and power in a single location. Scholars have called the most extreme cases "primate cities" to stress their overwhelming priority over other settlements in their areas. Bangkok, Jakarta, and Rangoon—all many times larger than their nearest competitors—are favorite examples. On the whole, city sizes in the larger western countries fall into an intriguingly regular order, with the largest city something like twice the size of the second largest, three times the size of the third, and so on. For that reason, North American geographers immediately take notice of the large share of all the urban population that Accra has in Ghana, Colombo has in Ceylon, or even Buenos Aires has in Argentina. Colonial history accounts for many of these primate cities. Today, countries exporting large volumes of raw materials are still significantly more likely than others to have their populations, activities, and power concentrated in a single metropolis.

Whether such a concentration helps or hinders is a matter about which regional planners argue furiously. Some point to the waste and danger of having all eggs in the same basket, but others reply that where there are few eggs, the only way to have an omelette is by putting them all together. In any case, the location and sheer amount of urban population have turned out to be a crucial policy issue for nations undertaking planned industrialization.

The policy problem appears in far more countries than the former colonial territories. For whether the cities already in existence grew mainly through trade, conquest, or something else, their organization differs from that of large industrial centers. Many sociologists make a fundamental distinction between the industrial and "pre-industrial" forms of cities or urbanization. As we have seen, this distinction could hardly gain its value from any extraordinary uniformity of the types of urban growth other than industrial. Rather, it makes sense because today the industrial form is practically superseding all others in most parts of the world, and because in sheer scale and rapidity it stands out from all the rest.

Up to two centuries ago, no country ever had much more than a tenth of its people in cities, and no city ever had much more than a million people. Today, England has only a tenth of its people left in the country, Italy alone has three or four cities in the million class, and by some definitions Tokyo and New York approach twenty million. With significant help from the growth of the modern nation-state, industrialization did it.

But just what did industrialization do? The easy part is to point out the effects of new technologies. Large-scale industrial production favors the agglomeration of producers, markets, and middlemen more than ever before, as well as producing a material surplus to support complicated specialties and institutions. Scientific agriculture sensationally reduces the number of men in the country needed to support 100 men in the city. Speedy, flexible transport and communication permit a single center to remain in contact with complex activities spread over vast territories. Organized sanitation and medical services reduce the odds that cholera or dysentery will decimate a huge city's population. And the techniques of city building themselves—steel frames, reinforced concrete, prefabricated housing—increase the possible pace and scale of construction.

Not that new technologies automatically and painlessly produce big, modern cities. Almost all industrializing countries extract a large part of their working capital from a more or less reluctant countryside. They do it by means of taxes, corvées, drafts, price controls, and outright seizures. Where the efficiency of agriculture is rising fast and the central government or the entrepreneurs adept at creating and then seizing the surplus, the extraction may work to the first advantage of the cities and the industrial establishment. England looks like such a case.

Often, however, the mobilization of surplus goes badly, and the hinterland evades central control. Indonesia has such problems. In any case the process means bitter rural-urban conflict and some form of expanding coercion from the city. To take an oddly relevant example, one of the powerful undercurrents of conflict during the French Revolution developed from the incessant demand for grain the primate city of Paris placed on the trading towns and villages within its grasp. The civilian "revolutionary armies" which marched out into the provinces from the capital had politics on their minds, but they gave their most persistent attention to assuring the grain supply. Many another country has discovered the same convergence of the needs of its revolution, the needs of its economic expansion, and the needs of its cities.

The struggle of city versus country occurs in all kinds of urbanization. Industrial urbanization simply exaggerates the process by its extraordinary pace, scale, demands for capital, and pressures for concentration. Many of the uniformities in industrial urbanization are of this sort: matters of scale rather than peculiarities of the process by which industrial cities grow.

Among other regularities in industrial urbanization, however, the "industrial" is probably more important than the "urbanization." As the process moves on, the division of labor in a nation's cities clearly becomes more complex, specialists in coordination, communication, and control more abundant, formal organization more prominent, the use of the city's space more differentiated, the rhythm of mobility more frenzied—at least up to a point. It is probably also true that in the industrial city the nuclear family of father, mother, and children alone gains new independence and importance as compared with the clan, lineage, or other larger kinship group; that the proportion of all people's lives spent in tight-knit groups of friends, neighbors, and kinsmen goes down; and that impersonal situations and channels of communication assume a larger part in everyday life, although these are points of hot debate and vigorous qualification.

The real question, however, is what part industrial cities and urbanization *as such* play in the major changes that do occur. For American sociologists of thirty years ago, much taken by Louis Wirth's labeling of "urbanism as a way of life," the big city itself was the villain or the savior. The mass of research since then has inconsiderately made the situation less clear by showing that it is more complicated. It has shown that in such highly industrialized countries as England, France, and the United States the big cities still contain large patches of presumably traditional social organization—transplanted villages, extended kin groups, and so forth. More important, it has traced the diffusion of the characteristic industrial forms of social organization far beyond the cities, and thus made us wonder even more how necessary is the connection between the one and the other.

What we *can* say is, first, the development of cities on an unprecedented scale is a normal part of industrialization; second, in the course of industrialization cities become even more crucial stations in the coordination and control of activities going on throughout the society; third, the characteristic forms of industrial society reach their fullest expression in big cities; fourth, cities play a special role in exposing people to the ways of industrial life, both by attracting and assimilating newcomers, by accumulating and displaying innovations, and by spreading the news outside.

The spread and exchange of life ways from city to city and city to country encourage a standardization of some crucial activities throughout the society. The imposition of uniform clock time is one example: things and people running on schedule. Something important lies behind the fact that Russia and the United States lead the world in studies of how people spend their minutes and hours.

Language provides another example of urban standardization: standard Italian over the last century has spread from cities like

Florence and Rome to replace (or at least coexist with) the countless dialects which used to break up the linguistic map of Italy; in Africa the linguae francae such as Hausa arose first as tribal languages, then became media of communication among different tribal groups in large cities, and finally spread as national and international tongues. Because the tempo of innovation, the degree of specialization, and the almost inevitable appearance of chinks, cracks, nooks, and crannies in very complex structures works against total standardization, standardization of some parts of life usually goes along with diversification of other parts. This confounds critics who see all of urban-industrial life marching toward gray monotony. The standardization is great enough to permit men to transport easily their accumulated experience, as well as themselves, from city to city. They do, increasingly.

In the early stages of industrial urbanization, when the death rate in the great cities more or less neutralizes their gains through births and there are few other cities to draw on, mass migration from the countryside supplies the new urban population. Some of it is permanent, some of it temporary. Much of it consists of villagers joining people already in the city to whom they are connected by kinship or common origin. The predominance of this sort of migration helps produce the city of tribal, regional, and national enclaves we discussed earlier. The Congo's Stanleyville, with its distinct settlements of Lukele, Bamanga, Bakusu, and other tribes, is a good example; so is the Chicago of fifty years ago, proud to be one of the largest Polish cities, one of the largest German cities, not to mention its concentrations of Czechs, Greeks, Italians, and many others. Gradually the rural sources of migrants diminish while mobility remains high, so exchanges of population among cities take on greater and greater importance. Nowadays three-quarters of the newcomers to American metropolitan areas come from other big cities or their suburbs.

As migration changes character, the rate of transmission of men and of messages from city to city and within big cities rises rapidly. The substitution of the transmission of images for the transmission of whole men, through such devices as telephones and television, is proceeding so steadily that one might expect the mobility of persons to level off while the volume of messages accelerated. So far (with jets, trains, and cars covering ever more passenger-miles) no country has yet seen that leveling off. Nevertheless, the most striking effect of the industrial city in the long run will probably be its impact on human communication. By its massing of people, information, and complex tasks, the industrial city has steadily overworked existing means of storage and transmission, and consistently stimulated the invention of new means, from the pneumatic tube to the text-reading computer. In a few generations, industrial urbanization has created a new type of man attuned to media of mass communication and regulating important areas of his life by those media.

It is important to avoid thinking that the general trends of industrial urbanization follow a single, inevitable track. While their experiences have some important common features, Japan is not simply recapitulating the history of England. The fact that other nations have already passed along the trail lets the latecomers examine a record and borrow a technology the first ones could not use. And the starting situation differs. Most countries now in the earliest stages of industrial urbanization are outside the Western European tradition, feel critical population pressures, face powerful competition from other wealthier nations, and have adopted substantially different political arrangements from the western countries which began the process earliest. Deliberate public policy is playing a larger part in the form of industrial urbanization than ever before. Controlled migration, careful land-use planning, the establishment of new cities, and governmental decisions about industrial location all make the developing nations today's chief laboratories of urbanization. It would not be amazing if the genuinely new ideas in urban organization began to come from their experiments, reversing the past flow of innovations from highly urbanized countries to the rest of the world.

Industrial urbanization will continue to transform the world for some time to come. Most likely we have even bigger cities in store, although it is conceivable that a new form consisting of carefully controlled, geographically separate settlements, lightning-linked by lines of power, transport, and communication, will emerge. Few countries will escape intensive urbanization. But the forms will again be various.

We have a great deal to learn about the processes of urbanization. Yet we know that industrial urbanization brings some standard changes into a nation's life, that the major activity stimulating urbanization seriously marks its character, and that every country plays its own variation on the common theme. Urbanization takes many forms—all the forms of man.

PART II

Methods of
Investigation

8 MEASUREMENT

Paul F. Lazarsfeld

Without knowing it, most of us have feelings or make decisions which imply measurements. We say that our mood is better today than yesterday. We hire a housekeeper by deciding that one candidate is more suitable than the others. Those of us who have children have to act as if we knew what balance of freedom and discipline were best for them. Most of the time, we do not need to be very precise in such matters. But the greater the social consequences, the more explicit do we have to be.

An admissions officer in a college has to develop careful criteria for selecting one candidate rather than another; the economic success of a factory may well depend upon whether the manager really knows what kind of supervision is most effective with teams of workers. If we are sociologists, it becomes one of our tasks to clarify the nature of measurement and quantification in matters where social relations are involved.

All of our initial examples implied the idea of ranking. One thing was preferable to another, a situation improved as compared with the preceding one, a certain type of organization is more efficient than another. Such rankings are indeed the core of measurement problems.

As a matter of fact, a good definition of the vague term "measurement" would be to call it a search for ordered classification. Around this core, we can then introduce all sorts of qualifications. It is useful to remember what we do with physical objects. A classical example of ranking is the arranging of minerals according to their hardness, which we say is their resistance to scratching. But sometimes we are concerned only with a "pass and fail" classification; we have a weight limit on jockeys and are interested only in whether the riders are above or below this weight. In other situations, we want much more precision than a ranking would provide; if we are on a diet, it makes quite a difference whether we lost half a pound or a full pound last week. It is advisable not to restrict the word measurement to any one of these procedures. If we first define it in a loose way, we can make finer verbal distinctions when they are needed. The term quantification is used wherever numbers are implied, but in fact it has the same meaning as measurement.

Once we have accepted a reasonable terminology and have abandoned loose comparisons with the physical sciences, we face the central problem of quantification in the social sciences: the complexity of the objects with which we are dealing necessitates developing "units" which are not immediately obvious, and there is a lack of "theories" which would right now permit a decision between equally reasonable alternatives. The following pages will illustrate these themes.

Let us start with a pervasive measurement problem in the social sciences, the stratification of society. We have a vague feeling that there is something like being higher up or lower down on the social ladder. But what do we really mean by this? Certainly money is involved, but money cannot always buy prestige, as anyone knows who has studied *The Social Register*. Certainly, prestige is also something we have in mind when we think of stratification. We could go on analyzing our imagery and would probably soon think of other elements in our minds —power, for one. But for the moment, it is sufficient to think of money and prestige as two "components" of stratification. The complexity which we mentioned before is already obvious in assigning an individual to a social class. How do we rank a member of an old distinguished family with little money left as compared to the upstart with ample means? No general answer can or should be given. It depends upon the special problem at hand. For some purposes the right thing is to average the two components of wealth and prestige, then the impoverished gentleman and the *nouveau riche* would be on the same level, with the wealthy prestigious person above and the impoverished anonymous man below. For other purposes, we would focus on what has been called status discrepancy. Taking people at the same average class level, we might want to know whether there is something peculiar about those whose average of prestige and wealth is the result of very discrepant components. People with great status discrepancy, for example, are more likely to vote for a radical party as compared with those whose rank on the same level derives from, say, higher prestige and lower income.

Clearly, we have done some cheating in the preceding paragraphs when we talked of averaging income and prestige. Income has a clear numerical measure, but how do we get numbers for prestige? There are many ways to go about this task, and two of them deserve special attention. One technique uses ratings expressed by people whose opinion matters. Prestige is a good example if we reflect on what we mean by it. Prestige is the feeling of respect and envy other people have toward a person. But as sociologists we do not think of one individual but of many people like him, and we know that in a modern society, it is the occupation of a person that chiefly determines his standing in the community. As a result, many studies have been done to find how occupations are ranked by the population at large. A small sector of such prestige ranking is as follows:

OCCUPATION	SCORE	RANK
Nuclear physicist	93	2
Banker	85	24.5
Bookkeeper	70	49.5
Bartender	48	83

We still wonder how the numbers in the "score" column of this table have been developed. One simple way is to ask people to judge occupations as having excellent, good, average, somewhat below average, or poor standing. We then assign arbitrary numbers to these ratings. Excellent = 100, good = 80, average = 60, somewhat below average = 40, poor = 20. We average the ratings from all respondents. A variety of statistical problems are involved in this rating procedure which we cannot discuss

95

here. But it is gratifying to report that such occupational prestige scales have turned out to be quite stable when studies were repeated after a period of ten years or compared from one western country to another.

One still might wonder how one adds up dollars and such a prestige rating to get at a stratification level, but that is not too difficult because one can convert dollars rather easily into a similar rating. We leave it to the reader to think of such methods when he faces the following task: he wants to rate the income of various academic levels from full professors down to the teaching assistants without revealing their actual salaries.

Sometimes it is difficult to apply ratings directly. In a dog show the judges might easily disagree if they judge the dogs over-all. More agreement is reached if separate ratings are made for posture, skin, ears, and so on; the average ratings then settle the final outcome. With very complex social objects it is often impossible to rate any aspects directly. One has to resort to indicators which are ultimately combined into scales. These so-called itemized scales are probably the most frequently used measuring instruments in sociological work and so they deserve special attention. We shall assume that someone wants to rank cities according to the degree of their integration. To develop a scale he is likely to go through four steps.

1. *Reflection on the Initial "Imagery."* The thought and analysis which culminate in a classificatory instrument begin with a rather vague image or construct. The investigator might perceive disparate phenomena as having some underlying characteristic in common. Or he may have observed certain regularities and is trying to account for them. In any case, the concept, when first created, is some vaguely conceived entity that makes observed relations meaningful. The investigator, concerned with "integration," might think of people who like each other, who co-operate in the improvement of their city, who walk in peace, and would hate to live elsewhere. He also will have different problems in mind. What accounts for degrees of integration? What consequences has it for the life of the citizenry? Whatever the starting point, after a while a second step will appear necessary.

2. *Concept Specification.* The originating imagery is specified by "aspects," "dimensions," and the like. In the case of integration of communities one might argue as follows. The elementary units of social groups are norms and people. Integration then has to begin with two dimensions: a cultural dimension which requires that the prevailing *norms* are not contradictory; and a personal dimension referring to relations between *people.* The latter are of two kinds: *discussion,* requiring the exchange of symbols, and *functional,* referring to the exchange of goods and services. Finally, it is necessary that people obey the prevailing norms, which brings out a *normative* dimension of integration. The next problem, then, is to find concrete indicators for these dimensions. This is the step at which "itemized scales" differ from ratings.

3. *Selection of Indicators.* How does one "think up" indicators? The problem is an old one. William James has written in *The Meaning of Truth*: "Suppose that we say a man is prudent. Concretely, that means that he takes out insurance, hedges in betting, looks before he leaps. As a constant habit in him, it is convenient to call him prudent in abstraction from any of his acts." James proceeds from an imagery to a series of indicators suggested directly by common experience. Actually one would not expect a "prudent" man to hedge in betting *always,* or to take out insurance on *all* possible risks; instead, one would talk about the *probability* that he will perform any specific act as compared with a less prudent individual. And one would know that the appropriate indicators might vary considerably, depending on the social setting of the individual.

To find indicators for the integration idea, the dimensional analysis gives good leads. What conflicts of norms—love thy neighbor but maximize profit—occur in belles-lettres, in court decisions, in personal conflicts? How much communication is there between people, how much prejudice between groups? To what extent does everyone's daily life depend upon what others produce, how often or how easily is the circulation of these services interrupted? How often do people violate norms (crime rate could be an indicator); how seriously do they take their civic duties, as indicated, for example, by their contributions to public charity? After indicators have been selected for each dimension, one has to recombine them because one cannot operate with all those dimensions and indicators separately. This leads to the final step.

4. *The Formation of Scales and Indices.* Many indices for the goodness of cities exist in the literature, some unidimensional, some multidimensional, and still others only concerned with a specific dimension. The final merits of such numerical computations often cannot be decided before a long time of use; all depends upon the value of the propositions to which the computations lead and how well the propositions in turn combine into larger systems. Often one hears discussions to the effect that a certain scale does not "really" reflect the intended concepts. This frequently helps in the considering of more convincing dimensions or of additional indicators. But no absolute decision is possible. What can be done is a sharp clarification of the procedures involved. A large number of mathematical models have been developed to clarify the combination of indicators.

Our summary gave, of course, an oversimplified version of the operation involved and leaves many problems undiscussed. But to highlight the main points the following remarks are pertinent:

1. The operations involved apply to individuals as well as to collectives and to inanimate objects. Whether one talks of temperaments of people or compares patterns of culture, there is the same task: one has to devise classificatory systems into which a concrete given object can be allocated.

2. These classifications are always intended or latent ones. Combinations of indicators are used in order to decide where an object is most likely to belong. The relation between manifest observations and latent classifications can best be demonstrated by its similarity to a medical diagnosis which uses a variety of tests to decide whether a patient has an infarction of the heart. Logicians have developed a general theory of disposition concepts of which the procedure under discussion here is a special case.

3. The relation between the manifest observation and the intended classification is a probabilistic one. A man might maintain his basic position, but by chance shift on an individual

indicator; or he might change his basic position, but by chance remain stable on a specific indicator. But if one has many indicators in a scale or an index, it is highly unlikely that a large number of them will all change in one direction by chance, when the man—or the group—one is studying has, in fact, not changed his basic position.

Itemized classificatory instruments, if compared with measurements in the physical sciences, have two disadvantages. First, they do not have a natural zero point as do measurements of length or width. But then neither does the measurement of heat where zero degrees Fahrenheit is chosen quite arbitrarily. Second, and somewhat more serious, is the problem of distance between the points on our sociological scale. No one can claim that on an ordinary measure of integration the distance between 30 and 40 is the same as the distance between 40 and 50. There are a variety of ways to alleviate this difficulty, but they are too complicated to be explained here. Actually it is not really serious, because in empirical work we are mostly interested in general relations rather than in very specific details. Thus it is significant to note that with increased education people score less on the famous F-scale which measures authoritarian personalities. At the present state of our knowledge, we really do not care how much difference one more year of education makes in this way. Or, in observing the work done by small groups, we find that people who have a tendency to talk more to their fellow members will also more often be asked their opinion and their advice. Such interrelations are expressed by so-called coefficients of correlation where the details of increase or decrease are neglected.

Many of the scales used in sociological research, especially those which deal with attitudes and opinions, are based on direct questions put to the people whom we are studying. It is at this point that one additional difficulty comes up. Our respondents might know what we are trying to study and give answers which are advantageous to them in specific circumstances. Techniques have therefore been developed which tend to disguise the purpose of our investigation. Here is an example of those projective techniques:

An investigator studying the industrialization of new countries often wonders whether people there are ambitious in a western sense and to what extent they are willing to work hard, if properly rewarded. To measure such levels of aspiration, a typical projective test would consist of showing pictures of somewhat ambiguous situations. An adult man might be talking to a boy, or a young man might be sitting in his shirtsleeves in front of a desk late at night. You then ask people to give their interpretation, to tell a story about those pictures. Will they say the grown-up man and the young boy are father and son, and the father is telling the boy that he should work harder in school, or will they say that the father and the boy are planning a fishing trip? Will they say that the man at the office desk in his shirtsleeves late at night is doing some hard work to get a promotion, or will they say that he is someone who is just trying to steal money out of the drawer of the desk in order to have an easier time? These interpretations are then used to get ideas as to the degree of aspiration, of achievement needs people have. It seems that in various not yet industrialized countries the level of aspiration so measured differs considerably and that the administrators of technical assistance have been able to make good policy use of such findings.

In principle, every characteristic of a person, a group, or an organization can be translated into some kind of measurement. An empirical study will consist of interrelations between such measures which we usually call variables. A considerable number of such variables is needed to arrive at meaningful findings. In the United States, for instance, when one uses a scale of political interest one can find the rather trivial result that people who are interested in politics are more likely to vote. This finding gets more interesting when we study men and women separately. The correlation between interest and voting is much lower for men than for women. But now we would like to understand this result better. Is it that for men the social pressure to vote is much greater so that they go to the polls even when they are not much interested? To test this interpretation, additional variables have to be developed. One possibility might be a questionnaire in which men and women are asked in a variety of ways whether they are conscious of the civic duty to vote. But we might also have recourse to techniques which do not involve any questioning at all—by observing, for instance, whether more voting propaganda reaches men in offices and factories than reaches women at home. Such observational techniques are sometimes called unobtrusive measures, the most famous example coming from the period of Prohibition; at that time, consumers would not readily have told how much they drank, but it was possible to count the number of liquor bottles discarded in trash cans.

There is scarcely an area of social life where one cannot find quantified data, and in many ways, the techniques of the sociologist have influenced other disciplines. Whereas the economists have been concerned with budgets as the way people spend their money, we now provide them with the idea of time budgets. A whole new field, the economics of leisure, is profiting from the large bulk of sociological data on what people read, what their TV preferences are, and so on. (Incidentally, mass communications research has been important in documenting how great the differences in tastes are among the various social strata.) Psychologists have always been interested in the formation and change of attitudes, but their evidence was based on small-scale laboratory experimentation. This can now be supplemented by the many large-scale studies done to evaluate advertising and political campaigns. These, in turn, have affected the work of the political scientist. We now have so-called panel studies where respondents are repeatedly interviewed as to their voting intentions. By this technique, people who change their party affiliations can be detected just at the time of their shift. As a result, tracing the role played respectively by party machines, propaganda media, and personal influence becomes possible. In the field of history, quantitative sociological techniques take two forms. Instead of quoting arbitrarily a newspaper editorial or a letter, historians are now likely to pick representative samples of such documents and to give a numerical picture of the distribution of opinions; as a matter of fact, such systematic content analysis has already entered the computer age. And secondly, election data which have been available as historiographical sources since the beginning of the nineteenth century are now being treated differently. The analytical techniques mentioned above have enabled the political scientist to consider an increasing number of variables and develop more sophisticated explanations of political trends.

Some aspects of this joining of forces deserve special attention. When quantitative procedures are combined into larger systems, formal mathematics begins to be an appropriate tool. This trend is only now developing and is too complicated to be presented here. Although one cannot claim that the social sciences have led to completely new mathematical ideas, they certainly have contributed to the interest in the development of algebra and probability, just as engineering problems have stimulated the growth of differential calculus.

Quantitative methods have also helped to break down the barriers between separated social science disciplines. The most outstanding example is the rapidly growing field of comparative research. The problems of underdeveloped countries and the competition between Eastern and Western political systems led to an intensified interest in studying large national units from every aspect—economic, political, and cultural. To transfer observations from one country to another and across institutional areas scarcely seems possible without constructing new yardsticks which will convert the small scales of sociologists to bolder dimensions.

Inventing ever more refined techniques to develop scales and combine them into ever more complex interrelations is the main task of the empirical sociologist. But how much is still to be done! A subtle piece of analysis might involve so many variables that they become empirically unmanageable, or a problem might be so complex that it is just too costly to approach it by quantified methods. Take, for instance, the question of which of two types of psychotherapy, Freudian or Adlerian, say, is more successful. We would first want to know what types of cases are channeled to doctors belonging to the two schools; we would have to separate the doctors' techniques from their general personality; rather clear criteria of cure are needed; and finally, this kind of study requires a long period of time to distinguish immediate from long-lasting success.

No wonder, then, that there are considerable controversies as to the importance of quantification. Fortunately, two extreme positions are quickly disappearing from this debate. The early pioneers at quantification argued that it made the social sciences more "scientific." Not only is this phrase an empty one; it can be downright misleading if it is meant to create a false sense of kinship with the prestigious natural sciences. Other opponents argued that social phenomena were so elusive that they could never be caught in the net of cold numbers. It is hoped that the preceding discussion shows the underlying misunderstanding. Many complex ideas can be translated into the language of variables and their interrelations; and just as no textbook on electricity will ever capture the full majesty of a thunderstorm, we should not expect that even the most subtle tables can fully reflect the complexity of the social fabric.

More moderate opponents of quantification sometimes fear a kind of imperialism which obscures the merits of non-quantitative methods. No one can deny that intuitive interpretation and broad historical perspective are crucial tools for the sociologist. As a matter of fact, there is much need for the clarification of these qualitative methods so that their relation to quantification can be more easily perceived. On the other hand, it is sometimes claimed that quantitative results are mostly trivial and establish only what is obvious to everyone anyhow. It seems appropriate to end these remarks with a short discussion of this problem of obviousness because it will permit the reader to form his own judgment.

During World War II, the American army conducted a large number of studies among soldiers in various battle areas and in training camps at home. After the war, the director of these studies, S. A. Stouffer, summarized the findings in a comprehensive four-volume report. The following paragraphs select a few of the quantitative results and then suggest why they might appear obvious to some readers.

1. Better-educated men showed more psycho-neurotic symptoms than those with less education. (The mental instability of the intellectual as compared to the more impassive psychology of the-man-in-the-street has often been commented on.)

2. Men from rural backgrounds were usually in better spirits during their army life than soldiers from city backgrounds. (After all, they are more accustomed to hardships.)

3. Southern soldiers were better able to stand the climate in the hot South Sea Islands than Northern soldiers. (Of course, Southerners are more accustomed to hot weather.)

4. White privates were more eager to become non-coms than Negroes. (The lack of ambition among Negroes is proverbial.)

5. Southern Negroes preferred Southern to Northern white officers. (Isn't it well known that Southern whites have a more fatherly attitude toward their "darkies"?)

6. As long as the fighting continued, men were more eager to be returned to the United States than they were after the German surrender. (You cannot blame people for not wanting to be killed.)

We have in these examples some of the simplest types of interrelationships which provide the "bricks" from which quantitative sociology is being built. But why, since they are so obvious, is so much money and energy given to establish such findings? Would it not be wiser to take them for granted and proceed directly to a more sophisticated type of analysis? This might be so except for one interesting point about the list. Every one of these statements is the direct opposite of what actually was found. Poorly educated soldiers were more neurotic than those with high education; Southerners showed no greater ability than Northerners to adjust to a tropical climate; Negroes were more eager for promotion than whites; and so on. If we had mentioned the actual results of the investigation first, the reader would have labeled these "obvious" also. Obviously something is wrong with the entire argument of obviousness. It should really be turned on its head. Since every kind of human reaction is conceivable, it is of great importance to know which reactions actually occur most frequently and under what conditions; only then will a more advanced social science develop.

If the reader wants to follow further the topics mentioned in this short chapter, he will have to consult a rather diverse number of sources. Leonard Reissman, in *Class in American Society* (Glencoe, Ill.: The Free Press, 1959, pp. 113–168), has an instructive chapter on the measurement of social stratification. There the reader will also find more details on the topic of occupational prestige ratings.

PAUL F. LAZARSFELD

The problem of how to translate concepts into all kinds of measurement operation has a long intellectual history. It has been traced by this writer in a contribution to *Concepts, Theory and Explanation in the Behavioral Sciences* edited by Gordon J. DiRenzo (New York: Random House, 1966, pp. 144–204). For a specific step of developing dimensions the integration of cities was used as an example. It comes from Werner S. Landecker and can be found in *The Language of Social Research* (New York: The Free Press of Glencoe, 1962, p. 19). The way indicators are chosen and combined into a classificatory instrument is most explicitly described in the book by T. W. Adorno *et al., The Authoritarian Personality* (New York: Harper and Brothers, 1950, pp. 222–290); there, the reader will also find more details on the F-scale.

Writings on projective tests are abundant in psychological literature. For the specific application to the study of underdeveloped countries, see David C. McClellan, *The Achieving Society* (Princeton, N.J.: Van Nostrand, 1961); Chapter 2 describes the technique, Chapter 3 some of the most important findings. The use of unobtrusive measures is engagingly discussed and exemplified in Eugene J. Webb *et al., Unobtrusive Measures* (Chicago: Rand McNally & Co., 1966). The role of repeated interviews to analyze change (panel studies) can best be gleaned from the study of an American election: Paul F. Lazarsfeld *et al., The People's Choice* (New York: Columbia University Press, third edition forthcoming).

American sociological journals are not often easily on hand. It is therefore fortunate that the Bobbs-Merrill Company, Inc., of Indianapolis, Indiana, in collaboration with the American Sociological Association, has provided a large number of reprints which are available at quite moderate prices. Especially for classroom teachers the following Bobbs-Merrill reprints are pertinent to the preceding discussion: (The reprint series number is given in parentheses after each title.)

ROBERT F. BALES, *A Set of Categories for the Analysis of Small Group Interaction* (S-56)
HOWARD S. BECKER, *Problems of Inference and Proof in Participant Observation* (S-337)
PAUL F. LAZARSFELD et al. *Some Functions of Qualitative Analysis in Social Research* (S-336)
GERHARD E. LENSKI, *Status Crystallization* (S-168)
S. S. STEVENS, *On the Theory of Scales of Measurement* (S-515)

The examples for our discussion of "obviousness" are taken from S. A. Stouffer *et al., The American Soldier* (Princeton, N.J.: Princeton University Press, 1950). This is a rich source of material which is now available in a paperback edition. A special case of measurement are the numerous tests used in all fields of education. Books on educational measurement describe specific problems, such as reliability and validity, which were not included in the present chapter. The most vigorous attack on these tests and more specifically on what the author calls "quantophrenia" can be found in

Pitirim A. Sorokin, *Fads and Foibles in Modern Sociology and Related Sciences* (Chicago: Henry Regnery Co., 1956, pp. 68–174).

A new phase in the development of quantification is already visible: How to classify complex organizations? Colleges vary in their "climate"; businesses have different degrees of centralization; hospitals may coordinate patients, medical staffs, administration and subsidiary services in various ways. A review of such measurement problems will be found in Allen H. Barton *et al.*, *Organizational Measurement* (New York: College Entrance Examination Board, 1961).

9 METHODS OF RESEARCH: THE NEW DEVELOPMENTS

Robert McGinnis

It would be misleading to suggest that a revolution is at hand among the methodologists of sociology. But there are clear portents of a coming change of major proportions in the methods that are used by sociologists to create and to test their theories. When it comes it will be the second great twentieth-century revolution in the field of sociology.

The last major change here occurred roughly during the decade of the 1930's. To oversimplify matters, this could be called the period of contest between humanists and empiricists. It was during this relatively recent period that sociologists cast off their European heritage of humanistic social philosophy. The goal of insightful understanding gave way to the goal of systematic knowledge. The arena of sociological activity shifted from the library to the field of on-going events. The scholarly procedures of historical investigation were discarded in favor of the tools of science. The grand-scale literary essay was replaced by the meticulous technical-research report.

For the greater part, this is where matters stand today. The sociologist is a gatherer of facts. His basic working tools are the interviewing techniques of survey research and statistical analysis. His greatest methodological concerns are with the validity and reliability of his observations and with related problems of measurement.

There is, of course, a second breed of sociologist—the theorist —but his number is infinitesimal when compared to the horde of empirical data gatherers. As a result, the American sociologist finds himself awash in a sea of facts but thirsting nonetheless for viable theories with which to organize them. There is a still deeper problem than that of imbalance between the volumes of fact and theory, and that is their disparateness.

An apt metaphor likens science to a continuing dialogue between theoretician and researcher. In this sense, at least, sociology must be judged second-rate science. In our field the languages of theory and research have become so alien to one another as virtually to defy translation. The theorist's "causation" is the empiricist's "correlation." In theory we have powerful organizing concepts—role, status, power, and the like. In research we have empirical categories, such as age, sex, and occupational title. The problems of reconciling and translating two such disparate languages are immense.

This is not intended to suggest that sociology is a moribund discipline. Quite to the contrary, it is a vigorous, growing field that today numbers more than 8,000 professionals in its American contingent. Sociological publications proliferate at a staggering rate. The problems that plague sociology today—too many data and too little viable theory—are by no means unique to it. They plague every field of science, especially the newer social sciences.

In recent years two developments have occurred that bear some hope for the revolutionary improvement in the quality of sociological methods. One of these developments is linguistic, the other a matter of hardware. Both are methodological, as the term is coming to be understood today. I refer to the imminent confrontation of sociologists with the language of mathematics and with the high-speed computer. The uses of mathematics and computers, especially as tools of the theorist, are by all odds the most important of the recent methodological innovations in sociology. The very conjunction of the terms "theory" and "method" may disturb some sociologists. In the past the word "method" was consistently associated with research, but seldom if ever with theory. Sociologists frequently have been accused of undue concern with their methods of research. To my knowledge, a parallel accusation never has been leveled against theory builders in our field. Perhaps in a deeper sense this is the nature of the impending revolution in sociological methods: the methodologist is becoming the technical assistant of the theorist as well as of the researcher. Let us consider the two major aspects of this new approach to sociological methods: first, the application of mathematics, and second, the uses of the high-speed computer.

THE USES OF MATHEMATICS IN SOCIOLOGY

Sociologists traditionally have been innocent of mathematics. Dr. Elbridge Sibley underscored this fact eloquently in his important recent study of *The Education of Sociologists in the United States.* Graduate students are exposed to chi-square, correlation, and a few other rudimentary tools of statistical analysis, but only rarely to more basic mathematical topics. Despite the absence of mathematics—one might almost say the aversion to it—in their traditional graduate curriculum, some sociologists are discovering it as a potential language for theory. They have become intrigued with the hope, possibly even the promise, that mathematics offers for improving sociological theory in the same way that mathematical statistics has benefited social research. Mathematics is a language that is rich without ambiguity, parsimonious yet consequential. To some, it is the ideal, indeed, the only really efficient language for theory. The contemporary folk language, even when generously laced with the jargon of sociologists, suffers important weaknesses as a vehicle for this purpose. Where mathematics is unambiguous, the similes and metaphors of natural language create innumerable false trails and logical snares. Mathematics yields up its rich consequences through deductive analysis. Its very beauty, its capacity for subtle nuance and symbolism make natural language enormously problematic as a tool of science.

In the physical sciences, the promise of mathematical analysis is proved beyond dispute. The behavior of a pendulum, of a body in free fall, or even of a celestial system, can be described and predicted with great accuracy through mathematics. The behavior of man is capable of vastly more complexity than even the most sophisticated of these physical systems. Thus, it taxes perhaps beyond its fullest capacity the characterizing power of mathematics. The proponent of mathematical theory in sociology does not deny the inescapable fact of human complexity. Rather, he seems to suggest a particular strategy for acquiring scientific knowledge about human behavior in light of this fact. His strategy consists of studying social behavior in its simplest forms and only much later of considering its more complicated aspects. It is in the simplest social behavior, such as playing games, choosing among alternatives, or simply being mobile, that mathematical analysis offers the most immediate promise. The promise is for unambiguous theories of social behavior, albeit the simpler ones, that yield deducible consequences which in turn can be tested against data.

Mathematical theories or models are not unitary entities. For instance, some are strictly descriptive where others offer predictions about future events. The so-called Theory of Dominance, for example, thus far is a descriptive formulation. It consists of a mathematical characterization of a set of actors bound together by a relation in which one of each possible pair of actors dominates, controls, or otherwise excels the other. One realization of this theory is provided by a tournament in which each entrant is pitted singly against every other one and in which no individual contest is permitted to end in a tie. As simple as it might appear, this is complicated social organization. If only eight actors are involved, more than 268 million different patterns of dominance are possible. Ten actors generate more than 35×10^{12} different dominance patterns. At present, there are several useful descriptive theorems about dominance structures, but little predictive knowledge. In contrast, theories of mobility, about which more will be said later, are predictive of future events.

Another axis along which mathematical theories can be distinguished is that of determinism versus probability. In a deterministic theory the behavior of individual elements is fully regulated by mathematical machinery. For instance, the location, velocity, and acceleration of a free-falling body in a vacuum are given exactly by the appropriate deterministic laws. Deterministic social theories have been advanced—but rarely tested against data—to explain a variety of phenomena such as the consequences of kinship rules or the flow of money. Probabilistic theories, on the other hand, do not determine individual behavior. Instead, they characterize the aggregate behavior of individual elements. Elementary behavior is determined by such theories only to the level of probabilities of occurrence. Statistical mechanics comprises a body of probabilistic theory in physics.

In the social sciences, theories that employ probability are more common by far than are deterministic theories. In part, this is a matter of individual taste, but also in part it reflects an ancient argument about the nature of the universe and about man's perception of it. At present, theoretical sociologists seem to concur that either social behavior is determined at most by laws that are intrinsically probabilistic, or that deterministic laws, if they exist at all, are so infinitely complex and multifaceted as to defy analysis.

Finally it is worth considering the dimension of time. To some, it appears ludicrous to invest time with the status of an analytical variable such as mass, pressure, or density. To them, time is at most a dummy variable to be eliminated in the final analysis of formal theory. To others, time is a real variable that should be accounted for fully and formally in any theory that is predictive. As with the question of determinism, this intriguing problem has roots that are deep in the philosophy of science. Formal social theorists can be found in both camps. Some sociological theories make no use at all of the temporal dimension, but in others it plays a central role. Many interactional models, such as the Theory of Dominance, eliminate time as a variable. Mobility and flow models generally rely heavily on it.

There is even now a wide range of substantive topics that are being studied through mathematical analysis. Interactional process analysis, coalition formation, mobility processes, and ecological patterns are but a few of the sociological phenomena for which mathematical models are available. One can get a sense of the extraordinary breadth of mathematical applications in sociology from works that have appeared in the past decade. Among these I would mention *Introduction to Mathematical Sociology*, by James S. Coleman; *Mathematical Models in the*

Social Sciences, by John Kemeny and Laurie Snell; and *Formal Theories of Mass Behavior*, by William McPhee. The range of mathematical forms that are employed in these studies also is wide. Nonetheless, many of the models are sufficiently simple to be mastered with no more than intermediate mathematical skills.

In order to illustrate the uses and limitations of mathematics in social theory, I should like to consider briefly the phenomenon of social mobility. Sociologists have long been occupied with various facets of this topic such as status mobility, movement through the family cycle, and human migration. It is a topic of varied aspects, each freighted with deep emotional content. Yet it is a subject that can be abstracted into the language of mathematics and developed as formal social theory.

The requisite machinery for building a mathematical theory of social mobility is really quite simple, but the way in which the machinery is used is another matter. The theoretical approach that I shall sketch is predictive, probabilistic, and explicitly temporal. The machinery consists first of a defined set of elements, ordinarily a specific human population, and a set of classes or categories, which the probability theorist calls states of nature. These states are such that each population element occupies one and only one of them at each point in time. The classes could represent social statuses, geographic locations, positions in the family life cycle, or any other division of the population in which elements can move from one state to another through time. Thus, we also need a time unit such as a calendar year.

Finally, we need two mathematical tools, the first of which is a vector, or ordered set, of m real numbers, where m is the number of states of nature. The second is a matrix of m^2 numbers arranged in m rows and m columns. The vector gives the fraction of the population in each of the m states at time t. Call the square matrix $P(t)$ and interpret the rows to represent location at time t-1 and columns to represent location at time t.

In this way the complex social phenomenon of mobility is abstracted and reduced to a sequence of mathematical matrices. The juice of human emotion and the nuances of motive are lost in the process, but the compensation for this loss is considerable.

Mathematical analysis can be brought to bear to unravel future consequences of alternative mobility systems in a way that would be out of the question for any less formal mode of analysis.

The apparatus is reasonably simple, but the way in which one treats it mathematically is another matter. The range of possible approaches is broad, each possibility involving a number of different simplifying assumptions about the behavior of the mobility system. The rules of orderly procedure suggest that the simplest approaches be investigated first. This is the strategy that was adopted about a dozen years ago by a team of analysts at Cornell University. They undertook a study of United States labor-force mobility among industrial positions. That is, they studied the process of workers changing jobs from one industrial sector such as steel production, to another, such as coal production.

The researchers initially employed just two simplifying assumptions, which together make up what is known as the Markov-chain model of probability. The first assumption demands that the probability of moving, for instance, from steel to coal production, remains invariant over the time intervals. In the short run, at least, this is not an extreme assumption. The second, however, is much more stringent in that it requires movement from one industrial location to another to be independent of any prior patterns of movement.

When the team of investigators tested the Markov model against data, it proved at best to be only moderately successful. The second assumption was unrealistic. The assumption requires that any two people in the same industrial location satisfy identical mobility schedules. People simply are not this uniform. Their prior relevant experiences differentiate them and subject them to different schedules of mobility.

The research team recognized this fact and accordingly divided their population of workers into two classes, which they called movers and stayers. The two classes were characterized by markedly different transition matrices. When these matrices were re-analyzed separately, the Markov model was found to predict the short-run mobility patterns of the labor force in a considerably improved fashion.

To some critics, research of this kind is nothing more than an exercise in actuarial statistics. "Where," they ask, "is the *theory* in all of this?" The answer is that the theory consists precisely of the simplifying assumptions of the model. When stated declaratively, these assumptions are theory. As such, they must be generated from the substantive sociological context rather than from mathematics, and they must be evaluated in the same context. In the preceding illustration, the theory consisted initially of two assertions that can be translated to say in English, first, that "mobility among states is constant in time," and, second, that "an individual's propensity to move is independent of any other characteristic that he may possess." As we saw, the second of these theoretical assertions proved to be flagrantly unrealistic and consequently was modified by a third theory sentence. In English, this third assertion was that "there exist two categories, movers and stayers, such that the second condition is true only within each category."

Recently, a second team of Cornell researchers has elaborated the third part of this theory. The second team began by reasoning that a human population simply does not fall neatly into the two categories of mover and stayer. Instead, it appeared to them that a myriad of factors in the interactions that occur between an individual and his environment determines the probability of his staying in it. They reduced this idea to what has since been called the Axiom of Cumulative Inertia.

Expressed metaphorically, the axiom likens an environment to a pot of glue that dries gradually about each new arrival, eventually cementing him firmly in his environmental state. Expressed more formally, the axiom asserts that the probability of an individual's remaining in a state of nature increases with each unit of his prior duration of residence in that state. The Axiom of Cumulative Inertia has a certain intuitive appeal, reflecting as it does such common notions as the sinking of roots and the gradual building up of bonds of habit and sentiment to a location or condition. Moreover, preliminary empirical tests of the results of this axiom have been encouraging.

When the axiom is imbedded in the Markov model, the mathematics become chaotically complicated. For one thing, time becomes double-barreled. In addition to the traditional representations of time as the history of the system, this axiom requires that it be represented separately as the history of individual elements in the system. This, in turn, gives rise to a system not with a single sequence of transition matrices, but with an entire matrix of matrices. The mathematics of the revised model is so complex, in fact, that the research team recently appealed for aid, not to expert human consultants, but to a high-speed computer.

COMPUTER APPLICATIONS IN SOCIOLOGY

The second fundamental component of the new sociological methodology is the introduction of computer technology into the field. As with the mathematical component, this innovation represents at least as much potential for the improvement of theory as it does for research. To understand this, it must be recognized that the computer is far more than a high-speed data processor. It is also a data generator and a logic machine.

In its most primitive conception, the computer is an ultra-fast desk calculator. Both receive numbers as inputs, process them through such conventional operations as addition, multiplication, or exponentiation, then put out the results in any of several forms of visual display, but the similarity ends there. Against the desk calculator's limited mechanical capacity is the modern electronic computer's ability, for instance, to add numbers together in about 1.4 millionths of a second. It should not be necessary to describe here the computer's remarkable capacity, speed, or facility in processing data. These features are the subject of innumerable popular accounts and bemused cartoons. It should be obvious by now that the sociological researcher, or anyone else with masses of data, can choose between rapid computer processing and laborious error-ridden clerical processing. By almost any standard, the computer wins out in this choice. But what fewer people recognize is that the computer can be equally invaluable to the scientific theorist who is unconcerned with problems of data processing.

The theoretical analyses of mobility that were described earlier included several dead-end streets. The goal was to discover whether eventually the proportional distribution in each state would settle into an equilibrium condition and, if so, what functional relations would exist between initial and equilibrium states. The mathematics soon proved to be impossibly complex, especially in light of the fact that the investigators had no idea what shape the end results might take. For these reasons the research team decided to simulate the behavior of their mobility system on a computer together with various initial conditions such as the number of states, the population fraction in each at time zero, and the initial transition matrices. The computer was able to reproduce in less than five minutes the behavior of the mobility system over a period of 1,500 time units.

The purpose of this exercise was less to generate numbers than to provide insight into the long-run behavior of the mobility system. In this sense the exercise was a success. A number of computer runs made clear that a state of equilibrium eventually occurs in this system and what determines its distribution. Many of these insights now have been verified through mathematical deduction.

By its capacity to simulate the structure and temporal dynamics of complex systems, the computer is a tool without precedent for the generation of theory. Social scientists already have conducted simulation experiments of such varied phenomena as the organization of the brain, community real-estate values with Negro population influx, the United States economy at the household level, human-choice behavior, and international political relations. The promise of these enterprises is for systemic quantitative theories with which to organize the masses of available data, and with which to organize more meaningfully the empirical research process.

To conclude as I began, the revolution in the development of sociological methods is not at hand, but that it is pending and the shape that it will take are reasonably clear. As with most intellectual revolutions, this one promises both rich rewards and heavy costs. Since I have dwelt on the rewards at length, let us consider briefly the cost to the field and to the intellectual tradition of sociology that will result from the new methodological tools of mathematics and computers.

The implications of these new developments are reasonably clear so far as the curriculum of sociology is concerned. Students in the field will have to master a working knowledge of the language of mathematics and acquire familiarity with the operation of electronic computers. In response to these needs, mathematics and computer science departments at leading American universities are offering an increasing number of courses that are especially tailored to the needs of social scientists. To a lesser extent the same is true in some engineering colleges, where social scientists are being encouraged to study modern systems of engineering methods. But these innovations are costly in the professional student's limited budget of time. More traditional sociology courses must give way if these newer topics are to be added to the curriculum.

Among established professionals in sociology, the new methods seem to pose the discomfiting prospect either of retraining or of being technologically and linguistically displaced. I very much doubt that the more traditional approach to theory construction ever will disappear. Nor should it. Its insightful contributions have been enormous. Nonetheless, these tides of change probably will create important new developments in the very organization of the field. Traditional areas of concern, the sociology of this and the sociology of that, may well wither and be replaced by altogether new organizing concepts. These changes may be costly in emotion and in the sense of orderly tradition, but they offer also the challenging excitement of intellectual exploration and of the creation of significant new knowledge. These are the promises of the new methods of sociology.

PART III

Functional
Subsystems

10 THE FAMILY AND KINSHIP

Ezra F. Vogel

Despite the inventiveness of man and the enormous variety of political and economic organizations from the simplest tribe to the most complex social structure, in virtually every society the nuclear family of parents and children has stood out as a distinct social unit. Even in societies so primitive that people are unaware of the biological contribution of the male in procreation, the child has a special social relationship with a father. In at least one social grouping, the Nayar military caste of India, the man did not regularly cohabit with a woman but lived separately in the all-male military organization. But even among the Nayar, where the progenitor played no role in raising the child, he was ceremonially tied to him and, according to our best ethnographic accounts, progenitor and offspring had certain mutual obligations.

It is true enough that man has been able to conceive of societies without nuclear families. In the mid-nineteenth century, for example, Friedrich Engels described the family as a bourgeois institution that would disappear with the advent of communism. According to his analysis, although woman was "enslaved" because of her economic dependence on her husband, with the advent of communism the common ownership of the means of production would free her. With the emancipation of womankind and community nurseries for children, the family would wither away. Engels was not the first revolutionary or utopian idealist to dream of the end of the family. Indeed, at the height of revolutionary fervor a certain contradiction exists between loyalty to the family and loyalty to the revolutionary group. For example, an Israeli sociologist, Talmon-Garber, who has studied intensively the Israeli rural collectives, the kibbutzim, has found that when revolutionary fervor is highest, loyalty to the family becomes weaker. Conversely, as the revolutionary ardor fades away, the attention and concern given to the family are greatly increased.

Although man has been able to conceive of the elimination of the family, no sizable society has been able to eliminate the family. In post-1917 Russia, as in some other revolutionary and utopian societies, an attempt was made to do away with the family. Women who filled out the necessary card at the local post office were automatically granted divorces. Pregnant women who were afraid that children might restrict their freedom were encouraged to have abortions. Yet, as we all know, the concern with developing a stable and ordered society soon led the Russian leaders to strengthen the family unit and to apply negative sanctions to those who failed to fulfill their responsibilities to their families. So every other successful revolutionary or utopian society—no matter how militant—has come to recognize some form of family organization.

Since the nuclear family has survived despite communalization, its existence cannot be a product of exclusively economic factors. How, then, can one explain the persistence of the nuclear family in every known society? Some have explained it as the only way of restricting an all-out competition between males for females and of females for males. As relationships between a given adult male and female are stabilized, their union is granted social recognition. This social recognition is commonly symbolized in ceremonies of engagement or marriage. The special link between mother and child is easy to understand because of the mother's giving birth and nurture to the child. But it is much more difficult to account for the regularity of the relationship between father and child. Some have argued that the regular occurrence of the social position of the father is derivative; it occurs because he has a special relationship with his wife and she has a special relationship with the child. Others have emphasized the importance of paternal economic and emotional support as well as authority. Malinowski has argued that the importance of father-hood lies in the placement of the child in the broader social context. At a minimum, it is the father who confers upon the child a legitimate status in the eyes of a wider society. Beyond this, the father's own status to some degree determines the child's initial status. In fact, societies having ascriptive status (those dominated by kinship or caste groupings) accept the father's standing as the critical factor determining the status of his child.

To be sure, the form of the ideal and actual family varies widely from society to society. Often a given society exhibits great variation in actual family units according to social class, stage of life cycle, occupation, and other idiosyncratic factors. Yet perhaps more striking than the variations between families is the fact that certain important features of nuclear family structure are almost universal. One is the incest taboo pro-hibiting sexual relationships between members of the family other than husband and wife. Again, many have advanced argu-ments for the virtual universality of the incest taboo. Some have argued that it is necessary to preserve the distinct social roles and the nature of relationships between members of the family. Others have pointed to the importance of the incest taboo in linking the family to the wider society and to preferential mar-riage as being important for the maintenance of ties between certain groups in the society. Not only do nuclear families every-where place some restriction on incest, but, as Parsons and Zelditch have pointed out, virtually all families everywhere have an internal distinction in authority based on age and distinct sex roles; the man takes a more instrumental role and the woman a more expressive role. Others have noted that the woman is inclined to spend more of her time in the family, the man more time outside of family affairs; even if both work, the husband is likely to have a firmer commitment and closer attachment to his work than does the wife; if one goes far from the home to a place of work, it is more likely to be the husband than the wife.

In this chapter I would like to concentrate on one particular problem: the relationship between familial organization and the broader societal setting. Generally speaking, in societies with a strong kinship system the nuclear family does not stand out as a relatively isolated distinct unit. In a patrilineal society, for example, maternal responsibilities may be shared with the father's sisters. In a matrilineal society, authority over children may be shared by the father's and the mother's brothers.

If one looks beyond the immediate kinship and community groupings to the relationship between family and broader economic and political forces, one is led to the conclusion that economic forces are much more critical than political ones in determining the dominant patterns of familial organization. Some have argued that there is a direct correspondence between familial relationships and a political system. In a major work on American civilization, for example, Max Lerner argues that the democratic political milieu and the more open and democratic family patterns broadly serve to reinforce each other. He contrasts this with prewar Germany, where the family and the political order were both more authoritarian. Perhaps the most common explanations given to support the view of consistency between familial and political patterns are psychological. Through the process of socializing the child, the family implants certain attitudes which are later reflected in his participation in the political institutions of society. Those who are psychoanalytically oriented have observed that attitudes originally held toward parents have been transferred to parent-like figures in the wider society. But the most that can be claimed is that these attitudes deriving from family behavior form one part of the attitudes toward authority. How important these psychological attitudes are is determined in part by the type of political organization—whether it is, for example, charismatic—the personal qualities of the leader (at least as interpreted by his followers) are very important—or a rational-bureaucratic type of organization, in which case the psychological factors have less importance.

Others concerned with the links between the family and political organization have emphasized the importance of values acquired in the family in determining political values. The argument here is essentially the same as for psychological factors: values acquired in the family will later be reflected in one's political values.

Within some limits, then, it is possible to find support for the thesis that attitudes and values acquired in the family later determine attitudes toward authority. In the Soviet Union, for example, when family authority had been greatly weakened as a result of the partially successful campaign to end the "tyranny of the bourgeois family," the government became a victim of its own success. Children reared in families with weakened authority did not show the proper discipline and respect for authorities in the government. The regime became sufficiently aware of this problem to set consciously about rehabilitating the authority of the family.

However, I would argue that the family's relationship with the government (acting in strictly political matters) is not so important as its relationship with the economy. Government is ordinarily at a considerable remove from the family; affairs of state have relatively little direct effect on family organization, and family organization has relatively little effect on political organization. While I am prepared to defend this as a general rule, such a conclusion needs several qualifications. In the first place, it assumes that the society has achieved a certain degree of stability. If a government has such difficulty in maintaining stability that the society in general is disordered, the disarray would obviously have an impact on family life and family organization. Furthermore, a government demanding an all-out mobilization for a national emergency requires individual sacrifice of an order that affects family behavior. The well-known cases of separations in wartime (for participation in the military, safety, defense, and so on) and the restrictions placed on travel, communication, leisure enjoyments, and so forth obviously have an impact on family behavior. To be sure, certain governmentally established patterns for forming and ending marriage relationships, inheritance laws, and other regulations provide certain limits on familial relationships, but such regulations generally set only broad guidelines and do not determine specific forms of family organization.

If one is concerned, not with families in general, but with the families in positions of power, it is much easier to make a case for the impact of family organization on government. If a governmental official is part of a very tightly knit kinship group to which he is expected to fulfill certain obligations, the kinship patterns may interfere with the manner in which he performs in the government. In such a case, fulfilling one's reponsibilities to the kinship group may be regarded from the official point of view as graft. On the other hand, scrupulous performance of government duty may be regarded, from the kinship group's point of view, as disloyalty. In many societies it is the higher-status families, the ones most likely to hold positions of power, that are more likely to have extended family organizations. This is likely to be true for a number of reasons. In a society where kinship groups are important, it often takes a relatively large and powerful kinship group to provide the necessary means (whether it be legitimation of high status, or connections, or military power, wealth, or supply of talented men) to achieve the positions of power. Furthermore, the children of a rich and powerful family are more inclined to remain close to their kin than are the children of those who are out of power.

In societies where those in power are members of large kinship groups, there are various ways in which governmental interests may be balanced with kinship interests. In some societies (as in imperial societies), the highest positions of governmental responsibility may be held by those within a single kinship group. Even within a clan, the positions of power in it may be dominated by a subgroup. In such cases, it is considered legitimate and even proper for the leading family to be supported and looked after by the government. While such privileges may be accorded to a leading or several leading families, obviously the same privileges cannot be extended to all families of governmental employees without being a serious drain on the government. Hence various pressures within government arise to limit the commitments of governmental employees to kinship groups. One of the most highly developed and formalized cases of limitations on these familial commitments was the case of Imperial China, where eunuchs were used as court officials and government officials were not allowed to serve in their own home area in order to ensure that they could not extend favored treatment to their families. The whole growth of civil-service regulations is obviously a very important development for preventing kinship obligations from interfering with governmental obligations. The problems are not so serious in a society in which the nuclear family maintains only weak connections with kin groups. Even in these societies, however, pseudo-kinship organizations and paternalistically organized factions and cliques may pose the same problem for the government that kinship groups would pose in societies where they are stronger.

It is probably true that if we go beyond the families of officeholders and examine the family organization of the citizenry, there are still some connections between family and political organization. For example, there is a certain difficulty in maintaining the strict subservience of women and children to the father if all adults are given full and equal citizenship rights. The contrast of this situation with that prevailing in countries where the government had contact only with the head of the household is striking. Dealing only with the head of the family and holding him responsible for the behavior of all its members serve to reinforce and solidify his power position. Moreover, other members of the household having legitimate claims on the government can assert them only through him. Granting women and adult children full citizenship rights, on the other hand, encourages their desire for minimal autonomy.

Despite these modifications, however, most families in a society are not directly affected by the political activities of their government. To seek out changes in family organization and behavior, it is much more important to examine economic stimuli, which have a much more direct impact on family organization. It is no accident that in the most thorough study yet undertaken of contemporary family organization around the world, Professor William J. Goode of Columbia University looks primarily to changes in economic organization to understand the changes in family organization.

Professor Goode has accumulated considerable evidence in his *World Revolution and Family Patterns* to indicate that certain basic patterns of family organization have proved to be broadly compatible with modern industrial and urban society. In his very careful study, Professor Goode makes it clear that even in the economic sphere there is no precise and necessary causal relationship between a given economic organization and family organization. Yet with some minor and perhaps temporary exceptions, world evolution toward a modern industrial society has been accompanied by the relative isolation of the nuclear family from larger kinship groups.

This does not mean that the nuclear family appears only as a concomitant of industrialism. Indeed, this same form, the relatively isolated nuclear family, is commonly found in hunting and gathering societies. If game and plants are limited, the members of a hunting and gathering society must disperse to maximize their food supply; the unit into which the group disperses is commonly the small elementary family. But again, one cannot predict family form only on the basis of this economic fact, for under conditions of warfare it is common for nuclear families in these hunting and gathering societies to band together to form extended families.

One family form which has had considerable stability and seems well adapted to relatively stable and well-settled agricultural societies is the stem family, a family form in which three generations live in the same household but with only one married son included. Other children leave home upon marriage. This family form maintains intact the family estate, since only one son remains living on the land and the property is not divided into plots so small that it is difficult or impossible to earn a living. In the stem family the fact that one son is to inherit the estate and others are not leads to further social distinctions within the family between the heir and his brothers and sisters.

The good fit between the stem family and the stable agricultural society does not mean that other patterns of family organization have not existed in agricultural societies. Another kind of family, the joint family, in which inheritance is divided among several children, may work well when land is in sufficient supply and population relatively stable. However, in periods of population growth, as family plots are divided among several children and become too small, the family often becomes impoverished and some form of recombination of land or migration is necessary even for minimal subsistence. On the whole, the stem family system generally has been better adapted to a stable or expanding agricultural society and in the long run has tended to persist in this kind of economy.

Similarly, the relatively isolated nuclear family has been shown to be best adapted to modern industrial society. Professor Goode, who has reviewed the evidence most carefully, has concluded that the following factors have constituted pressures toward the break-up of the bigger family units existing prior to industrialization: (1) industrial society requires physical movement from one locality to another, and this tends to limit the frequency and intimacy of contact between relatives; (2) industrial society makes it possible for some to rise socially more than others. This creates disparities between brothers and sisters in style of life, which tends to strain the relationships between siblings and reduce the amount of contact; (3) the growth in urban industrial societies of specialized facilities providing physical protection, welfare funds, and loans has undermined the need for relying on the family, again reducing the need for intimate contacts between relatives; (4) industrialization gives rise to a new system of values which stresses the importance of achievement more than birth—an individual is expected to make his own way and not to rely on his relatives; (5) because of the high degree of specialization and the growth of larger organization, it is statistically improbable that a person will be able to provide work for his relatives.

To say that the nuclear family is the dominant family in modern industrial society does not mean that nuclear family members have no contacts with relatives. Indeed, as a number of recent studies have shown, in the most industrialized countries it is very common to have relatively frequent contacts between relatives outside the nuclear family. The strongest ties between relatives in modern industrial societies tend to be between women, and especially between mother and daughters. If the man is separated for periods of time by war or other work, it is not uncommon for his wife and children to live with the wife's mother. In the Soviet Union and some other countries where the wife is frequently working, it is not uncommon for much of the work of child rearing to fall to the grandmother, who is likely to live with the family.

Of course, to what degree nuclear family members continue to live together depends in part on the availability of facilities provided by other agencies. If welfare is not provided by the government or by the husband's place of work or by some other community facilities, one may be forced to rely on the extended family for assistance, a factor which tends to draw the family together.

Economic conditions not only have very considerable impact on the extent of the separation of the elementary family from the wider kinship network, but also have a great deal to do with relationships within the family. If, for example, the father has difficulty in finding a good job, his position of authority within the family is greatly undermined. Extended unemployment also greatly affects his own feelings of confidence in relation to his family. Studies of less-privileged groups in a society, such as the lower-class American Negro, for example, have shown the lack of authority of the father in situations of prolonged unemployment or only marginal employment. Conversely, if better economic opportunities are available for the wives or the children, this also tends to affect their status within the family, as we have seen in some immigrant groups to the United States when patriarchal authority disappeared quite rapidly.

Employment conditions may also affect the husband and wife relationship. When national labor needs require that couples be separated over long periods of time, it not only weakens the relationship between them but lets authority over the children fall to the wife, who is likely to be the one to remain with the children.

It is impossible in this chapter to do more than suggest some of the connections between the family and the economic conditions of its society. Indeed, we who have conducted research on family organization have many problems which we do not sufficiently understand. But studies of family life are proceeding at a very rapid rate and there is no question that the economy has a profound effect on family organization. We know enough to say that the relationship is not by any means one-sided. It is clear, for example, that certain kinds of family relationships tend to be conducive to economic development. This is a problem that has been little studied but undoubtedly will be developed further by family specialists in the years ahead.

11 THE SOCIOLOGY OF EDUCATION

Martin Trow

One of the characteristics of scholarly and scientific disciplines is their tendency over time to develop special areas of study which provide a common focus for the work of those people in a discipline who share a common interest. One of the most rapidly developing areas of special study within the discipline of sociology is the sociology of education. This subfield brings together sociologists who are especially interested in the formal institutions devoted to education, that is, schools, colleges, universities, and the like; in the educational processes going on within those institutions; and in the relation of those institutions to other parts of the society in which they exist. In 1960 growing interest in these issues among American sociologists gave rise to the creation of a Section on the Sociology of Education within the American Sociological Association, and this group now numbers well over 500 members. In 1963 the Association showed its continued interest in the subject by assuming sponsorship of an existing journal in the area which under its new auspices took the name *Sociology of Education*.

The interest of sociologists in education is by no means a recent development. Many of the greatest figures in the history of sociology, such as Herbert Spencer and Emile Durkheim, gave educational institutions and processes a prominent place in their writings. And almost without exception the major figures in American sociology have written on educational issues at one time or another. What is new, since World War II, is the emergence of a special field of inquiry into educational forms and processes which a growing number of sociologists make the center of their professional studies, while retaining their professional and intellectual connections with men and work in other areas of sociology and other disciplines in the social sciences.

SOURCES OF DEVELOPMENT OF THE SOCIOLOGY OF EDUCATION IN THE UNITED STATES

The growth of this special interest in the sociology of education has been especially rapid during the past decade in the United States. And the reasons for this are themselves illuminating of the educational scene that sociologists study. In part the growth of the sociology of education has been made possible by the sheer growth in the number of trained and practicing sociologists since World War II—that is, as a part of the specialization of science and scholarship that accompanies the growth in knowledge and the numbers of scholars and scientists. But the study of education responds at least as much to external events and developments in the environing society as it does to developments within the scholarly discipline. In the United States a number of developments outside of sociology have drawn the attention of many within the discipline to educational institutions and processes. There was first the very rapid and sustained growth in college and university enrollments after World War II, a growth that we can now see as the first stages of the establishment of a system of mass, and eventually nearly universal, higher education. As recently as 1940, American colleges and universities enrolled only about one and a quarter million students, about 15 per cent of the population of college age, the eighteen to twenty-one-year-olds. By 1963 the number of students earning credits toward degrees in American colleges and universities had increased to 4.2 million, comprising about 40 per cent of the population of college age. Today college and university enrollments are over five million, and by 1970 will be seven million. This staggering increase in college attendance is sending shock waves through our educational system, and eventually through our whole society. Inevitably, it has raised a host of questions of interest to sociologists. Initially these have been questions having to do with the sources of the growth itself, the characteristics and aspirations of the large numbers of new students in our colleges and universities, the impact of their higher education on them, the organization and government of the new and expanding institutions of higher education, the problems of recruitment of staff to meet the new demands, and so forth. Many sociologists were drawn first to the practical problems of the very institutions in which they led their own scholarly lives, but stayed to study the more fundamental characteristics of education of which higher education is only a part.

In addition, while the numbers of students were growing very rapidly after World War II, the importance of higher education, especially in science and technology, was increasingly recognized as a major source of industrial and military power. In part under the spur of Soviet achievements in military and space technology, the federal government has become much more centrally concerned with the supply and training of technically skilled manpower. And this national interest, reflected in generous funds for research on these questions, has stimulated sociologists to study more closely the ways in which able youngsters are recruited to advanced training in science and technology. This problem naturally raised the question of the losses in ability and potential represented by students who leave formal schooling far short of the levels of education for which they appear to be qualified. And that question in turn directed attention to the secondary schools in which the basic foundations for scientific and technical careers are laid. At the same time it has become increasingly recognized that rapid social and technological changes are reducing the numbers of relatively unskilled jobs, as they increase the demand for more highly trained and educated people. And this has also stimulated interest in the extent and causes of early school leaving.

This last interest has gradually widened to a concern for the education of those groups in society who are socially and economically disadvantaged, for some as a result of past and present racial prejudice and discrimination. The major changes in the state of race relations in the United States over the past decade have stimulated an enormous amount of research on the special educational problems of children from the most deprived social and economic strata.

The growth of mass higher education, the concern for the relation of education to national power and prosperity, the interest in a reform of secondary education, and the more recent interest in the education of children from socially and culturally deprived homes are among the powerful external forces leading to the rapid growth of interest and work in the sociology of education. And a fair part of the work done in this area reflects the practical problems and concerns which have stimulated the growth of the field.

THE EXTENSION OF HORIZONS

But while the enormous growth of education, in size, in recognized importance, and in relevance for public policy has undoubtedly been the major stimulus for the increasing interest of sociologists in the area, their work is not therefore confined to the practical problems of education. The history of the sociology of education in the United States over the past two decades has been one of broadening horizons and the steadily growing range of problems, perspectives, and disciplines to which it attends. To a considerable extent these extensions of horizon reflect the wider interests brought to the study of educational institutions and processes by sociologists whose training and previous experience were in fields outside education. Before World War II the handful of men working in educational sociology was located mostly in schools and departments of education, devoted chiefly to the preparation of teachers and administrators for the public primary and secondary schools; many of them had themselves been trained in schools of education, and naturally focused their attention on the practical problems of teachers and administrators. But increasingly the subject has attracted men who were trained as sociologists, and teach and do research in university departments of sociology, or, if in schools of education, maintain their professional identification and intellectual ties with sociologists in other fields. This important shift in the professional training and interests of men working in the field has brought the sociology of education back into the mainstream of sociological thought, from which it had tended to become isolated while confined to the immediate problems of the schools.

Starting from the narrow and immediate problems of the classroom teacher and school administrator, which were the center of attention of all but a handful of educational sociologists before World War II, the field has in recent years extended its range institutionally, theoretically, and across national boundaries. Institutionally, sociologists have added to their interest in the public primary and secondary schools the study of colleges, universities, professional schools, and research centers, and, indeed, of other institutions where teaching and learning are organized activities. More important, sociologists have begun to look at the nature of educational systems and their functions in the larger society, and this has immediately brought them in contact with economists, political scientists, anthropologists, and historians who are approaching educational institutions from their own quite different perspectives. The problems of a large institutional complex like education are no respecters of disciplinary boundaries, and require sociologists of education to become much more widely knowledgeable about the many ways in which educational institutions and processes are affected, for example, by historical traditions, family patterns, the occupational structure, technological change, and political processes.

The theoretical resources of a line of inquiry are not the body of thought and knowledge that is potentially available to it, but that part of what is potentially available that actually informs work in a field. As the institutional horizons of the sociology of knowledge have grown, so also have its theoretical and intellectual resources. A major line of interest in sociology has been in social stratification, the study of the nature and bases and extent of social inequalities. One of the earliest and most persistent interests of American sociologists of education has been the influence of inequalities in social origins—largely stemming from the social and economic class into which a child is born— on school achievement. While social origins affect educational achievement, educational achievement increasingly determines the social position an individual holds in his adult life. Educational institutions work on one hand to translate social position at birth into achieved adult status; on the other hand, they are a major engine of social mobility in that they supply the avenues by which youngsters of modest beginnings can reach higher positions in society than their parents held.

The interest in the relation of education to social stratification meshes closely with current interests in the social psychology of learning and intelligence. The major external stimulus to this work has come from the movement to improve the social and economic position of American Negroes. We have long known that children from impoverished homes, who have suffered the effects of neglect, family disorganization, racial prejudice, and so forth, usually do poorly in their school work, have on the average lower IQ scores, and are more likely to leave school early to join the ranks of the untrained and unemployed adolescents on the street corners of big city slums. We are now coming to see that much of what we call "intelligence" or "academic ability" is itself acquired as a result of certain kinds of social experiences. A child's parents, his relatives and friends, and other important people and experiences of life influence his career in school in part through the way they shape his personality, in part through the encouragement and cultural and intellectual resources they give him. Some sociologists have focused on the differences in the linguistic resources of youngsters from different class and ethnic backgrounds, differences that greatly affect their later educational achievement. Others have looked more closely at the effects of racial prejudice on the child's feelings about himself, and the consequent effects of these self-concepts on school performance. Still others have focused on the effects of family structure, and particularly on the effects of the absence of a father (or fathering adult male) from the home. These and other studies are on the borders of the sociology of education, but as they illuminate the social and psychological forces that affect learning they touch on a central problem of our discipline.

These conflicting functions of education, both to transmit and to modify social statuses across generations, give rise to a variety of related kinds of investigation. Some sociologists focus not so much on the child as on the educational systems, in different times and places, which emphasize the transmission or the modification of social status. The movement in many European societies toward systems of comprehensive secondary schools, and toward the expansion of opportunities for higher education, can be seen as part of a world-wide movement toward the use of education as an avenue for social mobility and for the identification and training of talents and abilities wherever they may be found. In the United States we have long accepted that academic ability should be discovered and rewarded, whatever the social origins of the children who possess it. We are now beginning the more difficult task of learning how to create and nurture intelligence in the schools as well as to identify and reward it. And this requires attention *both* to the character of educational systems and to the nature and sources of intelligence.

The horizons of the sociology of education have been expanding in the range of institutions it studies and in the variety of theoretical perspectives and research techniques it uses in its inquiries. It is now also expanding across national boundaries. With a few exceptions, American educators before World War II paid relatively little attention to the educational institutions of other countries, but that situation is now changing very rapidly. This reflects the increased interest in education all over the world and the development of sociological work outside the United States which is of direct interest to sociologists of education in America. Thus there have been very important studies of social class and educational achievement in England, Sweden, and other countries, while scholars elsewhere have done valuable studies on university students, on the recruitment of teachers, and the like. In addition, American sociologists of education are interested in learning the extent to which, and under what conditions, the processes of education we can observe in this country are found elsewhere. For example, a very practical and yet theoretically challenging problem is whether children learn better if they are separated into different streams or tracks according to how well they perform academically, or whether they do better if children of various abilities are taught together. The evidence from American studies thus far is quite inconclusive, though the question is being examined in an important series of comparative studies of educational achievement currently under way.[1]

In addition to the valuable work of colleagues overseas, there is the growing interest of American sociologists in the relation of education to economic and political development. The fate of many of the new nations of Africa and Asia, as well as the developing nations of Latin America, is linked to their efforts to raise the standards of nutrition, of health, and of the general welfare of their populations. These efforts in turn call for a modernization of their industries, of agriculture, and of their systems of social administration. And in all these efforts the educational system is a crucial instrument of modernization, in many places extending literacy, in some countries providing a common core of experience, a common language and a common national identification, and everywhere attempting to provide the teachers, technicians, engineers, scientists, doctors, and administrators that are so sorely needed. Some developing countries have their own long-established systems of schools and universities; and there the new demands of rising expectations and rapid social change put great strains on traditional institutions. In other countries, especially those emerging from colonial rule, the educational systems are modeled on those of Western European countries, and very great problems arise in the transformation of those models to the different requirements of independent and developing nations. The comparative study of emerging educational systems and their role in economic and political development is an important, relatively new area to which sociologists of education have turned their attention.

DIFFERENT PERSPECTIVES IN
THE SOCIOLOGY OF EDUCATION

Sociologists of education approach their common subject in very different ways. Some start with practical problems of classroom and school system, and apply their sociological perspective and methods of investigation in an effort first to understand, and then to help solve, the problems that initiated the investigation. For example, pressures for the reform of American secondary education, its curriculum, modes of instruction, and forms of organization have grown sharply in recent decades. And sociologists have responded by studying such aspects of secondary education as the influence of the adolescent subculture, the work of school-guidance counselors and vocational advisers, and the efficacy of new modes of instruction such as automated and team teaching. The sociologist, along with the educational psychologist, has here the task of analyzing the nature of difficulties to which suggested reforms are directed, of assessing the probable effects of their adoption in specific circumstances, and then of evaluating the actual effects of those changes or innovations that are introduced. Without their help, the practical improvement of instruction and educational organization would necessarily be a matter of hit or miss, or of the experience of educators, an experience that is not always applicable to new reforms or circumstances. It would be wrong to suggest that most educational decisions are already firmly grounded in scientific findings. And since many educational issues involve political differences and value preferences, it is unlikely that they will ever be settled solely by reference to sociological or psychological discoveries. Nevertheless, sociologists have an important contribution to make to educational practice, and they are now beginning to make it.

While some sociologists of education start from the practical problems of the schools, others start from a somewhat more detached perspective, and attempt to increase understanding of educational institutions and processes by describing their development and present character more fully than has been done heretofore. By investigating the characteristics of schools and colleges, of students and teachers, of methods of teaching and forms of learning, and by studying changes in these elements of education over time, the nature of the relationships among these things becomes clearer. For example, a study of the growth of mass public secondary education in America during the first half of this century sheds much light on similar forces underlying the present expansion of our system of higher education. In this light we see that what is occurring now is a change not merely in size but in the functions of our system of higher education, as it becomes the chief instrument for higher occupational training in the society as well as the source of the social and scientific discoveries that are changing society. And this perspective also allows us to see how the growth and transformation of higher education is changing the functions of our secondary schools as well, forcing them to become increasingly preparatory schools for college and university. This enforced change in their historical role creates all sorts of difficulties and strains in the high schools which can only be understood in terms of these long-range changes in the relations of different parts of the educational system to one another, and of education as a whole to the society at large.

Still another approach taken by some sociologists is to start by identifying a number of basic functions performed by educational systems in all societies in which they exist. For example, everywhere schools and colleges and universities help transmit the culture of a society—its beliefs and values and skills—from one generation to another. In addition, they help equip youngsters to live in their society and to play the various roles that adults in their society are called on to play—for example, of husband, father, citizen, clerk, or engineer. With respect to some of these adult roles, of course, the schools supplement what a child learns from his parents; most children learn more about what it means to be a father in their homes than they do in school. But learning about other adult roles, especially those that have to do with earning a living, is in modern societies the special responsibility of schools. Very few children in modern societies follow in their fathers' footsteps and learn from them their craft or kind of work. And while youngsters still often learn much of their adult work skills in their first jobs, there is much that they must know even to get their first job, and that is learned in school. Even more important—though we tend to take it for granted—children learn in school that people outside their family tend to judge them by how well they do, and the importance of achievement is borne in on them increasingly the further in school they go.

Schools also play an important role in selecting and training and then placing people in different positions in society. An increasing number of occupations in modern society require high levels of skill and training, which are gained in high schools and colleges and universities. Not all youngsters are equally capable of acquiring these skills, in part due to what appear to be differences in general intelligence, in part due to differences in interests, motivations, self-discipline, parental encouragement, and other factors. Some of these differences show themselves quite early in the primary school years; in other cases a student gains an interest in his school work only in high school or even later. Nevertheless, while many teachers try to encourage their students to learn as much as they can, and to raise their capacities and performance, they are also responding to differences in these respects among their students. And the grades that students earn affect the kinds of schools they attend, what they study there, how long they stay, and what certificates or degrees they earn. And that in turn very heavily affects the kind of job they will have in adult life. Thus, in a society in which jobs calling for very high levels of education and training increase in number and importance, the importance of the school in selecting youngsters for the opportunities to gain that training is very great indeed.

A strongly held value of American society is that positions in society ought to be open to merit and ability without regard to a child's social origins; at the same time, we think it right and proper that parents should try to give their children "every advantage." The first of these values is reflected in the public educational system and in the rapidly growing public sector of higher education, which now enrolls some two-thirds of all college and university students. But in addition, these democratic values inspire a good deal of the work of sociologists of education, who are concerned with such questions as the social sources of educability and in the ways in which students from lower classes can be encouraged to continue their education through high school and into college, where the necessary training for the more skilled and responsible occupations is gained. Thus, in modern societies, schools and colleges help transmit the cultural heritage of a society, they help train and educate children for their adult roles, and they play a large part in selecting and placing young people in jobs which largely determine the positions they hold in adult society.

There is yet another task that educational institutions, but particularly the colleges and universities, perform, a task of increasing importance: that is, of creating new knowledge, and of applying this knowledge to all areas of social and economic life. The very rapid growth of scientific knowledge and its application to technology and to medical care are the most visible parts of a sweeping change in the role of knowledge in a society that is making change rather than stability the normal expectations of men. The search for new knowledge and new ways of using it has become a major activity of modern societies, involving large numbers of people and immense sums of money. Here the sociology of education is part of the very developments that it studies, as sociologists begin to study the organization of research, the recruitment of people to scientific and scholarly disciplines as well as to the professions, and the forces that give rise to innovations and their transmission to and adoption by various social institutions.

But for all the work and progress, sociologists have just begun to explore the world of education. Much more has been learned by sociologists about work and industry, politics, the family, and religion than about education and its institutions. Perhaps this is because so much was being done by educational psychologists, perhaps because only recently have we all become aware of the importance of education in modern society. Whatever the reason, the gap is being closed rapidly. Everywhere we turn there are new problems, as well as new possibilities for a contribution to both sociological theory and educational practice. A sociologist could not ask for more.

NOTE

1. Torsten Husén, *A Comparative Study of the Outcomes of Mathematics Instruction in Twelve Countries*, vol. 2 (Stockholm: Almqvist and Wiksells, 1966).

12 THE SOCIOLOGY OF ECONOMIC LIFE

Neil J. Smelser

ECONOMICS AND ECONOMIC SOCIOLOGY

The mere utterance of the phrase "the sociological analysis of economic life" raises an immediate and perplexing question: Since economic behavior is already the focus of the independent and highly developed discipline of economics, what do sociologists have to say about this kind of behavior? Or, to put the question more broadly, what are the differences between the approaches of the economist and the sociologist to economic activities and institutions?

The two approaches may be contrasted with each other in several ways:

First, the contrast may be made in terms of the subject matter to be explained. In many respects economists and sociologists ask different questions about economic behavior. Economists are interested in how people employ scarce resources to produce, distribute, and exchange goods and services for consumption. More specifically, they are interested in explaining the total level of production in a society; its composition in terms of different products—such as shoes, guns, and butter; the different combinations of the factors of production—such as land, labor, and capital; and the ways in which the rewards of economic activity—such as wages, rents, and profits—are distributed. The basic things to be explained in economics, then, are production, techniques of organizing resources, and distribution of wealth. Economic sociologists also are sometimes interested in these matters, but they focus mainly on other aspects of economic behavior. They treat it as a specific instance of general social behavior. Hence they are interested in studying economic behavior as complexes of roles and social organizations. In characterizing these roles and organizations, they focus on patterns of authority, status systems, networks of communications, and informal social groupings. In short, sociologists are interested in explaining variations in the social structure of economic activities and in explaining variations in behavior related to this social structure.

Second, the contrast may be made in terms of the forces impinging on economic behavior. Economists acknowledge that noneconomic variables—political, legal, and educational, for instance—influence economic life significantly. But in their discipline, economists usually assume that for purposes of economic analysis these influences are constant and thus do not modify economic processes; or, as it is often put, tastes and institutions are "given." Having thus simplified their view of economic activity, economists proceed to analyze the impact of economic variables upon one another. In particular, they are interested in explaining levels of output, price levels, wage levels, and so on, in terms of supply and demand factors in a market context. Economic sociologists relax, as it were, such stringent assumptions about the relations between economic and other social variables, and explicitly focus on explaining the ways these different types of variables impinge on one another. To illustrate: In studying wages, the economist concentrates mainly on the features of the market that influence wage levels—the supply of different types of skills in the labor force and the demand for these skills, which is in turn traceable to the existing level of technology and the demand for products produced by these skills. The economist may also wish to assess the impact of wage levels on the price level in general if, for example, he is interested in inflation. The sociologist, studying the same phenomenon of wages, inquires into a wider range of causes and consequences. If management, for instance, persistently tinkers with wage levels, this may strengthen informal cliques of workmen and incline them to subvert the authority of management, or it may foster the formation of a labor union or excite activity on the part of an existing one. Both these social consequences may then themselves feed back and influence the level of wages.

Third, the contrast may be made in terms of theoretical development of the respective fields. Because economists have limited the number of variables they study, and because they have been able to quantify most of their variables, they have advanced their science to a high level of theoretical sophistication. Very abstract and technical models of economic processes are available, and these are frequently expressed in precise mathematical terms. Of course, one of the costs of this theoretical excellence is that economists have greatly oversimplified the relations between economic and other social variables. The economic sociologist avoids this oversimplification by insisting that a multiplicity of social factors affects and is affected by economic activity. But in expanding his explanatory horizons the sociologist also pays a price: he is less able to organize his more complex subject matter into a theoretically adequate framework. Such are some of the theoretical tensions between economics and economic sociology.

In contrasting economics and economic sociology, I may have implied that economic sociology is a definite discipline that is formally organized, and taught and learned in specific courses of instruction. This is not the case. Economic sociology is rather a perspective in the process of emergence. Those who contribute to it go under many labels—labor relations experts, industrial sociologists, demographers, economic anthropologists, and those who study in those areas known as the sociology of work, the sociology of leisure, the sociology of economic development, and so on. Despite its looseness of organization and its diversity of sources, however, economic sociology does focus consistently on the application of sociological theory and research to the complex of activities concerned with the production, distribution, exchange, and consumption of economic goods and services.

In the remainder of my remarks I shall illustrate, selectively but scarcely exhaustively, the ways that the field of economic sociology has illuminated the relations among economic and other social variables.

145

AN ILLUSTRATION: THE PRIMARY GROUP IN ECONOMIC ACTIVITY

The primary group has long been a subject of interest among sociologists. It refers to a group that is sufficiently small to maintain frequent face-to-face interaction, and the ties within which are characterized by emotional intensity and diffuse loyalty. Examples of primary groups are nuclear families, cliques of friends, and small battle units such as airplane crews. In the past several decades, research by sociologists and others has uncovered numerous ways in which these small solidary groupings influence and are influenced by economic activity.

First, the primary group has come to be appreciated as a significant influence in the process of *production*. Until about forty years ago neither economists nor industrial sociologists were interested in the influence of workers' groups on output. The classical economists' version of worker behavior rested on the logic of supply and demand. It was assumed that the amount of work offered by an individual in the labor market is some function of the economic rewards available to him. On the job, too, the amount of work is a function of incentive schemes such as piecework and merit payments. Early in the twentieth century industrial sociology was characterized by a different but equally limited outlook. According to the main approach of the day— "scientific management," associated with the name of Frederick W. Taylor—workers in industrial organizations can be treated primarily as isolated neurophysiological organisms with definite capacities and skills; their efficiency, moreover, is largely a product of factors such as speed of work, amount of effort expended, and amount of rest allowed for recovery of strength. The scientific-management school more or less ignored the social-psychological determinants of morale and efficiency.

Recognition of the importance of solidary groupings within industrial organization was closely associated with the rise of the "human relations" approach in industrial sociology during the interwar period. When the famous Hawthorne experiments on productivity began in the Western Electric Company in Chicago in the 1920's, the initial emphasis was on the effects of various nonsocial factors—lighting and rest periods, for example—on worker performance. During the course of the experiments, however, it became apparent to the investigators that these "physical" factors were not nearly so important in fostering high morale and productivity as various "human" factors, such as receiving status, being accepted in a meaningful primary group, and being allowed to express grievances to a patient and responsive authority. The investigators, in short, isolated the solidary groupings as a determinant of economic behavior. Further experiments conducted in the Bank Wiring Room revealed that cliques of workmen could also affect productivity adversely by setting and enforcing their own informal standards of production rates, which were different from those established by management. These kinds of findings have given rise to a whole tradition of research on the diverse relations between the formal and informal organizations within a bureaucracy, and how these relations affect organizational functioning.

Turning to primary groups outside economic organizations, much research has shown how different kinds of family structure may facilitate or inhibit economic activity. Certain kinds of family structure—for example, primogeniture—may facilitate the formation of an urban-industrial labor force, since this structure ejects younger sons from the land and makes them possible candidates for other lines of employment. Research by Conrad M. Arensberg and Solon T. Kimball suggests that younger sons in rural Ireland constituted many of the migrants. Other features of family life, however, may inhibit economic activity. Kingsley Davis has pointed to the fact that the joint family system of traditional India, when combined with early marriage, discourages migration from the land and potential recruitment into other lines of employment. David Landes has argued that the peculiar structure of the French business family has kept the typical firm small and thus inhibited economic growth. In his study of the Chinese family, Marion Levy, Jr., isolated the factors of particularistic favoritism and functional diffuseness as features of Chinese kinship that constituted barriers to industrialization. And finally, many market arrangements show a kind of compromise between the demands of economic organizations and the demands of family life. A particularly clear example of this compromise is seen in the organization of many African labor markets in which male workers spend part of the year—or even several years—in urban employment away from their wives and families, and the rest of the time with their families in rural areas.

The relations between family life and economic activity are not a one-way street, of course. In fact, most of the research on these relations has been devoted to the impact of urbanization and industrialization on family life. Furthermore, the keynote for much of this research was set by the writings of a number of sociologists from the University of Chicago—especially William Ogburn and Ernest Burgess—the main thrust of which was to demonstrate that urbanization and industrialization have led first to the isolation of the family into a small, nuclear form and ultimately to its disintegration.

More recent research has challenged this simple and widely accepted thesis. Talcott Parsons has argued that the urban-industrial complex does not cause the family to deteriorate but rather gives rise to a more highly specialized and in some ways more effective family system. Other investigators have questioned whether the urban-industrial complex has caused the modern revolution in family relations. In the study of "pre-industrial" cities in Europe, China, and the Middle East, for example, Gideon Sjoberg found ample evidence of patriarchal, extended family organization; unequal rights for women; and kinship particularism—in short, all the features associated with the traditional *rural* family. Sjoberg's tentative conclusion is that urbanization as such is not responsible for modern family changes, but rather industrialization is the prime mover. Other investigators have called industrialization as a cause into question as well. William J. Goode has pointed out that modern family changes in the Muslim Middle East are moving in the same direction as changes in the West during the past two centuries, yet the Middle East has scarcely experienced an industrial revolution as yet. In her research on south Indian villages, T. Scarlett Epstein traced the decline of the extended family not to industrial changes but rather to certain types of new irrigation patterns and changes in land ownership. Arguing this kind of point from another angle, Eugene Litwak has suggested that while the demands of the modern occupational structure make for high family mobility, this has not destroyed the extended family. In fact, he asserts that modern communication and transportation systems permit the continued existence of visiting patterns and other contacts among extended family members, even if they are geographically removed from one another.

Clearly, then, the impact of urbanization and industrialization on family life is not so simple as originally portrayed by the Chicago school of family sociologists. Conditions other than urbanization and industrialization give rise to the more or less isolated nuclear or conjugal family; and not all instances of urbanization and industrialization create this kind of family system. More certain knowledge about these relations must rest both on more complex and sophisticated conceptualizations of industrialization and urbanization, and on an accumulation of careful comparative research.

With respect to *consumption,* not so much research has been done on the mutual relations between primary groups and economic activity, but it is apparent that primary groups influence consumption choices markedly. The life cycle of the family, for example, exercises a striking influence on consumers' spending and saving patterns. Consider the following regularities in the life of an American married couple. In the early childless period of married life, both husband and wife may be employed, but most earnings are spent on consumer durables, such as automobiles, furniture, and perhaps housing. During the early years of the children's life, the family is hard pressed to save or make big investments or to lay aside much in saving, since expenditures increase for children and income may decline as the wife quits employment. In the middle years—as the required support for dependents declines, the husband's income perhaps reaches its maximum, and the wife returns to work—the family is able to set aside considerable savings for retirement. In the later years, however, income drops radically with retirement and the family has to live in part on its past savings. In traditional sectors of societies such as India, enormous expenditures are made at critical points of the life cycle—such as wedding ceremonies, burial ceremonies, and feasts for the dead.

In addition to these life-cycle considerations, sex roles closely associated with marriage influence the family's expenditures. The demand for clothing in contemporary America is an example. Women, being relatively more involved in family entertainment and other "expressive" roles, demand a much more variegated line of clothing products, and actually spend more on clothing than men; men, being relatively more rooted in the impersonal occupational setting, demand a more limited line of "work clothes" and "business suits." Again, the sharp distinction between work and leisure for men in contemporary America is symbolized in clothing styles; hence the bifurcation of the demand for men's clothing into the more somber, solid styles to be worn at work and the more casual or even flamboyant styles to be worn in leisure.

One final example of the intrusion of primary group relations on consumption is in order. In an analysis of social processes leading to the purchases of foods and household goods, attendance at motion pictures, and changes in fashion, Elihu Katz and Paul Lazarsfeld isolated what they call the "two-step" flow of influence. Any given community has some citizens who are "influentials," and who maintain close touch with national and international advertising of products and services. The buying habits of the remainder of the consumers, who are normally out of touch with or uninfluenced by advertising, are nonetheless influenced *personally* by the "influentials," largely through informal contact in the community. Among other things, this research marks the discovery of the primary group—in which personal influence is the keynote—in the area of consumption, as it had been discovered in productive contexts by industrial sociologists.

FURTHER ILLUSTRATIONS: POLITICAL AND CULTURAL VARIABLES IN ECONOMIC ACTIVITY

I have dwelt at some length on the primary group, not because it is intrinsically most important but for two other reasons. First, I feel it is essential to explore a few illustrations rather than attempt a superficial coverage of the whole field of economic sociology. And second, the study of the primary group in economic life is very much an American product. Most theoretical innovations and empirical research have been supplied by American scholars. When we turn to other areas of economic sociology, however, we find that most of the major theories and even many of the contemporary research issues originated in European scholarship. This is especially noticeable with respect to the place of political and cultural variables in economic life. Most of the issues that are alive today in these areas of economic sociology trace to the contributions of—and conflicts between— two giants of the sociological tradition, Karl Marx and Max Weber.

The arguments of Karl Marx on the relations between economic activity and sociocultural structures are well known. For Marx, the key structures in any society are built around the organization of economic production. The general characteristics of the stratification system, the political system, the religious system, and the rest of society's superstructure are determined by the economic order. Furthermore, in any given system of production—such as the capitalist—the political system and the religious system are seen as weapons of the dominant bourgeois class in its struggle to subordinate the proletarian class. Much of Max Weber's sociology is devoted to studying the same general relations, but his formulations differ radically from Marx's. In particular, Weber was preoccupied with some of the noneconomic conditions under which industrial capitalism of the modern Western type would arise and flourish. One of his most famous arguments is that the rise of ascetic protestantism, especially Calvinism, established social and psychological conditions conducive to this particular form of capitalism. Another well-known argument is that bureaucracy provides the most rational form of social organization for perpetuating industrial capitalism. Weber also found many other conducive institutional structures in the political-legal complex, especially in property laws and monetary systems.

With this brief identification of themes in Marx and Weber, let us set forth a few examples of contemporary research on the relations between economic phenomena on the one hand and political and cultural factors on the other. Defined broadly, the term "political" encompasses the study of authority systems in organizations, the study of governments, and the study of competition and conflict among groups. The economic sociologist is concerned with studying the mutual relations between economic activities and these diverse political phenomena.

Most studies of authority systems within industrial firms involve the relations between the type of supervision (typically described in terms of an authoritarian-democratic dimension) and worker morale, productivity, and receptivity to innovations. The most common finding is that worker morale and productivity are higher under "employee-centered" leadership than under leadership oriented to technical standards of efficiency. Most of the experiments and field studies on supervision have been carried out in countries with democratic traditions—especially the United States and Great Britain. Societies with different political traditions might not display the same results.

Research on the political relations between economic organizations and other social units has advanced on a variety of fronts. Under the heading of the economics of imperfect competition, economists have studied a variety of political involvements of business firms—ways in which large firms are able to control and perhaps dominate prices and output under monopolistic conditions, ways in which wealth and power become concentrated in the economy, and ways in which government policies (e.g., antitrust policies) influence the structure and behavior of firms. Economists and sociologists have devoted a modest amount of research to the power relations between stockholders and managers and between consumers and business firms, but far more research has been conducted on the power relations and conflicts between business firms and labor unions. In particular, scholars have devoted much study to the causes of labor disputes. Some causes have been fairly well established: strikes occur more frequently under conditions of prosperity; more frequently in isolated industries with homogeneous worker populations; and less frequently under totalitarian governments and in periods of national crisis.

Finally, much contemporary research and discussion focuses on the relations between business and government. This research is shrouded by ideological controversy and confused findings. One school of thought, advanced by the late C. Wright Mills, argues that national political power has become increasingly concentrated in recent decades in the United States, and that the holders of power and makers of important decisions are constituted by a small group of corporate executives and military officials. This view, however, has been challenged on both substantive and methodological grounds. The empirical research on economic controls over local politics also shows a mixed picture. In a study of a southern community, Floyd Hunter concluded that the major decisions were guided by a small group of economically dominant individuals. Other research, for example that of Delbert Miller and Robert Schulze, indicates that the degree to which business groups dominate local politics varies considerably from community to community and over time.

As these few examples of research reveal, the issues raised so forcefully by Marx and Weber still dominate research relating to the mutual influence of economic and political factors—issues such as the conditions of effective authority in organizations, the conditions under which different economic interest groups become locked in combat with one another, and the degree to which the economic system dominates the political system.

The term "culture" refers to that complex of symbols that gives meaning and legitimacy to the conduct of social life. Concrete cultural items are cosmologies, values, ideologies, aesthetic productions, and scientific knowledge. The economic sociologist is preoccupied with the ways in which these symbols facilitate or inhibit various types of economic activity, and the ways in which economic behavior leads to modifications of cultural symbols.

Little research has been conducted on the role of cultural factors within economic organizations. What has been done focuses mainly on problems of effective communication. One of the persistent problems of bureaucracies, for example, is the disruption that occurs when necessary information is lacking altogether, withheld, distorted in passage, or too slow in arriving. Numerous studies of industrial bureaucracy have uncovered typical points of distortion and omission: subordinates "cover up" information they do not wish to have known by their supporters, and foremen "soften" orders from above out of sympathy with workmen.

Sociologists have conducted a more substantial amount of research on the relations *between* economic organization and cultural symbols. Some research, for example that of Robert N. Bellah on Tokugawa Japan, focuses directly on Weber's problem concerning the ways in which religious beliefs stimulate or inhibit economic development. Other scholars have inquired into the relations between ideologies and economic activity. The most thorough study of the ways ideologies are used as instruments of social control in industry is Reinhard Bendix's comparative research on managerial ideologies as they have developed in four industrializing countries—Great Britain, the United States, Russia, and East Germany. Bendix's main concern is with the justifications that managerial classes have generated in the process of inducing workers to submit to their authority. The effects of ideology in relieving role-strains are emphasized in the study by Francis Sutton *et al.,* of the American business creed; these investigators attribute the tenacity of the free-enterprise ideology among businessmen to strains in their roles; for example, their own ambivalence toward the phenomenon of bigness in the American economy is smoothed over by a defiant reassertion of the values of traditional free enterprise. Ely Chinoy's study of automobile workers also stresses the frustration-reducing elements of ideology, which often serves to rationalize the discrepancies between the expectations generated by the American Dream of equality of opportunity and the actual life situations of the workers.

Again, these examples show that the issues raised by Marx and Weber are very much in the forefront of contemporary research on culture and economic activity—especially the issues of whether cultural symbols should be considered as determined by economic roles, whether these symbols exert an independent influence on economic activity, or whether some kind of mutual interplay governs the relations between the two. The over-all impression gained from the research is that some kind of process of mutual interdependence obtains, but as yet sociologists have not produced an adequate theoretical formulation of this process.

In this chapter I have tried to sketch outlines of the growing field of economic sociology and to provide a sample of its issues and research. I have been able to cover the field only inadequately. If space permitted, I would summarize and assess the sociological work being done on occupational roles, on comparative economic structures, on the analytic relations among economic systems and other social systems, and—perhaps most important—on the relations between economic and other social variables in periods of change, especially as they have been studied under the label of "modernization." Finally, I hope this chapter has conveyed the idea that the field of economic sociology is in a fluid state of emergence. While much important research has been and is being conducted, many more empirical findings and much more careful theoretical formulations must come forth before the field reaches a point of adequate scientific integration.

13 POLITICAL SOCIOLOGY

Seymour Martin Lipset

Ever since the term sociology was first applied, the analysis of political processes and institutions has been one of its most important concerns. Sociologists argue and many political scientists agree that it is difficult to study political processes except as special cases of more general psychological and sociological relationships. In recent years many political scientists have elaborated and tested many politically relevant aspects of social science theory. The term "political sociology" has come to be accepted within both sociology and political science as encompassing the overlap between the two parental disciplines.

Within political science such work is often described as the behavioral or social science approach, but political sociology is of fairly recent vintage as a major subfield within sociology; there were few courses or books which used the term before World War II. Yet the linkage and overlap between sociology and political science date back, in fact, to the formal origins of both disciplines in the late nineteenth century. In Europe, the work of Weber, Michels, Mosca, Pareto, and Siegfried was relevant to the emerging concerns of what eventually became two fields. It is debatable whether various scholars were sociologists or political scientists. Thus, one review contends that the major sociologists in the late nineteenth century "were, for the most part, political sociologists, or, it may even be said, sociological political scientists."[1]

Political sociology can be defined most simply as the study of the interrelationship between society and polity, between social structure and political institutions. It is important to note that this definition does not imply casual priority to society over polity; political sociology is not, or not solely, the study of the social factors which condition the political order. For political institutions are themselves social structures, and hence are often the independent—that is, in the common-sense meaning, the casual—factors which affect other nonpolitical aspects of the social structure. For example, there is a considerable body of literature which asserts that the formal provisions defining the executive, the division of powers among different political units, or the laws which define the procedures for electing officials (elections systems, types of constituencies, and so on) have had powerful determining influences on the shape of the class structure; which groups have a sense of group consciousness; the lines of communications; the extent to which given nations have significant subcultures; and the like. Societal conceptions of proper authority relations may affect the power of officeholders, but the way in which the political institutions distribute political authority may influence orientations toward those in authority in a variety of structures. Politics, no more than economics, is an epiphenomenon of general social structures.

The polity may be viewed as that part of the social system which is responsible for allocating the resources and facilities of the society. Obviously the various subgroups within society are concerned with the way such resources are allocated. Decisions made by those in control of the state will necessarily bear unequally on groups and individuals. Consequently, there must be some mechanisms which lead individuals to accept the propriety of the decision-making system, which make them obey and even carry out decisions which they do not like. At the same time, since the various subgroups in the system will necessarily disagree about the policies to be followed, polities must formulate mechanisms through which such groups can maximize their ability to bring pressure on the decision-making structure. The analysis of the ways in which polities develop consensus about the rules of the game and handle the interplay among the diverse interests and values has been dealt with by political sociologists under the headings of legitimacy and cleavage.

LEGITIMACY AND EFFECTIVENESS

The stability of any given polity, its long-term ability to make decisions and secure adherence to them without the use of naked force, depends in large measure upon its legitimacy and effectiveness. Legitimacy involves the capacity of the system to engender and maintain the belief that the existing political institutions are the most appropriate ones for the society; effectiveness means actual performance, the extent to which the system satisfies the basic functions of government as most of the population and key powerful groups within it, such as the army and those who control the basic economic institutions, see them. While effectiveness is primarily instrumental, legitimacy is evaluative, linked to values.

The great German sociologist Max Weber suggested that there are basically three ways through which an authority may gain legitimacy, that is, an accepted "title to rule."

1. It may gain legitimacy through *tradition,* through "always" having possessed it. The title held by monarchical societies is essentially of this type.

2. *Rational-legal* authority exists when those in power are obeyed because of a general acceptance of the appropriateness of the system of laws under which they have won and held office.

3. *Charismatic* authority rests upon faith in a leader who is believed to be endowed with great personal worth: this may come from God, as in the case of a religious prophet, or may simply arise from the display of extraordinary talents.[2]

The contemporary world has many societies in which legitimacy is weak. A crisis of legitimacy is essentially a crisis of change. Crises of legitimacy have occurred in societies which are undergoing a transition to a new social structure, e.g., from feudal industrialism to capitalism, or from capitalism to some form of a socialist welfare or planning state. New nations such as those in Africa and Asia, and post-revolutionary regimes, like those of France in 1789 or Russia in 1917, obviously lack any claim to traditional legitimacy. Legal-rational legitimacy is weak in most such nations today, since to much of the population the law has been identified with the interests of a foreign or a domestic exploiter.

Severe crises flowing from the weak sense of legitimate political authority are likely to occur in such polities if (1) the *status* of major traditionally important groups is threatened during a period of structural change; and (2) not all the major groups in the society have access to the political system in the transitional period, or at least as soon as they develop political demands. To develop legitimacy, the new system must sustain the expectations of major groups (on the grounds of "effectiveness") for a long period, so that they may gain confidence in, and accept the propriety of, the "rules of the game" under which the new system operates.

Clearly, to incorporate basic structural changes while maintaining traditional legitimacy in political institutions would appear to be the best way to avoid political tensions. Thus it may be noted that if we divide democratic states as stable or unstable according to the criteria of whether they have had the uninterrupted continuation of political democracy since World War I *and* of the absence in them over the past thirty years of a major political movement opposed to the democratic rules of the game (i.e., no major fascist or communist parties), then we come up with the curious fact that ten out of the twelve or thirteen stable democracies in the world, those which fulfill these two requirements, are monarchies. Great Britain, Sweden, Norway, Denmark, the Netherlands, Belgium, Luxembourg, Australia, Canada, and New Zealand are kingdoms, or dominions of a monarch, while the only republics which meet the conditions to be defined as stable democracies are the United States and Switzerland, and possibly Uruguay.

In the first group, the preservation of the monarchy during the transition to a modern industrial society apparently retained for these polities the loyalty of the aristocratic, traditionalist, and clerical sectors of the population, even though these groups resented and resisted increased democratization and equalitarianism. In countries where monarchy was overthrown by revolution, and orderly succession was broken, the republican successor regimes have not been able to win legitimacy from all important

159

sectors down to the fifth post-revolutionary generation or more.

The second general source of loss of legitimacy during periods of drastic social change arises from the ways in which different societies handle the "entry into politics" crisis—the decision as to when new social groups shall obtain access to the political process. Whenever new groups become politically active, as for example when the workers first seek access to economic and political power, easy access to the *legitimate* political institutions has tended to win the loyalty of such new groups to the political system, and they in turn have permitted the old dominating institutions or strata, such as the monarchy or the aristocracy, to maintain their *status* while losing their power.

Political systems which deny new strata access to power except by drastic pressure or revolution also threaten legitimacy by introducing millennial (utopian or unattainable) hopes into the political arena. Groups which have to push their way into the body politic by force are apt to exaggerate the possibilities which political participation affords. Consequently, regimes born under such stress not only face the difficulty of being regarded as illegitimate by groups loyal to the *ancien régime* but may also be rejected by those whose millennial hopes are not fulfilled by the change. Today many of the newly independent states of Asia and Africa face the thorny problem of winning the loyalty of the masses to states which can do little to meet the utopian objectives set by nationalist movements during the period of colonialism and the transitional struggle of independence.

Given the legitimacy problems facing new nations and post-revolutionary societies, it is not surprising that many of them seem to find charismatic authority suited to their needs. Charisma, the cult of the leader's personality as a source of authority, is highly flexible and requires neither a long time to accrue nor a rational set of accepted rules. A charismatic leader is first of all the hero of the nation, who symbolizes in his person its values and aspirations. But more than this, he legitimates the new secular government by endowing it with his "gift of grace."[3] Charismatic authority, as exhibited in the leadership cults erected around Lenin and Stalin in the Soviet Union, Touré in Guinea, Kenyatta in Kenya, Nasser and Bourguiba in North Africa,

Castro in Cuba, and Mao in China, can be seen as a mechanism of transition, an interim measure which gets people to observe the requirements of the nation out of affection for the leader until they eventually learn to do it out of loyalty to the collectivity.

Sociologists have noted that polities characterized by charismatic legitimacy, however, are inherently more unstable than those possessing the other types. The charismatic leader is usually both the *source* and the *agent* of authority. In limited monarchies and constitutional democratic republics, however, the source, the king, figurehead president, or constitution, is not involved in responsibility for the actions of the given regime. The population is encouraged to differentiate between the *source,* which is to be venerated, and the *agent* and his policies, which may be *evaluated* as good or bad. In a charismatic system, discontents with the activities of the government will weaken the legitimacy of the polity and possibly result in the overthrow of the leader and his system. The downfall of charismatic leaders such as Syngman Rhee in Korea or Nkrumah in Ghana is an example of the relative brittleness of charismatic authority in the new states of Asia and Africa.

In *The First New Nation* I have argued that the early American Republic, like many of the contemporary new nations, was legitimized by *charisma,* although it also retained strong elements of rational-legal legitimacy carried over from the state governments.[4] We tend to forget that George Washington was idolized as much as many of the leaders of the new states of today. Unlike most of them, however, he resisted the pressure from those close to him to become an autocrat. However, he deliberately took on an aspect of a constitutional monarch, recognizing that his most important contribution to the new state was to give it time to establish a government of men under law, which we now call a rational-legal system of authority. He permitted the members of his cabinet to form hostile factions under the leadership of Hamilton and Jefferson, even though he personally disliked the views of the Jeffersonians. Washington refused to take full advantage of his charisma, even withdrawing from the presidency voluntarily and seemingly in good health; in so doing, he pushed the American polity faster toward a legal-rational system of authority than would have developed had he taken over the charismatic role *in toto*. The almost unique half charismatic-half rational-legal leadership had a powerful stabilizing effect on the society's evolution.

In new states or post-revolutionary regimes legitimacy must be won through demonstrated effectiveness. Loyalty to the system must be attained through developing in the various groups a conviction that the new government is the best—or at least an excellent—way to accomplish their objectives. The populace subjects even charismatic claims to a highly pragmatic test— that is, what is the payoff? For most such regimes today, demonstrating effectiveness means one thing: economic development. Given the "revolution of rising expectations," the payoff in terms of economic goods and living standards is more important than ever. Payoff, however, need not be defined only in economic terms.

The polity may win general acceptance through enhancing national prestige. Thus, the French Fifth Republic has won considerable acceptance among left-wing intellectuals because de Gaulle's emphasis on France's position as a major independent nation and his insistence on the supremacy of French language and culture strongly appeal to the educated strata. Various foreign observers have testified to the extent to which Red China's defeat of the United States in the Korean War has appealed to the emotions of anti-communist Chinese, who rejoice to see once humble China humiliate a major white power.

Various analysts have attributed the recurrent breakdowns in Latin America to the fact that few of these regimes have acquired legitimacy since their break with Spain and Portugal a century and a half ago. Lacking economic or symbolic effectiveness, they have failed to achieve legitimacy, and hence are unable to withstand crises.[5] The various military coups in 1965–1966 in East Asia, the Arab states, and Africa south of the Sahara also indicate the problems inherent in polities low in legitimacy which repeatedly face effectiveness crises. The political stability of those few Afro-Asian nations with traditional legitimacy, for example, Ethiopia and Thailand, stands out in sharp contrast to the situation in nearby former colonial territories.

As recent history has demonstrated, the political behavior of the military poses a special problem for nations weak in legitimacy. Only the military have the internal organization, the sense of group loyalty and authority, and, most important, the means to overturn the government quickly whenever they find its acts repugnant. The strength of the norms governing civil-military relations are therefore of crucial importance in any consideration of the social factors making for political stability. One may compare the need of the polity for powerful norms prescribing civilian control over the military to the need of the family for the incest taboo. Sociologists seeking to account for the universality of the latter, for the great repugnance felt everywhere against incest, have suggested that this taboo is a vital requisite for a human society. They point out that within a family the older members are more powerful than the younger, and that the more powerful—parents, older siblings—could take younger members as sexual partners. Since this is so, and the sex drive is also extremely strong, the only way to avoid the threat to the stability of the family posed by the possibility of incest is the existence of a norm more powerful than all others, which fills people with a sense of horror, of great sin or evil, if it is violated. And in a comparable vein, one may suggest that the military can overturn regimes at will, and hence destroy the possibility of stable government. Polities, therefore, require a strong norm to which the military adhere that insists on the separation of the political and military areas, no matter how much the military dislike the given policies of the government.

Inherent in the concept of legitimacy is military acceptance of civil authority. Hence, where legitimacy is weak, the taboo against military intervention in politics will also be weak, and one would expect to find the military taking part whenever the polity violates their concepts of right and wrong. Given this possibility, societies establish particularly strong norms which insist that officers must not violate their oath to obey the government. A considerable amount of symbolism and ritual is attached to the oath, the pledge of allegiance. The idea is drummed into the heads of professional soldiers that there is no higher virtue than obedience. (The emphasis on obedience, of course, is also linked to the need to make certain that men will obey their military superiors in times of actual combat.) And reports of the deliberations of officers who have considered or been involved in coups indicate that they have often long delayed such actions because of their feeling that by violating their oath they were committing a heinous crime, that they were repudiating the honor of the military. Many German officers, who despised Hitler and the Nazis, and who were morally incensed at the crimes committed by the Nazis in murdering millions of Jews and others, still could not bring themselves to violate their oath.

Where legitimacy is weak, where armies do not have a tradition of accepting the authority of civilians, where they have shifted allegiance from one regime to another in the recent past as a result of the nation's gaining independence or a revolution, the commitment to the oath will be weak. And if such regimes are not only low in legitimacy but are relatively ineffective in handling domestic problems or in dealing with foreign powers, one may expect to find, as we have already noted, recurrent military coups. This conclusion points up the need to consider the relationship between the exercise of force within political systems and the effectiveness of such systems.

Instrumental effectiveness and legitimacy are much more decisive for democracies than for autocracies, since democracy rests on consensus. Democracy involves the highest degree of access to the decision-making structure by various groups and individuals in the polity. And in complex social systems, as Max Weber and Joseph Schumpeter stressed, the distinctive way in which such access is made possible is through the formation of the political elite (the officeholders) in the competitive struggle for the votes of the electorate. In large-scale societies, democracy means an institutionalized competitive party system; in the absence of such a system, hardly anything limits the power of the political elite to ignore the desires of large segments of the population, or to use repressive methods.

Since democracy requires popular endorsement, it will also require prolonged effectiveness: that is, it must satisfy most of the people most of the time. Consequently it is not surprising that the most common generalization linking political systems to other aspects of society has been that democracy is related to the state of economic development. The more well-to-do a nation, the greater the chances that it will sustain democracy. From Aristotle down to the present, men have argued that only in a wealthy society with relatively few really poor citizens could the mass of the population intelligently participate in politics and develop the self-restraint necessary to resist irresponsible demagogues. A society divided between a large impoverished mass and a small elite results either in oligarchy (dictatorial rule of the small upper stratum) or in tyranny (popular-based dictatorship). To give these two political forms modern labels, tyranny's face today is communism; oligarchy appears in the traditionalist dictatorships found in countries like Paraguay, Haiti, Thailand, Spain, and Portugal.

A number of different scholars have pointed to the statistical relationship between the level of economic development and the existence of democratic stable polities. These studies show that the more economically developed and literate a country, the more likely it is to have a competitive party system.[6]

PARTIES AND VOTING

Perhaps the largest single field of inquiry in political sociology has been the study of voting behavior, partly because it is more easily researchable. Statistical data bearing on elections are available for many countries for long periods of time, and samples of the electorate may be easily interviewed, using conventional opinion-survey techniques. Concentration on electoral behavior is valuable, since voting is both a key mechanism of consensus in democratic societies and a major means of institutionalizing the conflicts among different groups. Students of elections, however, have been primarily concerned with the relationship between political parties and such types of cleavage as class, occupation, religion, ethnic group, and region, more as factors which generate political strife than as political consensus.

In contemporary democratic countries the most stable sources of party support come from factors related to stratification and cultural values. There are relatively permanent party alignments between higher and lower orders in status, income, and power, and also between specific groups which differ greatly in their views about the good society. The prototype of the first type of cleavage is the class party; the prototype of the second is the religious party. Differences rooted in stratification are preponderant in economically developed, stable polities in which the "politics of collective bargaining" is customary—fights over the division of the total economic pie, over the extent of the welfare and planning state, and the like.

Cultural or deeply rooted value conflicts are much more characteristic of developing countries with unstable polities. In addition to conflicts rooted in class differences, there emerge divisions between those adhering to values rooted in institutions linked to the pre-modern era, and those who accept orientations which are endemic in the processes of social and economic development, i.e., modernization. We see examples of cultural conflicts in the efforts to sustain the traditional position of historic religion, to maintain the status and privileges of higher social strata such as the nobility—whose position is a function of a pre-industrial society—and to protect the family pattern of a static rural society from the demands of a more universalistic system. Many of the variables which are associated with positions in a *Kulturkampf* (culture conflict) are linked not to stratification but to differential involvement in traditional or modern institutions (e.g., poor religious peasants may be conservatives, while well-to-do young professionals may be radical) and to generational experiences—the younger and better educated versus the older and the less educated. Sex, too, may provide a base for diversity where such issues are significant, since in most societies women's roles are more implicated in religious institutions, less in modern economic ones. Women are also less educated on the average than men and consequently they tend to be more supportive of traditionalist parties than of modernizing ones.

In many of the emerging nations that have developed some form of politics, party conflict has involved a division between modernizing and traditionalist elements instead of the left-right stratification more characteristic of the older, wealthier, and more stable polities. To a considerable extent, socialism and communism are associated symbolically with independence, rapid economic development, social modernization, and ultimate equality. Capitalism is seen as aligned to foreign influences, traditionalism, and slow growth. Hence, support for enhanced leftism is not only based on segments of the working class; it also secures considerable backing from the better educated who favor modernization.

I am not saying that stratification does not differentiate left and right in the developing nations. It certainly does. The support for mass communist or left socialist parties in some of these countries comes primarily from workers or impoverished sectors of the rural population. Although the Castro movement originated among university students, and drew much of its initial support from middle-class "modernizing" elements, the proportion of those with lower status and education who backed him increased after Castro came to power.[7] However, it is important to note that the modernizing-traditionalist division brings to the left heavy support from the better-educated and more privileged—students, military officers, civil servants, and executives—who associate leftism or socialism with rapid modernization.[8]

If we consider the developed countries next, it is clear from various sociological studies that in all of them there is a correlation between the leftism or conservatism of political parties and variables which can be ranked in stratification terms. The more liberal or left-wing parties are disproportionately supported by those with low incomes, by workers, by poorer farmers, by the less educated, and by members of low status, religious, racial, or ethnic groups. There are, however, many exceptions to these relationships, which the political sociologist must seek to explain.

The complexity (multidimensionality) of the stratification system of modern society itself helps account in large measure for the variations from the modal pattern. In the field of politics, deviations from the correlation between party support and any given indicator of class position help prevent the left from gaining the permanent majority which many nineteenth-century conservative opponents of adult suffrage thought was inherent in the fact that the poor seemingly outnumbered the well-to-do. Many are subject to politically conflicting experiences according to their position on different dimensions of the stratification system. Thus men may be high in power but disproportionately low in status or income; they may have high economic position and relatively lower social status, and so forth. Much research has shown that when men occupy incongruous social positions, the contribution of two discrepant statuses may produce responses different from the effects of either taken by itself, and also sometimes make for a more extremist reaction.

It may be suggested that, on the whole, conflicting stratification rankings contribute more to the support of the right than of the left. Men are constantly engaged in an effort to maximize their self-evaluation, their sense of status, and to reduce painful blows to their self-esteem. It seems natural that individuals should attempt to order their perception of the environment so as to maximize their claim to as high a status as possible. The man who achieves high occupational position, for example, is likely to drop his memberships in organizations which are lowly in status, to move to a higher-status neighborhood, and perhaps even to leave his low-ranking church for one whose members are higher in position, and in general try to take over the behavior pattern of higher social classes. When faced with the "choice" of acting out the standards of behavior inherent in different aspects of his positions in various stratification orders, he is more likely to opt in favor of those which are higher. All other things being equal, people are prone to see themselves among the more rather than the less privileged, if any option exists for them. Politically, this implies pressure to become more conservative. This is an example of a "conservative" bias inherent in stratification, which helps to counter the appeal of anti-elitist leftist parties to the resentments and aspirations of the numerous less-privileged strata.

There are, of course, many other relevant factors not directly related to stratification which sociological theory and research have specified as significantly affecting the behavior of the electorate. These range from the impact of diverse values to the effects of the mass-media and communications systems. The subtlety and complexity of the research on political behavior can only be hinted at in this chapter. And I particularly regret not being able to deal with the way sociologists have analyzed electoral systems as agencies of consensus.

CONCLUSION

The subjects discussed in this chapter clearly do not exhaust the interests of political sociologists. There is considerable literature devoted to the study of political participation at various levels. Many scholars have concerned themselves with the analysis of the conditions which foster the emergence of new social movements. Others have sought to understand the factors which affect the representative character of voluntary associations, e.g., political parties, professional societies, veterans' groups, trade unions, and so forth. Some have investigated the phenomenon of bureaucratization, seeking to specify the relationship between the formal structures of large social organizations and other elements in society. Most recently, political sociology like other branches of the field has become increasingly comparative in its methodology. A growing body of work seeks to relate systematically varying aspects of national polities to differences in the over-all social systems of which they are a part, such as their basic values.

NOTES

1. Albert Lepawsky, "The Politics of Epistemology," *Proceedings of the Western Political Science Association* (supplement to *The Western Political Quarterly*, XVII (September 1964), 32.
2. These are essentially the distinctions drawn by Max Weber. See H. H. Gerth and C. Wright Mills, eds., *From Max Weber: Essays in Sociology* (New York: Oxford University Press, 1946), pp. 78ff.
3. See Richard M. Morse, "Political Theory and the Caudillo," in Hugh M. Hamill, Jr., ed., *Dictatorship in Latin America* (New York: Alfred A. Knopf, 1965), pp. 62–67.

4. S. M. Lipset, *The First New Nation: The United States in Historical Comparative Perspective* (New York: Basic Books, 1963).

5. See Martin C. Needler, *Latin American Politics in Perspective* (Princeton: Van Nostrand, 1963).

6. See S. M. Lipset, *Political Man* (Garden City: Doubleday, 1960), pp. 48–67; James S. Coleman, "The Political Systems of the Developing Areas," in Gabriel Almond and James S. Coleman, eds., *The Politics of the Developing Areas* (Princeton: Princeton University Press, 1960), pp. 538–544; Everett Hagen, "A Framework for Analyzing Economic and Political Change," in Robert Asher, ed., *Development of Emerging Nations* (Washington: Brookings Institute, 1962), pp. 1–8; Charles Wolf, Jr., *The Political Effects of Economic Programs* (Santa Monica: The RAND Corporation, RM-3901-ISA, February 1964), pp. 19–34; Daniel Lerner, *The Passing of Traditional Society* (Glencoe, Ill.: The Free Press, 1958), p. 63.

7. That Castro's initial following was largely based on young, well-educated, middle-class Cubans has been documented by Theodore Draper. He points out that of Castro's eighteen cabinet members in 1960, every one was a university graduate, that they were of middle- or upper-class background, and professionals or intellectuals occupationally. Theodore Draper, *Castro's Revolution, Myths and Realities* (New York: Praeger, 1962) pp. 42–43. Draper also points out that the list of Cuban defenders of Castroism who were interviewed by C. Wright Mills in his effort to present the authentic voice of the Cuban Revolution for his book *Listen Yankee* did not include a single worker or peasant. "Without exception, his informants were middle-class intellectuals and professionals" (p. 21).

8. The appeal of left-wing ideologies to the intellectuals and other sections of the university-trained intelligentsia in the underdeveloped nations has been analyzed in some detail. See Morris Watnick, "The Appeal of Communism to the Peoples of Underdeveloped Areas," in R. Bendix and S. M. Lipset, eds., *Class, Status and Power* (Glencoe, Ill.: The Free Press, 1953), pp. 651–662; Hugh Seton-Watson, "Twentieth Century Revolutions," *The Political Quarterly*, XXII (1951), 251–265; John H. Kautsky, ed., *Political Change in Underdeveloped Countries* (New York: John Wiley, 1962), pp. 44–49, 106–113; Edward Shils, "The Intellectual between Tradition and Modernity: The Indian Situation," *Comparative Studies in Society and History*, Supplement No. 1 (1961), 94–108. Perhaps the most comprehensive treatment of the subject is Edward Shils, "The Intellectuals in the Political Development of the New States," in Kautsky, *op. cit.*, pp. 195–234.

14 THE SOCIOLOGY OF LAW

Leon Mayhew

The sociology of law proceeds upon the assumption that law occurs in a social context and can only be understood in that context. The word "occurs" is important here because, from a sociological point of view, law is not to be regarded as only a static set of rules, but as a process. Law occurs in courts, in administrative agencies, in law-enforcement agencies, in attorneys' offices, in business offices, and in negotiations between private citizens in all walks of life. It occurs as people use, interpret, apply, and create social norms with legally binding validity —that is, social norms which are enforceable by politically organized society.

The sociologist is concerned with explaining order and coherence in social life, and, to that end, sociologists often stress the importance of social norms, of the established social rules which serve to coordinate human activity. However, the sociologist cannot stop there, for he understands that norms do not operate automatically by their own power. People use norms, appeal to them, interpret them, and apply them. It is only by understanding this process that we can understand how legal norms function in social organization and how social organization shapes and constrains the legal process.

For example, it is not enough for the sociologist to know that there is, in the American legal system, a "right" to trial by jury. He wishes to know what sorts of people, from what social locations, are called on to serve on juries and how juries organize their deliberations. He wishes to know in what circumstances juries try to apply the formal law and when they rely on their intuitive sense of justice. The sociologist wants to know the consequences of trial by jury on the operation of the legal system and he seeks to understand how the organization of social life accounts for these consequences.

Thus the sociology of law has roots in sociology, for sociologists are interested in any human activity with a social character. At the same time, to understand the course of development of sociology of law in America, it is necessary to appreciate that sociological inquiry into legal institutions has occurred in the context of the discussion of intellectual issues that transcend academic sociology. The strengths and limitations of our efforts to bring sociological insight to the study of law derive from the fact that three polemical issues have animated discussion of the role of law in society.

1. America's historic experience with Prohibition and our current attempts to use legal tools to solve racial problems have placed the question of the relations between law and morality in very sharp focus. Concern with this problem leads to repeated posing of such questions as "Can law legislate morals?" or "Can law produce social change in the face of contrary attitudes in the community?"

2. American intellectual discussion has not escaped the world-wide battles between exponents of "conceptual" and "interest" or "functional" jurisprudence. Since the nineteenth century the critics of purely conceptual jurisprudence have alleged that law is not merely a system of logically related concepts and rules. To pretend that it is leads to failure to use law to achieve important social ends. Only by recognizing that judicial interpretation is a creative activity, necessarily responsive to social needs and pressures, can we channel and control this creative activity to make it serve crucial social functions.

3. American thought about law has been especially concerned with the concept of the rule of law. We have wondered how the legal process can be organized so as to ensure that the power of the state is controlled by law and the rights of citizens are protected in all strata of society.

There are several broad areas within the sociology of law, and progress in all of these areas has been affected by these three vital issues. It is convenient to divide the broad concerns of the sociology of law into four major categories:

First, there is the study of the functioning of legal agencies; second, the study of the development of legal order in the private sectors of society; third, the study of the impact of law on conduct; and finally, the study of law as a normative system, defining and contributing to the coherence of the major institutions of society. In each of these areas sociological investigation has revealed regularities and increased our verified knowledge of law as a social institution. At the same time, in each area many important questions remain uninvestigated and unanswered. As we look at these areas in more detail, we shall see that in a number of instances both the successes and failures of sociological inquiry can be attributed to the stimulation and the blind alleys provided by the surrounding intellectual controversies.

Students of the sociology of law have been most successful in illuminating the functioning of legal agencies. The "debunking" features of functional jurisprudence have supported interest in demonstrating nonlegal elements in the legal process. Those who would attack the sterility of conceptual jurisprudence are very receptive to the documentation of realistic influences on legal action. Again and again sociologically enlightened investigators have demonstrated the impact of social pressures on courts, attorneys, bar associations, juries, administrative agencies, and other legal agencies. Repeated investigation has shown that legal activity cannot be understood as a mere expression or reflection of legal concepts and rules. In some instances these studies have been merely polemical. It is relatively easy to show that legal officials are influenced by various realistic exigencies; the crucial task is to show that these exigencies are themselves systematically organized and understandable as elements in an ongoing, functioning system. Further, we have no reason to assume *a priori* that norms and rules do not play a part in organizing this functioning.

For example, in recent years students have developed very sophisticated mathematical techniques for isolating regularities in judicial decision making. Many of these studies have shown in a very rigorous manner that the variability in the way judges respond to situations cannot be accounted for by mere reference to legal rules and concepts. However, in many instances investigators have not gone beyond such explanatory concepts as "judicial attitudes" to elucidate the organizational sources and consequences of variations in judicial decisions. Such questions as "How are judges with particular attitudes recruited to the bench?" and "What are the consequences of variations in judicial decision on the operation of the legal system?" have not been investigated with an equal degree of sophistication and rigor. Nevertheless, efforts have been made to discuss problems of this type. For example, one student has shown that the amount of variation in opinion in the Supreme Court has not been constant over time and has suggested that increasing judicial dissensus is not necessarily a sign of breakdown of legal order but an indication of ongoing attempts to adapt legal norms to rapid social changes.[1]

The polemical character of work on the functioning of legal institutions can also be blamed for some of the limitations of sociological work on the legal profession. Although we have a growing number of works on the legal profession, we have had few empirical studies of the role of the attorney as an agent of social control. It has been suggested that the attorney, by transforming the client's concrete demands into normatively defined demands and by insisting that clients face reality, acts as an agent of social control.[2] Most of the work on the legal profession has been more concerned with the non-normative influences operating on legal practice. It is as if investigators were worried lest they be charged with a naïve conceptual jurisprudence.

The failure of sociological research to articulate clearly the normative elements in the functioning of legal institutions should not blind us to the real achievements of sociological research in this area. We are beginning to see an impressive body of documentation of some principles of general significance. For example, numerous studies provide support for this general proposition: At each point at which the legal system is linked to the larger society the legal processes at that point reflect the structure of the larger society—that is, the larger society is structured by a division into social strata with varying layers of prestige. At each point where the law is linked to the larger society the legal process shows the impact of stratification. Thus the jury is an institution designed to link the legal process to the community; it is specifically conceived to provide protection from arbitrary action by unresponsive officials. Research indicates that although the jury is conceived as a democratic institution, the stratification of the community is reproduced in the jury, and through the jury the stratification system of the society affects the legal process. Middle-class persons are more likely to be selected to serve on juries, and, once selected, they are more likely to be elected foreman and more likely to have disproportionate influence.[3] Stratification has also been shown to influence the legal process at other points at which the legal system is linked to the larger society. The selection of members of the legal profession and the selection of claims to be litigated are both influenced by social stratification, and for this reason stratification shapes the entire legal system by shaping the raw materials with which it operates.[4]

It is important to recognize that social influences on the legal process are not limited to the social pressures brought to bear on the makers of legal decisions. Sociologists have been equally interested in the forces that determine which claims are to be litigated. It has been shown that organized group interests play an important role in determining the issues that come to be presented to legal agencies, and the forms in which these issues are presented. Thus the field of race-relations law in the United States has been heavily influenced by the strategic plans of the National Association for the Advancement of Colored People. This association has selected cases quite carefully in order to present pioneering claims in a cogent sequence and has then placed considerable resources behind its strategic claims.

There is no guarantee that important social interests will be well represented by the group organization which is essential to their effective legal presentation. Thus a crucial task of sociology is to undertake studies designed to show how some claims come to be more effectively represented than others. The sociologist is interested, for example, in the impact of the professional ethics of attorneys, which often prohibit the organized channeling of personal-injury cases by arrangements between unions or hospital employees and lawyers specializing in personal-injury litigation.[5] Does the prevention of such arrangements lead to a situation where insurance companies are more effectively organized to suppress claims than are injured parties to press them?

At this point we can clearly see the intimate connection between the study of the functioning of legal agencies and the problem of the rule of law. Sociologists tend to be skeptical of the power of rules or norms to achieve social ends without the support of social organization. One of the major concerns of political sociology has been to examine the sociological supports that make democracy possible. In this respect, students of politics have stressed the importance of a rich associational life to ensure the maintenance of political education and concern, and the effective protection and representation of a broad range of social interests. By the same token the rule of law is not guaranteed by the mere existence of a written constitution or an accepted tradition of the supremacy of legal norms. An operating rule of law requires the organized representation of claims in order to ensure that they are brought to the attention of legal agencies and effectively presented. In the legal context one type of organized group is particularly important—the organized legal profession. To what extent can a well-organized legal profession ensure adequate training for legal practitioners, the maintenance of professional standards, the maintenance of a qualified and ethical judiciary, and adequate representation of the legal claims in all strata in the society?

Again the debunking tradition has not found it hard to demonstrate the failings of the American bar. There are glaring examples of the use of bar associations to restrict legal practice or to oppose the appointment of qualified judges for political purposes. A number of studies have shown that the bar is itself stratified.[6] Law schools, law firms, and types of legal practice are arrayed in strata of varying prestige in such a way as to ensure that highly placed interests are well represented. The same system of stratification also tends to place lawyers of low social status in positions where they face great pressures to engage in professional practices of a dubious nature. There seems to have been less interest in documenting the role of professional organization in supporting the rule of law. Accordingly the mechanisms by which legal ideals have been realized to some degree are not well understood. Again we see the weak side of functional jurisprudence as a stimulus to sociological research on law. The notion of a rule of law presumes that legal rules or concepts can in fact guide legal decisions so as to ensure a degree of protection for citizens against the organized centers of power in society. Approaches that stress the sociological limitations on conceptual jurisprudence appear to contradict approaches which search for the organizational supports that permit conceptual rules to operate in legal life.

Fortunately we are beginning to see the emergence of careful and balanced studies of the problems of professional organization. For example, one recent study carefully demonstrated the measure of success which the American Bar Association has achieved in reducing the political elements in the selection of federal judges. But the same study also shows that the Association's success has given more power to the upper strata of the profession in order to ensure the selection of candidates who conform to their interests and values.[7] At the conceptual level the problem has been attacked by attempts to draw a more careful distinction between "legality" and "legalism." The former concept refers to the establishment of procedural fairness and normatively regulated decision making, while the latter refers to the ritualization of the pretense of logical certainty and the consequent insensitivity to pressing social demands and problems.[8] The sociological problem is to outline the social conditions that support responsible autonomy and the conditions that permit intrusions on the independence of the legal system on the one hand, or unresponsive ritualism on the other.

Sociological interest in the rule of law has not been limited to the role of the law of the state in the total society. Spurred by an interest in bureaucracy, sociologists have studied the development of analogues to legal procedures in large-scale organizations. In studying such phenomena as the establishment of grievance procedures, the sociologist can attempt to illuminate the functions of legal rules and formal procedures. Such work can be illustrated by a recent study indicating that the more bureaucratic an organization is, the more its employees see themselves as protected by rules.[9] Studies of this type show that we have made progress in demonstrating that the development of systems of rules may enhance rather than prevent freedom for the participants in organizations.

These studies come under the heading described earlier as the study of the development of legal order in the private sectors of society. Interest in this range of problems has also been enhanced by functional jurisprudence, for in one of its forms (the sociological jurisprudence of Eugen Erlich),[10] this brand of jural thought insists that any viable legal order must reflect the "inner order" of society as it emerges in social groups and associations. Attention is now turning to concrete studies of the development of "living" normative orders as they develop within and between the associations and groups which form society. Such studies become particularly interesting when they include investigation of how private groups use the law of the state as a tool in the course of negotiating private legal orders. One current student of the use of legal instruments has provided us with an extensive documentation of the relations between automobile manufacturers and their dealers.[11] His investigation shows that private, informal systems for planning relationships and settling disputes were prevalent and could not be ignored by any student seeking to understand the effect of the formal law. At the same time, the organized efforts of the National Automobile Dealers Association brought about changes in the law which dealers were able to use effectively as counters in informal negotiation and which influenced the forms of private arrangements. Additional studies of this type are crucial, for if we are to understand the influence of law on human relations, we must look beyond the use of law in official agencies to the use of law in private interaction. Indeed the very issue of the rule of law might be redefined as a problem of whether the official legal structure is organized so as to lend powerful support to the use of legal norms as effective weapons in private negotiation between unequal parties.

For similar reasons the study of the use of law is also important in the study of the impact of law on conduct. The impact of a law is not confined to the results of enforcement by official agencies. It is necessary to see whether private groups are utilizing the existence of the law as an instrument in securing their interests. It is surprising that sociological study has paid so little attention to mechanisms of this type. The weaknesses of our accounts of legal impact must be ascribed to the effects of the historic polemic on law and morality. The argument has been so intense that the participants have been driven to surprisingly extreme positions, including, for example, the view that law can only ratify norms or patterns of behavior that are already established. Thus, sociologists find themselves required to expound such elementary propositions as that the American federal government would probably not be able to maintain its present level of activity on the basis of voluntary contributions. Nevertheless, sociologists are now coming to realize that the question is not "Can law affect conduct?" but "Under what conditions does law affect conduct and by what mechanism is the influence of law established?"

There is mounting evidence that the effectiveness of law in changing patterns of conduct does not depend entirely on the degree to which law corresponds to attitudes in the community or on the severity of the sanctions used to enforce law. In the first place it is clear that the notion of community attitudes is a complicated one. We must distinguish between community beliefs as to the necessity or desirability of a law, the fairness of a law, the right of the lawmaker to pass the law, and the fairness of the law as applied to particular instances.[12] The willingness of the community to obey the law must be distinguished from its desire to obey the law. People may not like to pay taxes, but the right of the government to impose them is not generally challenged in the United States. Adequate explanation of patterns of noncompliance must involve reference to patterns of belief about the illegitimacy or unimportance of particular provisions and patterns of loopholes in the organization of enforcement.

Further, it is important to recognize that the community is

not a homogeneous set of individuals but a complicated network of variegated interests, beliefs, and patterns of conduct with varying degrees of organization. What to one segment of the community is an illegitimate and onerous demand is to other segments a necessary condition for the effective and ethical functioning of the community. Hence, any meaningful account of the effect of law on conduct must try to isolate the relevant features of the organization of the community in order to answer such questions as whether certain specialized groups have an interest in implementation of the law, whether such groups are organized to press demands for enforcement, and whether if they are organized they have clear channels of influence on the administrative machinery of the state. By the same token it is necessary to specify the location in the community of groups of potential violators and the access of such groups to defensive strategies. In sum, the inadequacy of defining the problem of law and conduct as a problem in whether law can act against community attitudes lies in failure to recognize that law *is* a response to attitudes somewhere in the community. Thus the task is to determine the degree to which ethical and political leverage is available to the supporters of a law as a consequence of their position in a network of social organization.

Even if one is examining the problem of enforcement from the point of view of an enforcement agency, social organization is the crucial object of study. We cannot, for example, understand the success of the United States government in collecting income taxes in terms of such simple concepts as public acceptance. The government's high level of success has clearly depended on the development of highly organized systems of access to taxpayers through the systematic withholding and reporting of the income of other people by private citizens at major control points in the society.

In three of the four major areas of sociology of law the combined impetus of sociological interest in social organization and jural interest in functional jurisprudence has stimulated sociological investigation of law, but in the fourth area, the study of law as a normative system, these sources of stimulation have had a contrary effect. This effect has involved more than framing issues in inappropriate ways. In their zeal to show that law is more than a system of norms or rules, sociologists have tended to ignore the sense in which law is a set of norms, and in consequence the study of law as a normative system has suffered. Investigators have become so sensitive to the dangers of taking enunciated rules for granted, without reference to how they are used and interpreted by legal agencies or whether they correspond to the living law actually in force in society, that they have neglected to examine the content and function of sets of legal rules. How do various types of organizational problems lead to different sorts of legal rules? How do the values of society affect normative solutions to organizational problems? It is unfortunate for sociology that such problems have been neglected, for the founders of sociological theory were very interested in broadly comparative problems in the structure and content of law as a normative system.

Fortunately, with the growth of our knowledge of the uses of legal norms and the functioning of legal institutions it is becoming easier to recognize how general statements of the contents of legal rules must be qualified. Given this capacity, students may feel more free to develop accounts of the significance of the contents of systems of rules. Indeed, one influential student of legal institutions has seen that functional jurisprudence is not, in the last analysis, a mere critical attack upon rigid conceptualism, but a positive attempt to understand how legal rules function to implement social aims through the imposition of normative controls. Guided by this insight, Professor J. W. Hurst and his students and associates have been producing monographs which describe and interpret trends in the development of legal norms. Professor Hurst, a teacher of law by profession, has pointed the way for sociological study with stimulating accounts of the development of law in the United States. His work may be illustrated by his interpretive discussion of the relations between law and the conditions of freedom. American law has continually reflected a fundamental valuation of the release of human creative energy, but the conditions for the release of creative energy have changed as the organization of society has changed. Thus, as large-scale organization and concentrations of wealth became more prominent in America, American law shifted its emphasis from a concern with control over the environment to a concern with control over social power.[13] Hurst did not come to this conclusion by merely speculating as to the meaning of the content of legal rules. He studied the origins and the uses of rules in different sectors of society and the political contexts in which rules emerged.

From the sociological point of view, law is to be understood as a social process, but it is becoming increasingly clear that to understand law as a social process is to understand the operational meaning of legal norms as they are used, applied, interpreted, and ultimately, through regular patterns of use, embodied in the institutional structure of society.

Indeed, sociologists hope that the sociological study of law will ultimately make its most important contribution by illuminating the structure of the institutions of modern society. A complex society such as the United States is organized around fundamental institutions which provide coherence to organized social life. The institutions of political authority, property, contract, incorporation, and marriage provide ready-made means of establishing purposive and binding relationships among men. These institutions are defined and regulated by law. It is the task of sociology of law to provide an account of how legal agencies and private groups use law to establish and regulate conduct through the formation of social institutions.

NOTES

1. Eloise Snyder, "Uncertainty and the Supreme Court's Decisions," *American Journal of Sociology,* LXV (1954), 241–245.
2. Talcott Parsons, "A Sociologist Looks at the Legal Profession," in *Essays in Sociological Theory* (rev. ed., Glencoe, Ill.: The Free Press, 1954), pp. 370–385.
3. W. S. Robinson, "Bias, Probability, and Trial by Jury," *American Sociological Review,* XV (1950), 73–78, and Fred L. Strodtbeck *et al.*, "Social Status in Jury Deliberations," *American Sociological Review,* XXII (1957), 713–719.

4. Leon Mayhew, *Law and Equal Opportunity* (Cambridge, Mass.: Harvard University Press, 1968).

5. The emergent response of the law to this sort of problem can be seen in Brotherhood of Railway Trainmen v. Virginia ex. rel. Virginia State Bar 377 U.S. 1, 1964. See Kenneth Reichstein, "Ambulance Chasing: A Case Study of Deviation and Control within the Legal Profession," *Social Problems*, XIII (1965), 3–17.

6. See, for example, Jerome Carlin, *Lawyers on Their Own* (New Brunswick, N.J.: Rutgers University Press, 1962), and Jack Ladinsky, "Careers of Lawyers, Law Practice, and Legal Institutions," *American Sociological Review*, XXVIII (1963), 47–54.

7. Joel B. Grossman, *Lawyers and Judges* (New York: John Wiley and Sons, 1965).

8. Jerome H. Skolnick, "The Sociology of Law in America: Overview and Trends," *Law and Society*, supplement to *Social Problems* (Summer 1965), p. 38.

9. Phillip Selznick and Howard Vollmer, "Rule of Law in Industry," *Industrial Relations*, I (1962), 97–116.

10. Eugen Erlich, *Fundamental Principles of the Sociology of Law* (Cambridge, Mass.: Harvard University Press, 1936).

11. Stewart Macaulay, "Changing a Continuing Relationship between a Large Corporation and Those Who Deal with It: Automobile Manufacturers, Their Dealers and the Legal System," *Wisconsin Law Review* (1965) pp. 483–575, 770–858.

12. See Harry Ball, "Social Structure and Rent-Control Violations," *American Journal of Sociology*, LXV (1960), 598–604.

13. James Willard Hurst, *Law and the Conditions of Freedom in the Nineteenth-Century United States* (Madison, Wis.: The University of Wisconsin Press, 1956).

15 SOCIAL STRATIFICATION STRUCTURE AND TRENDS OF SOCIAL MOBILITY IN WESTERN SOCIETY

Bernard Barber

One good way of understanding the social stratification structure of Western society is to consider its dynamic processes and its patterns of change. Accordingly, after briefly defining some of the several different dimensions of that structure, I shall sketch what has changed in each of these dimensions during the course of Western history since medieval times and I shall further show how these changes have affected mobility processes and trends. Of course, there always have been, and there remain, some national differences in these changes, processes, and trends, but for my present purpose I shall ignore the differences and emphasize the overriding similarities that already exist and that will continually increase.

The first among the several equally important dimensions of stratification we shall consider is occupational prestige. In all societies the male heads of families (and their immediate kin) are differentially evaluated in terms of the functional contribution they make to society in their relatively full-time "productive" roles. Such roles always make larger and smaller functional contributions, and accordingly are differentially evaluated—that is, awarded differential prestige. Nowadays we call all such roles "occupations," but in the past some of these roles—for example, religious or military roles—might not be so defined. But the principle still held. Even if the landholding-and-management functions of a nobleman were not called an "occupation," still these noblemen were in fact evaluated in terms of their relative success in their "productive" contribution to society. This could most easily be seen in the case of those who failed disastrously in these functions of their noble role and consequently lost their prestige.

During the last six or seven centuries there has been a basic change in the structure of occupational prestige in Western society. Earlier, the military, landowning-and-managing, governmental, and religious-official roles were somewhat more highly evaluated than the commercial, industrial, scientific, teaching, and various other professional roles. This is not to say, as the established ideology of the time sometimes put it, that these latter roles carried *no* prestige at all. But because they were relatively less valued, men sought to move themselves or their sons into the former roles as soon as they could. In modern times, in general, the latter roles carry as much prestige as the former. Consequently, there is more social mobility through the latter roles now than there used to be, and those who are mobile in this way are usually as content to stay in these "modern" roles as to move to the traditionally more prestigious ones.

There remains some small residue of preference for the older roles as against the newer ones in some of the nations of Western society. But, as comparative data for Western Europe and Russia collected by Professors Inkeles and Rossi show, there is large cross-national consensus on the relative prestige ranking of all types of occupational roles, and this consensus does not express any preference for the older as against the newer type of role.

A second dimension of stratification structure is made up of authority and power rankings. Authority may be defined as the legitimate capacity for achieving goals in social systems, power as its *illegitimate* counterpart. Both obviously have functional (and, under some circumstances, dysfunctional) parts to play in all social systems, large and small. In all societies some roles have more authority or power, others less, and so a stratification of their structure results. Until very recently in Western society the stratification of authority and power was quite peaked, with very large shares of each in the hands of the higher nobility and clergy. Authority and power struggles tended to take place among segments of the nobility (including the monarchy), not between the nobility and the bourgeoisie, as some would have it. Mobility in the authority and power structure for individual members of the bourgeoisie usually meant getting into noble roles as individuals, not joining up with other bourgeois as a class against the noble class. Gradually, however, and more suddenly in some places—e.g., France—a greater share of authority and power moved from governmental, clerical, and landholding roles to the more modern roles. Also, with the gradual enfranchisement of the majority of the population in Western society, authority and power became still more widely shared, with the lower white-collar and working-class groups increasing their relative influence. When most men can vote, and where there is a genuinely democratic political and social process, the middle and lower masses can pool their individually small pieces of authority and wield a total influence great enough to have at least a countervailing and sometimes a predominant influence over those in the higher social classes. This new pattern of authority and power structure provides greater opportunities for mobility for men in the middle and lower orders of society both in this structure itself and in other types of stratificational structure insofar as these are affected by the authority and power dimension.

A third dimension of stratification structure consists of income or wealth. Different occupational roles in a society have different capacities for earning income and for accumulating capital wealth. There are similar differences, owing to family connections, in the chances for inheriting wealth. Sometimes highly prestigious and authoritative roles—for example, the Pope—can earn or accumulate little money. Sometimes roles of low prestige—e.g., thieves—can accumulate large amounts. The resulting stratification of income and wealth may be either pyramidal or diamond-shaped in form, and more or less peaked in either case. On the whole, Western society has moved from a more pyramidal to a more diamond type of stratification structure for income and wealth, although considerable peakedness, perhaps as much as ever, remains even with the new shape. There also remains a considerable negative peakedness of distressing poverty at the bottom of the structure, although on the whole the several nations of modern Western society have been continually raising the minimum welfare standard for those at the bottom of the income and wealth structure.

Income and earned or inherited wealth have always been instruments both for the acquisition of more money and for the purchase of access to more highly valued roles, as in the purchase of education, or of titles of nobility, or of marriage partners (e.g., when rich daughters were married to poorer but prestigious noblemen). Thus, in the past as well as in the present, money has played its part in several processes of mobility. But this part may be diminishing in Western society as access to education and to highly valued roles themselves becomes more directly dependent upon the display of achievement. We may be moving toward what Michael Young has called a "meritocracy," in which money has very little part to play in the processes of social allocation and mobility. As he has also only half-playfully pointed out, such a society is not without its own peculiar social strains and dysfunctional effects.

A fourth dimension of stratification structure can be seen in education or knowledge. Men in society have always had differential access to education and knowledge, with important consequences not only for their performance of the different roles to which they were assigned at birth but for their opportunities to move into those other roles, often more prestigious, for which their "natural" talents best suited them. The stratification of education and knowledge in Western society has been markedly pyramidal until quite recent times. Only since the nineteenth century has universal literacy been considered a socially necessary and morally desirable goal; and even now, full equality of opportunity for education remains, despite all the progress in this direction, more a hope than a fact. In the period since World War II there has been an especially noticeable lag between the capacity of countries in Western society (with the likely exception of the United States) to provide the educational opportunity that was necessary for the national welfare and desired by individuals striving to make themselves useful to their society and to rise in the social hierarchy. But the social requirements of running highly specialized industrial societies, as well as increasingly strong egalitarian norms, push toward more and more equally available educational opportunity. Again, there looms on the social horizon the prospect of a "meritocracy" which has gained its place in the more prestigious and more authoritative parts of society through its right of equal access to educational opportunity and through its demonstrated ability to make the most of that opportunity.

Religious or ritual purity defines a fifth dimension of stratification structure. In terms of the functionally significant religious ideas that prevail in every society, individuals may possess more and less of the valued characteristic of religious or ritual purity. In Hindu society, so far as this dimension of stratification structure is concerned, there has been a marked inequality, with considerable consequences for the other stratificational dimensions as well. In Western society, where the Christian belief *ideally* has been expressed in such terms as "the brotherhood of man in God" and "the priesthood of all believers," a considerable consequence has been to reduce actual inequality in this dimension very far and even to provide some basis through this conception of equality of religious and ritual purity for a more far-reaching social, economic, and political equality. In actual social fact, inequalities in the other dimensions of stratification have probably always frustrated the realization of the Christian ideal of complete equality in the religious and ritual-purity dimension, more so perhaps in the past than in the present, although we have still not entered the Kingdom of God in this respect. But the ideal of Christian and so-called secular equality (which is derived in part from the Christian belief) has been a radical one and has had far-reaching effects upon all dimensions of stratificational structure in our society, most particularly in the last century or two.

Kinship and ethnic group rankings constitute our final dimension of stratification structure. In all societies, kinship groups— and their extensions in the form of ethnic groups—perform independent and essential functions; procreation; socialization of children; and provision of psychological, social, and moral support between and among the parents and children, the parents themselves, the siblings, and the other kin that make up the extended forms of the family and the ethnic group as a whole.

Kinship and ethnic groups, by virtue of the way they perform these and other functions for the national and local communities in which they are located, are differently evaluated, *qua* kinship and ethnic groups, all apart from their occupational prestige, authority, or power, or income or wealth. The result is a stratification of kinship and ethnic groups wherever ethnic heterogeneity exists. These rankings influence the way in which members of particular families view themselves and are treated by others.

In the past history of Western society this differential evaluation of kinship and ethnic groups was not only recognized, but even glorified, as a support for the stability of society. More recently, however, as egalitarian norms have spread and been strengthened in Western society, there has been some tendency both in fact and in moral ideal to play down the role of the kinship and ethnic groups. The particularistic character of affiliation with kinship and ethnic groups has been repugnant to the universalistic norms of Western society. Nevertheless, the indispensable functions of kinship and ethnic groups have persisted and have had to be acknowledged even in the face of their incompatibility with an absolute realization of universalistic norms. Affiliation with particular families and ethnic groups is still an asset or a liability in social interaction of many kinds and in access to opportunities for social mobility of all kinds. Until the functions of kinship and ethnic groups have been replaced by universalistic functional alternatives—and so far they have not been—these groups will continue to be differentially evaluated and some pattern of accommodation between these evaluations and the demands of universalistic norms will continue to exist. If the family no longer has its older, glorified place in Western society, it still has some honor and some significant consequences both as a structure of stratification in itself and for other stratification dimensions and processes.

Although not themselves an independent dimension of stratification structure in the sense that the six dimensions we have discussed are, the institutionalized norms about mobility that prevail in a society have an important independent effect on the amount and degrees of mobility that occur in that society. Of course, other factors, such as the relevant opportunity structures, are also important determinants. We know something about these different norms as they have prevailed at different times and places in past periods of Western society and as they were expressed in the writings, usually ideologically self-serving, of the well-educated upper classes. But we know little, directly, of how people in the lower orders felt. It is probably a safe guess that these people on the whole shared the sentiments of their superordinates, else Western society would have been much less stable even than it has been. For the present, if we would, through the use of polls that surveyed a representative cross-section of national populations, we could discover what norms about social mobility the different social classes actually have. But even such research remains to be carried out on a systematic and comparative basis.

As we have suggested, despite the existence of the Christian ideal of the equality of all men, the predominant type of norm concerning social mobility until quite recently in Western society has been what has been called the "caste" norm—that is, a norm disapproving of social mobility. One might wish for social mobility for oneself, but it was not approved of in general, as a moral good, for everyone. Only in the last century or so has there been a shift toward the predominance of what has been called the "open-class" type of norm, which approves *in principle* of mobility. The older type of norm was supported by an organic ideology of society which justified not only the relative fixity of the social structure as a whole but the place of each individual within it. The open-class type of norm is justified by an ideology which prefers "change" or "progress" in society and which asserts that individual mobility based on merit is both a prerequisite of that progress and an inalienable right of the individual. The open-class type of norm is obviously one factor which favors an increase in the amount of mobility in the recent history of Western society.

What has come to be called the "style of life" in sociological analysis is, again, not so much an independent dimension of social stratification as an *indicator* (to use Lazarsfeld's term) of one or more of these several dimensions we have discussed. That is, a style of life is composed of the things men do and the possessions they have which are construed by themselves and others as indicators of, or symbolic of, the place they occupy in one or another stratification structure. Almost any kind of behavior or any kind of possession or ornament can become an indicator, or part of a set of indicators, of a class-typed style of life. Highly visible consumption items, however, are likely to be the ones that are most easily noticed and most frequently remarked on. That is why, when he was talking about social-class differences in styles of life, the American sociologist-economist, Thorstein Veblen, spoke of "conspicuous consumption." In the most general sociological sense, applying to all societies, all classes consume conspicuously.

Because of the pyramidal distribution of wealth and the relative scarcity of consumer goods in earlier times in Western society, the differences in styles of life of the different social classes were considerably more marked than they are today. Also, under the influence of caste norms disapproving of mobility, the upper classes tried to control access to those items of their style of life which they thought peculiarly characteristic of their behavior, so that parvenus or upstarts might only with so much the greater difficulty be admitted to the higher social classes in which their demonstrated merit or acquisition of wealth or authority entitled them to be placed. Thus, the wearing of fur was often legally restricted to the nobility, and there were other forms of sumptuary legislation with effects on class-related styles of life.

During the last century or so in Western society, despite the emergence of mass-consumption economies, class differences in styles of life have not disappeared but have become somewhat more subtle than they used to be. That is what we mean when we speak nowadays of "inconspicuous consumption," by which we mean not wholly invisible consumption but only relatively less visible consumption. Under the influence of egalitarian norms, more people at present than in the past try to reduce at least a little bit the relative conspicuousness of their class-related consumption, though we are far from realizing any utopia of aspiration or performance in this regard. In general, we may say that some form of conspicuous consumption or differences in class styles of life will continue to exist but that the trend has been and continues toward what I have called *the pattern of gross equality and subtle inequality*. This trend reflects and strengthens similar changes in the stratification structures themselves. If it looks as if differences of prestige, of authority, of income, or of style of life are no longer present, this is usually an illusion which is dispelled by closer inspection of actual social reality.

Now let me speak more directly of changes in amounts and types of mobility in Western society. Social mobility, upward or downward, occurs when a male head of family (and his immediate kin) comes to occupy a higher or lower place than his father did in the structure of relative rankings for any one of the several stratificational dimensions. Upward and downward mobility seem to have existed in some amount in all societies, and certainly there was no lack of either in Western society throughout its long course. Because of the recently expanding opportunity structure of Western society, probably there has been more upward mobility recently than in the more distant past, but this is a question of degree, not of absolute differences. In both periods, past and present, most mobility has been of small degree —that is, movement upward or downward affected only a few ranks in the whole scale of ranks of any dimension of stratification. But in the past as well as in the present there has also been a certain amount of mobility of very large degree, that is from the very bottom, or near it, to the very top, or near it, and vice versa. Whether the amount of mobility of large degree has increased considerably in the present is still an open empirical question. In any case, for the present as well as for the past, mobility of large degree is a phenomenon that happens to relatively small proportions of those who are mobile in any degree. Of course, these relatively small proportions—under 10 per cent if one includes both upward and downward mobility as indicated in various studies of mobility among American business and professional elite groups—may involve what is in absolute terms a considerable number of individuals and their families.

The processes or channels of social mobility have also changed somewhat during the course of history in Western society. As we have suggested earlier, there has probably been relatively more mobility recently through the more modern occupational roles, although the traditional roles, such as the religious, the military, and the governmental, have continued to serve as channels of mobility in modernized form. For all roles, the one constant is the increasing importance of educational performance in the processes of mobility. As egalitarian norms have increased equality of access to educational opportunity, and as the society has increasingly required more highly educated people to man its altered structure, educational systems and processes have become ever more important determinants of social mobility. As a result, there have been continual and ever more urgent calls for expansion of the educational system at all its levels, both in the more modern countries of Western society and in the rapidly modernizing countries in other areas of the world.

I can discuss only one last subject: changes of shape of Western stratification structures. When each of the male heads of families (and their immediate kin) in any society are measured along any one of the several dimensions of social stratification, there results from the set of measures a distribution of relative rankings which can be conceived of as having a structured shape, for example, as the Gaussian normal distribution curve is represented by a bell shape. For a variety of reasons having to do with such matters as the needs of social systems and the distribution of talents in the individuals who fill positions in social systems, the structures of relative ranking possess some greater or less degree of hierarchy—that is, of more or less steep tapering toward the top. Given the fact of hierarchy, the two basic shapes that appear in the distributions of stratificational rankings are the pyramid and the diamond. The two shapes indicate that there is always a minority ranked toward the top, an "elite" or set of "elites." But in the pyramidal shape there are also relatively few people in the middle ranks, the mass of the population being in the lowest ranks. In contrast, for the diamond shape there are proportionately more people in the middle ranks than in the lower ranks, although there remain enough in these lower ranks to constitute the tapering at the bottom that exists in the basic diamond shape.

Although of course we have no precise data, it seems to be the case that Western society has moved during the last century or so from an essentially pyramidal type of structure in its various dimensions of stratification to an essentially diamond type. As the specialization of the division of labor has increased, and as the average levels of skill and responsibility in the different "productive" or occupational roles have risen, the proportion of middle-ranking roles has increased in Western society. Through associated processes of social evolution there have come into existence proportionately more middle-ranking positions in such stratificational dimensions as those of authority and power and income and wealth. This is what is usually meant when it is said that Western society is now "middle class"—namely, that the greatest proportion of the population is ranked in the upper, middle, and lower parts of the middle orders rather than at the highly peaked top or bottom of the stratificational pyramids. So large is the proportion of people in the middle ranks that some writers about society, especially those opposed to this recent trend of change, have spoken of the "middle mass." In the modern type of society, of which Western society is the chronological and typological forerunner, the great majority of people will tend to be middle-ranking and their positions will often be symbolized by their "white collars." We do not mean to suggest that all differences of relative evaluation have been eliminated; far from it. As always, differences of ranking are made, both of oneself and one's fellows, but these differences are smaller and more subtle when many people are clustered closely together in the middle ranks.

The change from an essentially pyramidal to an essentially diamond shape in the stratification structures of Western society has meant a continual enlargement in the opportunity structures for individuals in the lower orders of society. As the relative number of positions in the middle ranks has kept increasing, there have been, *ipso facto,* an increasing number of opportunities for upward social mobility, opportunities created by the changing shape of the social system, all apart from such opportunities as can be created by individuals themselves in even a relatively static type of stratification structure. Some downward mobility exists, now as in the past, but probably the relative amount of upward mobility has increased as the opportunity structures in Western society have been expanding. These expansions have occurred at different rates at different times in different countries, and although such expansion would seem sociologically finite, it probably still has some distance to go in most parts of Western society. But the basic trend is there.

PART IV

Sociology of Culture

16 THE SOCIOLOGY OF SCIENCE

Norman W. Storer

If we were to sketch a map of American sociology today, we would find that the sociology of science occupies a relatively small part of it. However, it borders on the sociology of knowledge, the sociology of education, and the sociology of professions, and is by no means isolated or without allies. In addition to these three neighboring areas, it also has close ties with studies of formal organizations and of creativity. While there are probably no more than a score of American sociologists who claim the sociology of science as their major focus of interest at present, their number is increasing steadily. Certainly the increasingly practical importance of science in both national and international affairs has been partly responsible for this growth, but the intrinsic interest to be found in viewing science as a distinctive area of social behavior is becoming more widely recognized as well.

As with any special field in sociology, someone who says that his work is in "the sociology of X" is indicating that the behavior of people who are concerned with "X," or who are *in* "X," or are influenced *by* "X," makes up the focus of his interests. The sociology of science, then, is the study of the patterns of behavior in which scientists engage, the factors which influence their behavior, and the consequences of their behavior for the larger groups and societies to which they belong. Science is thus conceived as a social institution, a complex of patterns of behavior and interrelationships having sufficient internal coherence to enable us to distinguish it from other areas of social behavior.

Given this initial framework, the sociologist of science asks about the nature of the relationships that exist among scientists, the ways in which people become scientists, and how it is that they learn and support the patterns of behavior that characterize them as scientists. He asks further about the relationships among the rules that govern the behavior of scientists and how they are related to the over-all goal of science. This goal, which Robert K. Merton of Columbia University has termed "the extension of certified knowledge," provides a baseline against which to measure the "social health" of science and also a foundation for the analysis of how scientists come to want to engage in these patterns of behavior and to support the norms and values that guide them.

Beyond these fundamental questions, of course, are many which may have more practical import: What are the factors which stimulate or which hinder scientific creativity in various settings? How may young people be encouraged to seek careers in science? How will the scientific community be affected by the increasing amounts of material support that society provides for it, and by the increasing esteem which is accorded to scientists? That the sociology of science is concerned with questions having both fundamental theoretical significance and relevance to important practical problems suggests that the field will experience considerable growth during the next few years.

The sociology of science did not achieve this perspective overnight, nor can I say with assurance that my colleagues in the field would agree in all respects with this capsule description of our work. Simply to apply the knowledge we have of the development of other new scientific specialties, we know that in the beginning there may be a good deal of disagreement in a field over the definition of its central interests and questions. The passage of a decade or more is often required before a general definition of this sort can develop and be accepted by all those involved in the work. My own guess is that the sociology of science is somewhat past the halfway mark in this process, although much remains to be done before a broadly acceptable perspective can emerge.

Incidentally, I might remark that one of the peculiar characteristics of this field is that it cannot avoid being highly introspective at times. Occasionally the task of speaking about one's own speech, or analyzing one's own analytical processes, can become rather confusing. To carry out research on the process of research, however, only adds to the challenge, and offers as well the implicit promise that one may come to understand oneself better as a scientist while studying science more generally.

Once a new field of scientific interest has achieved an identity of its own, it is able to look backward and to trace the men and the lines of work which may now be seen as its forerunners. Although this process sometimes involves a re-evaluation of the importance of several men's work, it will be worth while to look briefly at the pioneers in the sociological study of science. It is impossible, of course, ever to pinpoint the first man who can be said to have studied science in a sociological perspective, but we can safely go back at least as far as the German political economist and sociologist, Max Weber, who pointed out in 1921 in his studies of world religions that certain configurations of societal values may encourage or discourage the development of science within a society. Well before this time, people were writing about science and its relations with other parts of society, but it is difficult to argue that discussions of "the warfare between science and religion" involved a genuinely sociological view of the topic.

Until the 1930's, science tended to be viewed primarily as something which might or might not develop in a given society, or else as the unexamined source of knowledge that had various consequences for the rest of society. Such studies came generally under the heading of social change, or else were seen as a part of the sociology of knowledge. Pitirim A. Sorokin saw empirical science as particularly symptomatic of what he termed the "sensate" system of truth, in a broader theory of cyclical social change, and William Fielding Ogburn thought of science as a prime factor in producing "cultural lag" in society. Marxian scholars were at work, too, and devoted considerable attention during the 1930's to the relations between economic structure and the rise of science.

Perhaps the culmination of the social-change approach to science came in 1938 with the publication of Robert K. Merton's

Science, Technology, and Society in Seventeenth-Century England, and the appearance in 1946 of Ogburn's *The Social Effects of Aviation* marked the high point of studies stressing the implications of scientific and technological advances for society. Work in these areas continues, of course, but since then the sociology of science has tended to focus upon more specific problems having to do with the internal structure and dynamics of science.

Interestingly enough, the first important work in this new vein came also from Merton, at the same time that his *Science, Technology, and Society in Seventeenth-Century England* was appearing in print. This was a paper on "Science and the Social Order," delivered in 1937. This paper and one in 1942 on "Science and Democratic Social Structure" laid out the guidelines which have largely been followed since that time by other investigators.

It was quite natural before the late 1930's that the sociology of science and the sociology of knowledge were paired, or that the former was seen as a subspecialty within the latter. This was due to the view that science is primarily of importance to society because of its output of empirical knowledge. I suspect that the sociologists' failure to look more closely at the internal structure of science was due also to their having accepted, or wishing to protect, the internal myth of science that it is somehow different from other fields of human activity and untainted by the difficulties that beset them. So long as the search for knowledge is supposed to be carried out according to rational procedures and without the interference of such irrelevant factors as personality differences and political considerations, there was obviously little of interest to be found in the social structure of science.

But with the growing maturity of sociology and the increasing need on the part of society to improve the productivity of science—especially during World War II and after—it was recognized that the social relationships among scientists are not necessarily those described by the "pure" rules of scientific procedure. Accordingly, attention has turned more and more to the internal characteristics of the scientific community, with the "ethos" of science being more correctly viewed as a set of *ideal* norms and values rather than as a direct reflection of reality.

CURRENT ACTIVITIES

Rather than attempt a thorough review of the present state of the sociology of science, which would require far too much space, let me take up three major topics with which the field is concerned as illustrations of its scope and current interests. First, there is the central problem of the dynamics and structure of science: the energies which keep it going and the ways in which these energies are channeled. Second, there is the more practical realm of questions concerning the morale and productivity of scientists in various settings. Finally, we shall look at the relations between science and public policy, concentrating on the problem of how the advice and the technological achievements of scientists can be harnessed to the over-all goals of a society.

The Structure and Dynamics of Science

The sociological analysis of the social and cultural structure of science may be said to have begun with Merton's work in the late 1930's. This was a natural consequence of his earlier interest in how the values characterizing seventeenth-century Puritan England were so favorable to the rise of science in that country. Now he went further in conceptualizing the components of the ethos of science and in making a start toward explaining their functional importance for science. Briefly, the ethos was described as composed of four fundamental values. These were *universalism* (the faith that natural phenomena are everywhere the same, and that the truth of statements about them is independent of the speaker); *communism* or *communality* (the principle that knowledge should be shared freely); *disinterestedness* (the scientist should not exploit his findings for personal gain—financial, honorific, or otherwise); and *organized skepticism* (the responsibility of each scientist for assessing the goodness of the work of others, and for making known his evaluations).

As it turns out, these values, *mutatis mutandis,* are necessary in any field of scholarship whose aim is the production of truth, whether this be empirical, aesthetic, or philosophical. Without the patterns of behavior and the interrelationships among scholars indicated by these values, the collective search for truth would be undermined by the self-seeking tendencies which are a part of every man. Truths would be sold to the highest bidder, men would hesitate to criticize each other's work for fear of reprisals, and scholars would design their research in order to produce the greatest personal gain rather than to be most useful in extending a body of public, generalized knowledge.

Merton did not stop here, but went on to pick up another aspect of science and to make it an equally significant part of the picture. This was his analysis of controversies over priority in scientific discovery, which he presented as his Presidential Address to the American Sociological Association in 1957. Drawing upon cases from the history of science, he pointed out the fundamental importance of professional recognition as the legitimate reward for achievement within science. To be a good scientist, one must contribute to the extension of knowledge, which means that one must make discoveries. Since only the first man to make a discovery receives credit for it, contests over priority in discovery are to be found throughout the history of science. Merton's interpretation of these contests is that they indicate how important to the scientist is the professionally competent indication by his colleagues that he has indeed contributed substantially to the progress of science. These indications, which make up what we call professional recognition, range from simply being footnoted in another scientist's work to the receipt of such a world-renowned honor as the Nobel Prize.

Seen in this perspective, the scientist's deep commitment to the advancement of knowledge makes understandable both his interest in professional recognition and his continued support of the values of science. In the former case, professional recognition confirms his hope that he is living up to the requirements of his role, and in the latter he supports these values because they are necessary if the extension of knowledge is to continue.

Another interpretation of these phenomena has been proposed by this writer. It is based on the assumption that creativity is a natural human drive and that the competent response of others to one's creations is needed before the creative act is really felt to be completed. Certainly creativity is the *summum bonum* in scientific endeavor, and it seems to me that the scientist's desire to continue to be able to receive competent response to his work provides an alternative explanation of why scientists continue to support the ethos of science, and of why the general advancement of knowledge is taken to be their goal. From this point of view, the scientist's interest in professional recognition is actually his interest in obtaining competent response to his contributions, and when favorable response is expressed formally, it constitutes professional recognition. A scientist's allegiance to the ethos of science may thus be seen as his support of a social structure through which it is possible for him to obtain competent response to his creative efforts.

Further, once it is accepted that knowledge somehow exists apart from individual knowers, it acquires a universal quality—and creativity must be measured against the universal standards embodied in "the literature" or in "the state of the art." Thus, the desire to create becomes at the same time a desire to extend the body of knowledge with which the scientist is concerned.

This is not to suggest, however, that scientists are openly anxious to acquire professional recognition. Indeed, their extreme ambivalence toward its receipt is another topic which Merton has found to be extremely revealing of the social dynamics of science. He cites instance after instance of scientists' first denying any interest in professional recognition at all, and later passionately claiming it for themselves or defending the recognition they have received already. The norm of humility in science seems to account for this ambivalence, and the possibility that an open expression of interest in gaining recognition might itself injure the quality of the response one receives is probably another reason for the scientist's ambivalence toward it.

Here, then, we have in ideal form the social institution of science, its participants collectively engaged in the extension of knowledge and guided in their activities by a system of norms and values that simultaneously ensure the validity of their contributions and sustain their motivation.

In larger perspective, we may view science as a profession, a career based upon the command of a specific body of knowledge. The most basic attribute of any profession is that its members are responsible for a specialized body of knowledge—for its maintenance, transmission, extension, and application. Science is thus generally comparable to other professions such as law and medicine, except that its emphasis is upon the extension of knowledge while the emphasis of the "service" professions is largely upon the practical application of knowledge.

Just as medical doctors cannot afford to have laymen telling them how to do their jobs, so scientists must be free of outside interference if they are to be most effective in their work. Although the majority of American scientists are employed by government and industry rather than by universities, the invidious distinction sometimes made between "pure" and "applied" research seems to reflect the fact that a scientist who is hired expressly for his research abilities must be subject to the demands of his employer. Consequently, he cannot be entirely free to select his research problems solely on the basis of their relevance to the extension of knowledge, and is in this sense less "effective" as a scientist. He is unable to behave entirely as the ideal scientist ought to, and suffers in comparison with the university scientist and his greater freedom.

Morale and Productivity

This brings us to the general problem of scientists' morale and productivity—the study of those things which are particularly important in determining whether or not a scientist is satisfied with his position and his work, and which may thus have an influence upon the quantity and quality of his work. This topic, understandably, has been the subject of much investigation in recent years, and the findings have been generally in accord with what we would expect on the basis of our description of science as a social institution and as a profession.

Like other professionals, scientists are not expected to be motivated primarily by economic considerations. If this were the case, professionals would be likely to exploit their special expertise at the expense of their clients and would quickly lose the trust of their clients; in the case of science, where creativity is most highly valued and scientists do not have clients in the usual sense, competent response to creativity rather than monetary reward is the appropriate *quid pro quo*. The money that a scientist earns is thus viewed as facilitating his work rather than as the goal of his activities, and so long as his income is adequate to his family's needs (in terms of what he thinks necessary in his social position), his morale will be mainly influenced by other, more specifically science-related factors.

One of these factors is directly related to the dynamics of science: the extent to which he feels that his work has received adequate recognition. Perhaps more so in the universities than in industrial and government laboratories, a sense that one has received proper credit from one's peers for what one has accomplished will affect the scientist's general satisfaction with his position, his plans to stay or move on to a new one, and even the quality of his work. Barney G. Glaser has found, in analyzing data from a large government laboratory, that those scientists who express some dissatisfaction with the amount of credit they have received for their work are indeed less satisfied with their place of work, more prone to think about seeking another position, and tend to be somewhat less productive as their dissatisfaction mounts. Such findings seem to represent on a small scale the reactions of scientists who find that, unknown to them, their discoveries have been made previously by others. Merton cites several historical instances in which the disappointed scientist actually left science altogether or else became bitter and unproductive thereafter.

In organizational terms, the potential conflict between the scientist's need for professional autonomy and his employer's need for predictability and control in the organization has also been found to be a factor in scientists' morale. This is essentially the conflict posed by trying to obey two masters, the value system of science and the employer. In the university, naturally, this conflict is minimized since the scientist ordinarily is paid for teaching rather than for the research he carries out, and his employer's interest in his research tends to be limited to a concern that it be meaningful to his own colleagues. A university is pleased to have a Nobel Prize winner on its faculty, regardless of the nature of the work for which the prize was awarded.

But in industry, and to a lesser extent in government laboratories, the scientist is usually expected to work on those problems that are of importance to his employer—product development and improvement and other things that will be of benefit to the company rather than to science as a whole. There are often restrictions on the scientist's freedom to publish his findings, too, since they can be an important advantage in his company's competition with other firms.

Perhaps a part of such conflicts can be minimized by the "style" of the research supervisor. The work of Donald Pelz and his co-workers at the University of Michigan suggests that a kind of "participatory" style of management is most effective in sustaining the scientist-employee's satisfactions, while both authoritarian and laissez-faire management are less effective. Independent support for this contention is provided by Gerald Gordon of the University of Chicago, who found that the highest percentage of "most innovative" projects in medical research (those rated in the top fifth by a group of professionally competent judges) came from hospitals rather than from universities or health-research agencies, and that this was because in such situations there tended to be a much higher proportion of researchers reporting that they had both a great deal of freedom in designing their own projects *and* a good deal of discussion of these projects with their organizational superiors. Where either discussion with superiors or individual freedom was absent, innovation was appreciably diminished.

Scientific productivity is difficult to measure, largely because of the difficulties involved in estimating the quality of an article or a book. Simply to count a man's publications, perhaps considering a book to equal four or five articles, is certainly the easiest way to arrive at a scientist's productivity, but this runs into the objection that there is no direct relationship between the number of a man's publications and the significance of his work for the development of knowledge in his field. Assessing the extent to which a paper or a research project is "innovative" is one alternative to the simple counting technique, but it is a more laborious measure to develop and also fails to take account of those materials whose real impact might not be felt for twenty years or more. Within the sociology of science, then, while the concept of productivity is generally taken to be of critical importance, there is little agreement upon how it is to be measured. Still, it may be hoped that what has been accomplished thus far by using relatively crude measures is of some value.

For instance, Pelz found that the quality of a man's work (as evaluated by his colleagues and superiors) seemed to be enhanced when he had frequent contact with both a colleague who shared his orientations and interests and a colleague who differed in some appreciable way; in this particular study, those scientists who had close contact with others who had both "local" and "cosmopolitan" viewpoints tended to do work of higher quality than that carried out by men who did not have this mixture of support and challenge in their personal relationships within the laboratory.

Since science is a collective, cumulative enterprise, productivity is also influenced to a considerable extent by the efficiency of communication within science. Within the last ten years or so, increasing attention has been paid to the problem of how to get useful information to the right people with a minimum of delay; how real the increasing difficulty of achieving this goal is cannot be precisely measured, but there is a growing awareness on the part of scientists that the steady increase in the rate of scientific publication is becoming a serious obstacle to adequate, effective communication.

Conservative estimates indicate that there are at least 30,000 scientific journals published throughout the world today and that together they carry more than a million articles each year. Derek Price, a historian of science at Yale University, has found that the amount of scientific material published annually doubles every fifteen years, and that this rate of increase has held steady over the last three hundred years. It would thus seem that what we today call the "publication explosion" is not really a new phenomenon, but rather a problem that has been growing steadily until at last we have defined it as a kind of crisis.

The problem posed by this plethora of publications is of such immense practical import that attention to it has by no means been confined to sociologists; in fact, the sociologists of science have barely begun to look into the various functions performed by scientific communication and to analyze the factors which influence the modes, speed, and consequences of communication among scientists. Besides carrying information, for example, the communication system of science also carries professional recognition, so that its performance is crucial both to the substantive progress of science and to the continued morale and motivation of scientists. This is certainly one of the most promising areas of the field for investigation and we may expect a marked increase in work on it in the near future.

Science and Society

We come finally to the relations between science and the rest of society, a topic which by virtue of its complexity and size has perhaps been slighted by the sociologists recently in favor of smaller and more easily limited problems. But as soon as we begin to look at the products of science—ideas as well as technology—we must be concerned with the arrangements through which they are transmitted to the larger society. A part of this topic, of course, is handled by the analysis of the part that scientists play in industry, from the development of new products to quality-control operations. Here, however, I wish to focus attention upon the more general problem of the relations between science and government, and particularly the consequences for both science and democratic government of their increasing interdependence.

Whether or not science will in fact be able to solve the major issues facing individual nations and the world as a whole today, it is clear that governments are turning to scientists more than ever before for assistance and advice in solving problems that range from health and economic development, through communications and transportation, to national defense and worldwide disarmament. Here we find writ large the same problems that the patient faces when dealing with his doctor, or the client in hiring a lawyer: how to be sure that the services acquired will be of highest quality, and how to be sure that the professional will not exploit his expertise for personal advantage.

Certainly scientists tend to be adequately rewarded in financial terms by their governments, but at the higher levels of policy-making there is the ever-present possibility that scientific advisers will, consciously or not, bias their advice so that the political ends they prefer may come closer to realization. C. P. Snow's discussion of the relationship between Sir Winston Churchill and his chief scientific adviser during World War II, F. A. Lindeman (Lord Cherwell) may be cited as the forerunner of widespread concern with such problems. This, however, has been defined as something primarily of interest to political scientists and to historians, and the sociologists of science have paid almost no serious attention to it. Indeed, fewer than a quarter of the thirty-nine articles included in a recent volume on *Science and Society*, edited by Norman Kaplan of the George Washington University, are by sociologists. It is possible, too, that the virtual necessity of making value judgments and offering practical advice in this area may have made it appear less appropriate as a subject of sociological inquiry.

Christopher Wright, director of the Institute for the Study of Science in Human Affairs at Columbia University, has estimated that out of the quarter-million scientists in the United States, perhaps one thousand of them make up what he calls the "science affairs community"—the group of scientists who regularly participate in government councils and serve to mediate between the scientific community and the government. He has analyzed the mechanisms through which scientists become members of this informal and changing but highly influential group, and suggests that while a high level of scientific competence is prerequisite for such membership, previous acquaintance with governmental processes and considerable skill in administrative work are also necessary. There is thus to some extent a self-perpetuating establishment involved, a consequence more of the limited number of men available who possess the desired combination of talents and interests than of any self-seeking and exclusionist tendencies.

To go a bit further with this aspect of science-government relationships, we may ask also about the implications of government-by-experts for traditional democratic ideology. This is the question of how the lay citizen, lacking the specialized knowledge that seems increasingly necessary in order to make sound policy decisions, can still retain ultimate control of his government. Don K. Price, Dean of the Kennedy School of Public Administration at Harvard University, has suggested that the problems here are not so much that the policy-makers will become the captives of the experts as that they will allow themselves to give up their constitutional responsibilities in return for the assumed certainties of expert advice. At base, this is apparently not a problem that can be solved by passing laws, but must depend instead for its solution upon the enlightened and informed wisdom and responsibility of those involved in all aspects of government.

To return once more to the more legitimate concerns of the sociologist, there is the reciprocal problem of how closer ties with the government will affect the institution of science. A basic plot in novels dealing with creative people of any sort concerns their temptation to give up their own artistic or scientific standards for the sake of public acclaim and financial security. In one sense, this is also a problem now facing the scientific community as a whole. When large research grants come to symbolize scientific excellence, when an invitation to advise the government comes to represent professional recognition, and when practical discoveries receive more and more public recognition, there is the possibility that the value system upon which science is based will become distorted.

It must be admitted, though, that the sociology of science is not yet at the point where such tentative speculations can be supported by thorough knowledge of the social processes involved and extensive factual information. Common sense, rather than established sociological knowledge, suggests that the scientific community will slowly adjust itself to these changes in its social environment so that it may continue to be a vital force in society. If this is true, science will continue to construct broader and more valid pictures of the forces which govern the natural and social universes, and to play its special part in helping the governments of men make more rational and humane decisions.

It may be, in the end, that the sociology of science will play a crucial role in bringing this to pass. The admonition, "physician, heal thyself," may someday be a reasonable description of what the knowledge developed by this small and relatively new field of basic sociological inquiry can do for itself and for the scientific community of which it is a part. For the present, though, we must look upon the sociology of science largely in terms of its promise rather than its accomplishments—for its major achievements, both pure and applied, lie mainly in the not-too-distant future.

17 THE SOCIOLOGY OF RELIGION

Robert N. Bellah

Men have probably thought about sacred things from the time they began to think at all, but thinking about why one thinks about sacred things is a relatively recent enterprise. Those few instances in which pre-modern man tried to explain religion—the Greek Sophists, Hsün Tzŭ in ancient China, Spinoza and other Western philosophers in the seventeenth and eighteenth centuries—occurred in societies in which traditional religious systems had been eroded and spiritual confusion was on the rise. Periods of religious stability have not stimulated serious intellectual inquiry into religion.

In our own day, when the restless inquiry of the scientific mind concerns itself with virtually everything, so that we could expect religion to become an object of study, the atmosphere of ideological conflict and religious doubt—as it has in the past—conduces to such a study. But also as in the past resistance to such study is strong, both overtly and unconsciously. Sacred things are by definition most deeply inner, most highly reverenced, most carefully respected by those for whom they are sacred. The objective or scientific study of the religious life has seemed to many a contradiction in terms, a mere act of violence on the part of the scientist toward a sphere of life he does not understand. Other astute objectors have found the scientific study of religion only pseudo-scientific, only a cover for something which is itself more a form of religion, even if a misguided one, than of science. Both of these objections are serious, and while they cannot be dealt with adequately in this chapter, consciousness of them must form the first step in any effort to understand religious phenomena.

One way out has been to assert that what the scientist studies is the human aspect of religion, not the divine—he studies man, not God. But that implies that we already know what is man and what is God and what is the difference between them. Such a claim can hardly in itself be scientific. It is perhaps better to assert that we have a human obligation to learn all we can about the entire universe, including ourselves, and that no sphere, not even religion, is exempt from this obligation. Such an assertion seems to be part of the inherent ethic of science, though it may well be close to the religious dimension of science itself, for the obligation has something sacred about it.

Current theories of religion tend to see it either as an answer to certain general but inescapable problems of meaning or as a response to a certain kind of experience, above all, an experience of limit, giving rise to the sense of a beyond, or as a combination of these. The experience of death, evil, and suffering gives rise to profound questions about the meaning of it all which the everyday categories of cause and effect do not answer. Religious symbols provide a context of meaning within which these experiences can be dealt with by placing them in some grander cosmic economy and providing emotional solace—even if it is the solace of renunciation. And religious symbols may be used to express the experience of the limit and source of all human power and meaning, an experience which may arise just when problems of meaning are most pressing.

One difficulty with these theories is that they are in a sense circular. It may be religious-symbol systems that give rise to problems of meaning which would never have arisen spontaneously. It is certainly the case that religious symbols and ritual forms have often induced psychic states interpreted as encounters with the divine. But on consideration this apparent difficulty tells us something important about religion, namely its profoundly relational and reflexive nature. Long ago Durkheim pointed out that nothing in the world is sacred in itself. The sacred is a quality superimposed on the sacred thing. For the Mahayana Buddhist every stick and stone contains the

Buddha nature, but he is experientially aware of this only in the moment of enlightenment. The sacredness emerges only when he is in a certain kind of *relation* with reality. We are forced to conclude, then, that religion is not simply a reaction to some fixed parameter of human experience, not simply a means to cope with anguish and despair. Rather, religion is a symbolic form which shapes human experience, both cognitive and emotional. Religion may create anguish and despair as well as allay them. Nor do I mean here simply that religion has "functions" and "dysfunctions," for in some contexts it is the creation and heightening of tension and anxiety which make religion most functional.

Man is a problem-solving animal. Religion is concerned with what to do and what to think when other forms of problem solution have failed. It is concerned not so much with particular problems as with the problematic nature of man, and with the particular problems, such as death, which most immediately imply that problematic nature. Religion has to do not so much with the experience of particular limits as with limitation in general. To some extent, then, religion can be seen as based on second-order reflective experience higher in generality than in particular experiences. This does not mean that the religious experience may not be concrete and intense, but that it is intense about that which transcends or lies behind the particular. The reflective nature of religion, even the most primitive, is obscured by the tendency to concrete symbolization and anthropomorphism, which are the natural accompaniment of strong feeling. But for even the simplest primitive the religious realm is somehow different even though very close, if heard is not seen, if seen is only glimpsed. The transmitted religious symbols also provide us with meanings when we did not ask, help us hear when we were not listening, help us see when we did not look. It is, then, this shaping and molding capacity of religious symbols, with respect both to meaning and feeling, and on a relatively high level of generality transcending particular contexts of experience, that gives them such power in human life, both personal and social.

We have gradually in the last few paragraphs been building

up a definition of religion as a set of symbolic forms which relates man to the ultimate conditions of his existence. There is of course no such thing as religion in general except in an analytic sense. There is no one set of symbolic forms which performs the function of religion for all men. Rather, there are a great many diverse forms. It is perhaps the central function of the sociology of religion to discover and classify those forms and discern the consequences for action which adherence to them entails. In this task the symbolic and psychological study of religion must go hand in hand with the sociological, for the social consequences of religious orientation are explicable only when we understand the symbolic structure of the religion and its mediation through individual personalities.

One dimension for the classification of religious systems which has recently been revived after a period of neglect is the evolutionary. I have proposed a five-stage classification based on degree of differentiation of the religious-symbol system. I do not argue that development through the five stages is inevitable nor that earlier stages cannot coexist with more advanced ones in the same society. Nor do I overlook the great diversity of types which can be found at any one level of complexity. Rather, I would stress the differences, especially in terms of capacity for development to higher stages of differentiation. I have called the five stages primitive, archaic, historic, early modern, and modern.

The religious-symbol system at the primitive level is characterized by Levy-Bruhl as *"le monde mythique,"* and Stanner directly translates the Australian aboriginal word for it as "the Dreaming." The Dreaming is a time out of time, or in Stanner's word, "everywhen," inhabited by ancestral figures, half animal, half human. Though they are often of heroic proportions and have capacities beyond those of ordinary men as well as being the progenitors and creators of many particular things in the world, they are not gods, for they do not control the world and are not worshiped.

One feature of this mythical world is the high degree to which it is related to the details of the actual world. Not only is every clan and local group defined in terms of the ancestral progenitors and the mythical events of settlement, but virtually every mountain, rock, and tree is explained in terms of the action of mythical beings. All human action is prefigured in the Dreaming, including crime and folly, so that actual existence and the paradigmatic myths are related in the most intimate possible way.

A second feature related to this penchant for particularity is the fluidity of organization of the mythical material. The fluid structure of the myth is almost consciously indicated by the Australians in their use of the word "Dreaming." This is not purely metaphorical, for as Ronald Berndt has shown, men do actually have a propensity to dream during the periods of cult performance. Through the dreams they reshape the cult symbolism for private psychic ends, and what is even more relevant, dreams may actually lead to a reinterpretation of the myth which in turn causes ritual innovation. Both the particularity and the fluidity help account for the hovering closeness of the world of myth to the actual world.

Primitive religious action is characterized neither by worship nor by sacrifice but by identification, "participation," acting out. In the ritual the participants become identified with the mythical beings they represent. The distance between man and mythical being, which was at best slight, disappears altogether in the moment of ritual when "everywhen" becomes now. There are no priests and no congregation, no mediating representative roles and no spectators. All present are involved in the ritual action itself and have become one with the myth.

At the primitive level, religious organization as a separate social structure does not exist. Church and society are one. Religious roles tend to be fused with other roles, and differentiations along lines of age, sex, and kin group are dominant. In most primitive societies age is an important criterion for leadership in the ceremonial life. Specialized shamans or medicine men are found in some tribes, but they are not a necessary feature of primitive religion.

As for the social implications of primitive religion, Durkheim's analysis seems still to be largely acceptable. The ritual life does reinforce the solidarity of the society and serves to induct the young into the norms of tribal behavior. We should not forget the innovative aspects of primitive religion, that particular myths and rituals are in a process of constant revision and alteration, and that in the face of severe historic crisis rather remarkable reformulations of primitive material can be made, as in the so-called cargo cults or nativistic movements. Yet on the whole the religious life is the strongest reinforcement of the basic tenet of Australian aboriginal philosophy—namely, that life, as Stanner puts it, is a "one possibility thing." The very fluidity and flexibility of primitive religion are barriers to radical innovation. Primitive religion gives little leverage from which to change the world.

Here we can treat archaic religion, the second stage, only briefly. As I use the category, archaic religion includes much that is often called primitive, namely the neolithic systems of much of Africa, Polynesia, and much of the native New World. It also includes the Bronze Age religions of both old and new worlds. The characteristic feature of archaic religion is the emergence of true cult with the complex of gods, priests, worship, sacrifice, and in some cases divine or priestly kingship. The myth and ritual complex characteristic of primitive religion continues within the structure of archaic religion, but it is systematized and elaborated in new ways.

Both the primitive and the archaic stages have a monistic view of the world, though in somewhat different ways. For both of them the sacred and the profane are different modes of organization of a single cosmos. But with the third stage, what I have called the historic stage, an entirely different realm of reality, having for religious man the highest value, is proclaimed. All the historic religions are in some sense transcendental and they are all—at least latently—world-rejecting, since relative to the supreme value of the transcendent this world is devalued.

In one sense historic religions represent a great "demytholigization" relative to archaic religions. The notion of the one God who has neither court nor relatives and who is the sole creator and ruler of the universe, the notion of self-subsistent being, the notion of an absolute negativity which transcends all oppositions and discriminations, are all enormous simplifications of the ramified cosmologies of archaic religions. Yet all the historic religions have, to use Voegelin's term, mortgages imposed on them by the historical circumstances of their origin. All of them contain, in suspension as it were, elements of archaic cosmology alongside their transcendental assertions. Nonetheless, relative to earlier forms, the historic religions are all universalistic. From the point of view of these religions a man is no longer defined chiefly in terms of what tribe or clan he comes from or what particular god he serves, but rather as a being capable of salvation. This is to say that it is for the first time possible to conceive of man as such.

Religious action in the historic religions is, above all, action necessary for salvation. Even where elements of ritual and sacrifice remain prominent, they take on a new significance. In primitive ritual the individual is put in harmony with the natural divine cosmos. His mistakes are overcome through symbolization as part of the total pattern. Through sacrifice, archaic man can make up for his failures to fulfill his obligations to men and gods. He can atone for particular acts of unfaithfulness. But historic religions convict man of a basic flaw far more serious than those conceived of by earlier religions. According to Buddhism, man's very nature is greed and anger, from which he must seek a total escape. For the Hebrew prophets, man's sin is not particular wicked deeds but his profound heedlessness of God, and only a turn to complete obedience will be acceptable to the Lord. For Mohammed the *kafir* is not, as we usually translate it, the "unbeliever," but rather the ungrateful man who is careless of the divine compassion. For him, only Islam, willing submission to the will of God, can bring salvation.

Partly because of the supreme value of salvation and the many dangers and temptations in the world leading men astray, the ideal of the religious life in the historic religions tends to be one of separation from the world. The early Christian solution which, unlike the Buddhist, did allow the full possibility of salvation to the layman, nevertheless in its notion of a special state of religious perfection idealized religious withdrawal from the world. In fact the standard for lay piety tended to be closeness of approximation to the life of a monk.

The historic stage sees a differentiation of religious organization from other forms of social organization to a degree previously unknown. While few of the historic religions attained a degree of differentiation comparable to that of the Christian church, all of them had some independence from other structures, particularly the political structure. This meant that the political realm did not contain the principle of its own legitimation (as would have been the case with Bronze Age divine kingship) but was dependent to some degree on the religious hierarchy for legitimation. The greater the degree of structural independence of the historic religion, the more likely was it that movements of social and political reform would arise on the basis of religious values. In all cases the historic religions did develop conceptions of the good society which exerted long-term pressure on societies in which they existed toward greater value realization. It should be remembered, however, that the main concern of the historic religions was with the drama of salvation and that they had no concern with social change for its own sake. Rather, they abhorred change, and when urging reform usually did so in the name of some prior paradigmatic social order to which they wished to return.

Early-modern religion, which finds its most developed instance in the Protestant Reformation but which was anticipated in a number of other cases, such as the Jodo Shin sect in Japan, represents a definite shift to this world as the primary sphere for religious action. Salvation is not to be found in any kind of withdrawal from the world but in the midst of worldly activities. Of course, elements of this existed in the historic religions from the beginning, but on the whole the historic religions as institutionalized had offered a mediated salvation. Either conformity to religious law, or participation in a sacramental system, or the performance of mystical exercises was necessary for salvation. All of these involved to some extent a turning away from the world. Further, in the religious two-class systems characteristic of the institutionalized historic religions the upper-status groups—the Christian monks or Sufi *shaykhs* or Buddhist ascetics—could, through their pure acts and personal characteristics, store up a fund of grace that could then be shared with the less worthy. In this way, too, salvation was mediated rather than immediate. But with the Reformation the whole world, in Max Weber's words, became a monastery. Especially for the Calvinists, work in the world became the chief means for the glorification of God. Thus, without breaking through the symbolic structure of historic religion, early-modern religion managed to reformulate it so that the discipline and drive of the religious motivation became available for the transformation of the secular world. In the case of ascetic protestantism the results were dramatic not only in the field of economics, which Weber stressed, but in politics, education, science, law, and so forth.

Most recently and again mainly in the West, the symbolic structure of the historic and early-modern religions has begun to be questioned, especially the cosmological dualism which is fundamental to all of them. The shape of religion in a post-dualistic world is not clear, but such religion must take account of the tremendous growth of human knowledge leading to a relativization of the place of man in the natural cosmos through the growth of natural science and the relativization of man in the cultural world due to the increasing knowledge both of history and of other cultures. Man is as problematic as ever, and inescapable problems of meaning continue to confront him. The process of secularization involves a change in the structure and role of religion rather than the end of religion itself. But these are matters which we are only beginning to understand.

If this evolutionary sketch has any cogency, then it would suggest two main areas on which the sociology of religion might concentrate in the contemporary world. The first area is the shift from historic to early-modern religion, from primarily other-worldly to primarily this-worldly religious concerns, of which the Protestant Reformation was the harbinger but which is now going on in virtually every major religious community, notably in the Roman Catholic. This problem is particularly acute in the so-called developing nations. The second area is the shift from early modern to what I have called modern religion, which is taking place mainly in the most advanced Western countries but also perhaps in Japan. A word about each of these problem areas will conclude this chapter.

In almost all of the developing countries the stimulus to

change has been to an important degree external, ranging from brutal military assault to relentless economic pressures, to the more insidious forms of ideological subversion. This means that in most cases the need to defend has been prior to and stronger than the need to change. The logic of the situation, however, has been that it is impossible to defend without changing. Religion has been deeply involved in this pattern of attack, defense, and change. Christian missionaries were often the shock troops of the Western impact, making a direct assault on the religious and ethical beliefs of the non-Western people. Even without this direct challenge from an alien religious system, the experience of social and personal failure, which has been so general in the early stages of Western impact, inevitably has raised the problem of identity. Religious symbols have, in most of these societies, provided the basic terms for thinking about personal and social action. In a situation of crisis the relevance of these inherited patterns became problematic.

A common early reaction everywhere has been apologetic and defensive. The superiority of the indigenous tradition, Islam or Hinduism or Confucianism, to Christianity and the whole of Western culture was asserted in the most sweeping way. Some Muslims argued that Western science and philosophy were derived entirely from medieval Islamic culture, and thus everything of value in the West really came from Islam. Some Hindus argued that Western values are purely materialistic and that India is the only home of true spirituality. Some Confucians claimed that the West understood science but had no appreciation of the truth about human relations, which could be found only in Confucianism. But the early defensiveness was almost never unmixed with an impulse to change and reform. Even where the change advocated was a return to an earlier, allegedly purer state of the non-Western tradition, the intention, implicit or explicit, was that through such change adaptation to the modern world would be furthered. Occasionally non-Western intellectuals became so disillusioned with the inadequacy of their traditional culture to meet the problems of the modern world that they abandoned their ancestral faith for Christianity or some secular Western ideology. All of these positions are characterized by a balance between the need to defend and the need to adapt. Where defensiveness became absolute, the capacity to deal with the treacherous conditions of the modern world failed. Where adaptation led to total rejection of the traditional culture, the intellectual found himself isolated and irrelevant. Let us consider an ideal solution which would transform the historic religious tradition into an early-modern type and thus contribute maximally to the modernization process.

Above all, the historic religion must be able to rephrase its religious-symbol system so as to give meaning to cultural creativity in this-worldly pursuits. It must be able to channel motivation disciplined through religious obligation into this-worldly occupations. It must contribute to the development of a solidary and integrated national community which it seeks neither to dominate nor divide, though this certainly does not imply sanctioning the nation as a religious ultimate. It must give positive meaning to the long-term process of social development and be able to value it highly as a social goal, again without necessarily taking social progress itself as a religious absolute. It must contribute to the ideal of a responsible and disciplined personality. As part of the new balance between religious and secular in modern society it must be able to accept its own role as a private voluntary association and recognize that this is not incompatible with its role as bearer of the society's ultimate values. This list of requisites is, as we have said, an ideal typical construction. Certainly no religion of historic type has transformed itself in such a way, and probably no religion of historic type could have done so completely. Some religions, by the very nature of their religious-symbol system, would rather be destroyed than change. But if modernization is to be successfully accomplished, either traditional religion must make this transition, at least in large part, or it must be able to withdraw from major spheres of life and allow secular ideologies to complete the transition.

A few examples will suggest the problems and contradictions involved. In Japan an essentially archaic Bronze Age divine-emperor cult was effective in channeling motivation into this-worldly spheres and in furthering national solidarity and unity.

It failed, however, to develop either voluntary organizational forms or any stress on the independently responsible personality. Thus it was easily distorted into what some Japanese scholars call "emperor system fascism" in the 1930's and early 1940's. In India, Gandhi, following a long line of Hindu reformers, showed how Hinduism was compatible with the dignity of all callings and with a national unity transcending caste. His deeply ambivalent feelings about many aspects of modern society and his misgivings about industrialization did, however, undoubtedly deflect to some extent the development of an effective early modern form of Hinduism. In Turkey, traditional Islam was brusquely shunted aside in favor of a nationalism emphasizing pre-Islamic Turkish culture. The new ideology, however, was able to capture the enthusiasm of only a relatively small elite group and an unreformed Islam has continued to hold sway in the countryside. In China, traditional beliefs were rejected in favor of an intensely charismatic communism with many of the characteristics of early modern religion. However, it remains to be seen whether the trauma suffered by the traditional cultural identity will not have serious consequences and whether the charisma can be successfully routinized. Lastly, we see in the Second Vatican Council an evident move on the part of the Catholic Church in the direction of early-modern characteristics, but very serious problems about authority and tradition remain to be solved. At any rate, every one of these cases needs intensive sociological research which would yield both practical and theoretical results far richer than the rather parochial concentration on such subjects as ever more refined typologies of church and sect which seem to dominate much of American work in the sociology of religion.

Finally, let me turn briefly to the religious situation in the most advanced societies. Here the chief difference from the developing nations is that external problems, though not by any means absent, are less pressing. The general level of material well-being is high, even though pockets of poverty and injustice remain. The level of education is constantly rising so that the percentage of college graduates in some sections of the United States may approach 50 per cent in the not distant future. The exposure to information about the world from a variety of media is unprecedented, even though there are important communication blockages. While in the developing nations the immediate economic and political problems absorb most of the available emotional energy and cognitive sophistication, in the most advanced societies the question is more apt to be what is the meaning of life once such problems are solved. In the developing nations stark religious or ideological formulations—communism, nationalism, religious revivalism—with relatively clear and simple world views and an immediate imperative to action, are most appropriate. While such tendencies are not absent in the most advanced societies, they do not appeal to the best-educated and most cosmopolitan segment of the population. For this constantly increasing and ever more influential group, subtle, self-conscious, and undogmatic systems of thought are necessary. Religious groups can no longer take traditional commitment for granted. Everything handed down from the past is subjected to searching scrutiny and motives for acceptance are carefully considered, especially by the best-trained minds of the religious groups themselves.

One partial solution, in the United States at least, has been a preoccupation with the problems of poverty and injustice remaining in the society and which are all the more salient because so many objective problems have been solved. The tremendous fervor for the civil-rights movement in the most sophisticated religious and intellectual circles is an indication of this. Preoccupation with the rest of the world in its efforts to develop may serve a similar function. But the point is that fervor on particular issues does not mean commitment to an over-all ideology of early-modern type by such groups. Indeed, such ideologies are held in great suspicion, which is one reason for the claim that ours is an age of the end of ideology. But of course most of the world is in an intensely ideological phase and many groups in the most advanced societies are susceptible to ideological appeal. In fact, the relatively small group for whom ideology has ended would hardly seem worth considering if it were not that it seems to be the advance guard of a very general and large-scale sociocultural transformation.

It is still too early to discern the shape of religion in a post-dualistic world. But it does seem clear that metaphysical dualism is not being superseded by a flat, materialistic monism. Rather there is an increasing awareness of a multiplicity of worlds partly given, partly built up in the complex network of interactions between self and reality. The major mode is personalist and individualist but not asocial or apolitical. In fact, it is increasingly recognized that only a very complex institutional structure, including a particular kind of family, school, and church, could produce and sustain a person able to operate in a world where everything, even one's deepest ideals, is radically open to choice. The possibilities of derailment are enormous, but so are the possibilities for growth. The German theologian Bonhoeffer has spoken of "man come of age." By this is not meant the self-deification of man, for it is the infant who believes in the omnipotence of wishes. Man come of age is aware of his inescapable limitation. He is not deterred thereby; rather, he is challenged to realize the fullness of his humanity.

But we must always remember that even in the most advanced societies the substratum of the primitive and the archaic is still powerful, dominating the lives of many and present in the psyches of us all. Any large modern society is a laboratory for the study of every imaginable type of religious orientation. In Japan, for example, we can find the age-old ritual of the peasant village, the half traditional half ultra-modern revivalistic new religions of the urban lower classes, the aesthetic Zen cult of upper-class intellectuals, and the anguished search for personal meaning on the part of those to whom none of the existing religions speak. But if there is immense diversity in these societies, there is also present as one dimension of religious life a civil religion that provides more or less coherently a framework of religious unity for the society even where religious pluralism is most pronounced. In the United States, for instance, we can think of the Deistic symbolism which is an essential part of our public ceremonial, a ritual calendar in which Thanksgiving Day and Memorial Day are more central than the Fourth of July, and a roster of saints headed by our martyred President, Abraham Lincoln. The Kennedy memorial at the Arlington National

Cemetery is only the latest major shrine in the national faith. I am not speaking satirically nor do I think this can be called "American Shinto," since Shinto is fundamentally quite different though equally deserving of study in its present situation. The American civil religion is a serious religious tradition which must be analyzed as such, including both its profound and its aberrant aspects. And every other one of the great modern societies presents similar materials for the analyst. Here, too, there is much unfinished business for the sociologist of religion.[1]

NOTE

1. This chapter is based on two recent articles of mine: "Religious Evolution," *American Sociological Review*, XXIX, No. 3 (1964), and the Epilogue in Robert W. Bellah, ed., *Religion and Progress in Modern Asia* (New York: The Free Press of Glencoe, 1965). The ideas briefly sketched here are considerably more elaborated in those articles.

PART V

Strain, Deviance, and Social Control

18 DEVIANT BEHAVIOR AND ITS CONTROL

Albert K. Cohen

The aim of this chapter is to introduce you to the sociology of deviant behavior and its control. One way of doing this is to review the development of theory and research in this area, but I have chosen another, which I consider more suitable for a brief introduction to this field. This will be a set of sociological observations on deviance in one country—the United States—with only occasional reference to theories and their authors. By doing this, we sacrifice a proper appreciation of the scholarly work that has gone into the building of the modern sociology of deviance. This method will, however, convey in a concrete way the flavor of the sociological approach to deviance—namely, the attempt to understand a society's deviance in terms of the social structure of that society.

The United States has a reputation for very high rates of crime, delinquency, violence, sexual profligacy, corruption in business and government, and general moral decay. Whatever the reality may be, it is extremely difficult, in the present state of our knowledge, to make precise statements about the prevalence of any particular form of deviance in any country, and still more difficult to make scientifically tenable comparisons among countries. In no country do rates of officially recorded offenses constitute an accurate measure of the actual prevalence of the respective behavior; there is always a "dark figure," the obscurely known or altogether unknown residue of behavior that does not become part of the public record. The gulf between the known and the unknown varies for different kinds of offenses, and for any type of offense it varies from one country to another. In any sphere of conduct where valid knowledge is not available, the imagination tends to create its own images, which may be only imperfectly related to the facts. This is especially so in the field of deviant behavior, where, on the one hand, the facts are exceptionally obscure and, on the other hand, fear, anxiety, the need for formulating some kind of public policy, and sheer fascination with the lurid and sensational provide exceptionally strong incentives to the exercise of the imagination. Before we attempt some cautious generalizations about the actual prevalence of deviance on the American scene, and its causes, it will be worth our while to comment on some aspects of American attitudes toward deviance, both because these help to account for the imagery and because they have some bearing upon the forms and frequency of deviance itself.

One notable feature of American culture is a reluctance to accept, with philosophical resignation, the imperfections of man and society. This American attitude does not typically take the form of revolutionary movements, but it does typically express itself in a passion for locating and exposing evil and in the demand for reform. In the conservative image, the evil that stands out is the vice and wickedness of the great city, its politicians and racketeers, its hedonism and sensuality. Its causes tend to be attributed to personal moral defect, irreligion, the lack of discipline, the decline of patriotism and the decay of the ancient virtues; the remedies tend to be seen in the area of religious revival, moral instruction, example, discipline, and the stern enforcement of the laws. In the liberal image, the evil that stands out is the corruption of business and government, the ruthlessness of the powerful governed by their vested interests, the neglect and suppression of the poor. Its causes tend to be attributed to the defects of social institutions, the unequal distribution of wealth and opportunity, the existence of prejudice and discrimination; the remedies tend to be seen in the area of the reform of social institutions, the expansion of opportunity and the extension of political power to the disadvantaged classes, the vigorous intervention of government in the control of economic institutions, and a humanitarian, non-punitive, "therapeutic" approach to the treatment of the deviant. On both sides, however, the orientation is activistic: do not temporize with evil but root it out.

In consequence there are few aspects of American society that escape censure, few forms of deviance that are not exposed and denounced and endlessly documented. Another consequence is an enormous amount of concerted activity, both private and governmental, for the control of deviance. It is well known that Americans are much given to participation in voluntary associations, many of them purely social or professional, but many of them consecrated to public service and civic virtue, and one celebrated form of civic virtue is the exposure and repression or correction of other people's vices. The criminal law is freely used to control types of behavior that in many other societies are likewise regarded as deviant but are left to be regulated by other social institutions and the informal processes of public opinion. Such legislation includes the repressive laws that make crimes of the so-called vices—prostitution and other forms of sexual deviance, gambling, the use of marijuana and drugs of addiction, and still, in some American jurisdictions, the use of alcohol. Most countries have some criminal legislation affecting these areas of conduct, but few try so hard to use the cumbersome machinery of the criminal law as a major means of repressing so wide a spectrum of deviant behavior.

It must be realized that these vices, whatever their moral status, are activities from which human beings derive profound satisfactions which require, as a rule, the active collaboration of other persons, and for which, if need be, people are prepared to pay well. Therefore we are speaking of the production and consumption of goods and services. Because the demand for these goods and services is widespread, and because their recipients are not victims in the ordinary sense of the word but rather beneficiaries, the laws prohibiting them are enforced fitfully and largely ineffectively. They do, however, contribute importantly to criminal statistics. Furthermore, by making these goods and services unavailable from lawful sources, and attaching stigma and risk to the traffic, these laws tend to reduce the supply without correspondingly reducing the demand. For those willing to take the risks, therefore, the traffic provides opportunities for great profits, and the more vigorous the enforcement, the greater the profits. In the special case of narcotics, where the punishment for selling or use is, in this country, especially severe, but the demand especially inelastic, the cost of indulgence becomes exceptionally high and addicts are compelled to steal to support their addiction. Thus the zeal to stamp out nonconforming behavior by criminal legislation tends to transform non-crime into crime, to foster the creation of illegal forms of business enterprise, and to encourage the pursuit of certain forms of crime in order to make others possible.

You will observe that I have said nothing about the individual offender, his idiosyncrasies and psychology. My point, and the point of the sociological approach to deviant behavior, is not that these are irrelevant, which is manifestly absurd, but that the study of the characteristics of individuals alone is not enough to explain the occurrence and scale of deviant, and especially criminal behavior.

But the war on deviance is not limited to repression through the harsh medium of the criminal law. The social services of the state as well as private and quasi-public social-service agencies not only render assistance to families and individuals in distress but also share importantly in the task of social control. They are staffed largely by social workers, a numerous and specialized profession with a distinctive philosophy, vocabulary, and technology, strongly influenced by psychiatry. The social-work profession tends to see deviance as a problem of mental health, blocked opportunity, or personal emotional immaturity, calling for sympathy, patience, support and counsel, and frequently for psychiatric and psychological therapies. To enlarge on this theme for a moment, there is a world-wide trend, but nowhere more marked than in the United States, especially among the highly educated, to redefine many types of deviance as medical rather than as police problems, as sickness rather than as sin or crime. Homosexuality, alcoholism, and drug addiction are cases in point. However, this is nowhere the dominant view, even in the United States.

In addition, some social workers and a number of sociologists have developed programs aiming at the reduction of deviance through massive changes in social organization at the community level, with emphasis on the enlargement of employment opportunities among the poor and a greater voice for the poor in the governmental and civic decision making affecting their interests. The theory behind these programs is that deviance is a product of frustration, helplessness, despair, and alienation from conventional institutions, resulting in turn from the inability of the poor to control their own environments and destinies. An excellent example is the multimillion-dollar experiment in delinquency prevention in New York City called Mobilization for Youth, financed largely by funds from the federal government.

The tendency to seek out deviance and to make its control a matter of governmental responsibility is seen also in the field of juvenile delinquency, which is here more broadly construed than in most other countries. The juvenile court, which was established in this country in 1899, has jurisdiction not only over the criminal behavior of young people but over a wide range of behavior that would not constitute crimes if committed by adults. Sexual misconduct, truancy, running away from home, the defiance of parental authority, and other kinds of misconduct once the responsibility of the family alone constitute a significant part of the business of the juvenile courts and contribute to the official statistics of juvenile delinquency. Because these statistics include such a wide variety of behavior, and because the juvenile courts differ strikingly in their practices, it is exceedingly difficult to make comparisons among different jurisdictions with respect to the frequency of different forms of juvenile deviance, and still more difficult to make comparisons with other countries. Juvenile delinquency is certainly a serious problem in the United States, as it is in all advanced countries and in countries and regions undergoing rapid social change. Some forms of delinquency, notably fighting among street gangs, are probably more prevalent and serious in the United States than in most other countries, but even this form of delinquency, romanticized in the musical comedy *West Side Story*, is largely localized in a few metropolitan cities, is probably nowhere so extensive as it is commonly thought to be, and seems now, for reasons not at all clear, to be declining.

Finally, it is important to add that the United States is a very wealthy country and can afford to indulge its passion for ferreting out and waging war by all manner of devices on all sorts of deviance. Few countries could afford so large and expensive an apparatus for the social control of deviant behavior.

A final note concerning the institutions of social control. This rich and varied picture we have drawn is also one of turbulence and conflict, reflecting the varied and inconsistent philosophies and techniques to which I have alluded. For example, the dominant attitude toward drug addiction is that it is a vice, a police problem, and calls for ruthless repression and drastic punishment. At the same time the view is gaining ground that it is essentially a medical problem that is only aggravated by police methods, and we have a number of experimental treatment programs based on this view. The treatment of drug addiction is therefore a subject of violent controversy and drug addicts are dealt with in radically different ways. In general, it may be said that every conception of the nature of man and society is reflected in a characteristic approach to the problem of the control of deviant behavior, and in no country are so many of these approaches embodied in actual programs of control.

Many of these programs are premised upon essentially sociological conceptions of the nature of deviance. Among these conceptions is the view that most deviance is not a simple expression of personal pathology but that it is learned behavior, acquired in large part in interaction with others who provide models both for the techniques and the supporting beliefs and ideologies; that deviant behavior, like most human behavior, requires both material and moral support from communities of like-minded persons; and that, in general, the processes that generate and maintain deviant behavior are not very different from those that generate and maintain conforming behavior. In the field of social control these assumptions are increasingly reflected in programs that seek to alter the behavior and beliefs of the individual by changing the cultures and social organization of the groups of which he is a member.

Now, before I discuss some sources of deviance in American society, let me make clear that by "deviance" I understand not only crime and delinquency but any behavior that violates widely accepted rules of conduct. It is a very mixed bag. It includes the illegal use of violence, of which alone there are numerous varieties, ranging from the murder of a spouse in the heat of passion to the carefully planned assassination of a political leader. It includes indulgence in a variety of distinct vices as well as the business operations that cater to these vices. It includes all forms of corruption and misconduct, illegal or merely unethical, among law-enforcement and government officials. It includes the violation of laws and customs regulating the activities of business enterprises, professional persons, tradesmen, and artisans. It includes suicide, the evasion of taxes, false insurance claims, and cheating on examinations. Is there anything that one can say that is relevant to this whole vast, variegated field? This itself is a much-disputed question in the sociology of deviance. One position is that there can only be, at best, a sociology of prostitution, a sociology of embezzlement, a sociology of drug addiction, and so forth. I do not agree with this extreme view, but I cannot review the arguments here. One thing, however, is clear: the manifold varieties of deviance are not simply diverse expressions of some single, generalized, protean propensity to deviance. Where one kind of deviance thrives, another may be rare. Societies that are highly productive of certain kinds of deviance may be relatively free of others. Therefore, not only must the following remarks be taken as tentative, in view of the present state of our knowledge; insofar as they are valid, they cannot be equally relevant to the whole spectrum of deviant behavior.

The United States is a dynamic, growing, prosperous, more or less democratic industrial society. Many of the features that make this possible are also fertile sources of deviance. All of them may be found in other societies, but in few do they exist together in the same degree.

It is a characteristic of an expanding industrial society that it is an insatiable consumer of skills. New industries and new technologies grow up almost overnight. New occupations appear, vast new organizations spring up, and old organizations expand. Millions of new positions are created and old ones vacated at every level of government, economy, and scientific and educational organization, vastly more than can be filled by an established elite. In a number of ways such a society tends to produce high levels of aspiration, a hopeful reaching out for a better life, for success, for social and material advancement.

Such a society must be a more or less open society. It must man its positions with qualified persons and must seek them at every social level. It must, then, be a society of opportunity. But it is not enough that opportunity be objectively there; people must also be stimulated to seek these opportunities, to believe that these opportunities are for them, and that by dint of ambition, drive, and preparation they can attain them. The dominant ideology of American society, however imperfectly it may be realized in practice, emphasizes the virtue of seeking to better oneself; it denies the legitimacy of fixed orders, to each of which a certain station in life is appropriate; it encourages each man to compare himself with a wide universe of others of greatly differing social origins. The educational system is perhaps the principal vehicle for the transmission of this ideology, and in many ways it strives to keep open, as late as possible, the opportunities for acquiring the qualifications for escaping from the social class of one's origin and moving up. The economy of such a society requires a population able and eager to consume its products, and a large part of its energy goes into the stimulation of wants. Wealth is, in fact, widely dispersed and highly visible, a constant reminder to people of what is desirable, and that the desirable is possible. Such a society is the scene of a continuing revolution of rising expectations.

These features of American society are calculated to maximize ambition and hope and to provide the incentive to train oneself, to work hard, to seek responsibility. These ever-rising levels of aspiration help to account for the astounding productivity of American society. They help also to produce discontent, discrepancy between what one seeks and what one has attained. Indeed, the dynamism of American society is premised to a large extent upon this discontent in the present coupled with confidence and hope in the future. But where confidence and hope fail, where legitimate avenues to the achievement of one's goals appear blocked or one's personal resources insufficient, discontent can turn to disappointment and frustration. Most people, of course, make a tolerable accommodation to their situation, and a certain amount of frustration is the lot of most of mankind. Most people learn eventually to temper their aspirations to what they can attain. However, the ubiquitous pressures to the escalation of goals make for a certain restlessness and instability, and impatience at constraint and discipline. It is the thesis of the American sociologist Robert K. Merton that American society, to an exceptional degree and in all classes of men, produces such discrepancy between what one is led to desire and what is legitimately obtainable, that this leads to a weakening of the rules and institutions that regulate and discipline men's conduct, and ultimately to the rejection of the authority of the rules and to various forms of deviance.

It is certainly the case that opportunities are inherently limited and unequally distributed, whereas the stimuli to the expansion of aspirations, by comparison, operate more or less indiscriminately. This poses a fundamental dilemma of any dynamic, democratic society: how to have a contented people, respecting themselves and one another without regard to their worldly success, and at the same time create the motivation to high levels of production and growth. Or, to put it differently, how to raise men's hopes so that they will strive to attain them, and in the process turn the wheels of a prosperous society, without reaping a large harvest of failure, disenchantment, and rebellion.

The sense of despair and futility and the ineffectiveness of conventional institutions of social control are especially marked among the poor of the great urban agglomerations. It is also a characteristic of a dynamic industrial society that it attracts vast numbers of migrants from areas of chronic poverty—typically from peasant societies and underdeveloped areas within the same society—to its great metropolitan centers. In the United States this would include both whites and Negroes from the American South and a large influx of migrants from Puerto Rico. Here they congregate in vast slums along with the residue of previous migrations, with the failures and rejects of the economy, with the casualties of technological change.

239

But it is not enough to note that they are poor. The poor of other societies, or even of American society, are not necessarily especially prone to crime and deviance. For that matter, the poverty of these American poor, measured in absolute terms, may be less than that which they knew in their previous homes. They are poor people in the setting of the American metropolis and transplanted from another culture. They are subject to the unsettling stimuli of the mass media, of the spectacle of great wealth, of the example of the minority of their countrymen who have managed to flourish in the new setting. They are handicapped by prejudice and discrimination. And they are typically ill equipped to utilize and exploit the opportunities of an urban, bureaucratic, impersonal social structure. Their traditional methods of adaptation to economic insecurity, which rely heavily on extensive networks of kinship and patronage, are of little avail here. Their frequent dependence on the social services of the state is wounding to their sense of dignity. They live in rapidly changing, loosely organized areas with few stable, indigenous institutions that command authority, especially among the young. They live in a society where economic success, or even survival, is to an exceptional degree dependent upon educational achievement. Their traditional cultures, however, place little value on such achievement; they provide their children with little orientation to academic success; the young absorb little from the schools and drop out early, to enter the labor market in the most menial, unstable, and poorly rewarded employment. Here we find, on a massive scale, frustration and disillusionment, apathy and alienation. Of all classes of the population, these people feel they have the least stake in the social order because the rewards they draw from it are the most fitful and meager, they understand it least, and they are the most removed from the centers of power.

One way of summarizing the implications of all this is the following. Society may be seen as a set of games, governed by certain rules. These rules define the proper methods of play and the criteria of success. Positions in these games provide participants with public identities—that is, they define to others the kinds of persons they are—and with self-conceptions. If they value these identities, then the players have an incentive to play hard and to subordinate to success in these games impulses and interests that jeopardize the credibility of these identities. In this way, they provide a basis for self-discipline and a coherent and stable life organization. Where the games are poorly understood, there the possibility of successful participation is perceived as feeble. People tend, if not to reject the games, to become indifferent to them, to be unresponsive to the rules governing these games, to minimize, in their life schemes, the importance of the identities growing out of these games. They tend, especially if their circumstances are shared with many others, to devise or to seek out other games within which they can find, or hope to find, identities that are more rewarding, although they may bring recognition only within the limited circles within which they move. Failing this, their lives become unstable, erratic, responsive to the opportunities and impulses of the moment.

In the impoverished areas of which I am speaking, the serious games of the conventional world, organized around work, education, and service to the community, are games in which it is difficult to compete effectively. People therefore develop only weak investments in their involvements in these games and the identities they provide, and acquire only weak incentives to conform to the standards of conventional and respectable conduct that are expressive of such identities. It would be a gross caricature to describe these areas as anarchic, chaotic, and devoid of conventional discipline. However, they do provide a setting productive of high rates of deviance, especially among the young, who are of all groups the least firmly anchored to identities that demand for their validation the demonstration of the conventional and bourgeois virtues. But even most of them, as they grow into adulthood, marry and come to participate, even though marginally, in the occupational system, acquire investments in the conventional virtues, and become, in the main, reasonably law-abiding citizens.

In recent years, American sociology has become increasingly interested in so-called white-collar crime, which was first subjected to serious sociological study by the American criminologist, Edwin H. Sutherland. White-collar crime does not refer to all crimes committed by persons of high social status. It refers rather to crimes committed by businessmen and corporations in the normal conduct of their business. It would include, for example, violations of governmental regulations prohibiting cartels, monopolies, and other conspiracies and combinations in restraint of trade; violations of pure food and drug regulations; false and misleading advertising; illegal operations on the stock market; and so on. Complaints alleging such violations are usually handled by administrative agencies, and only rarely by criminal courts. Therefore they do not contribute significantly to criminal statistics. Furthermore, the offenders are seldom seriously stigmatized and they continue to enjoy positions of respect and influence. However, the acts of which I am speaking do violate criminal statutes and are, therefore, as Sutherland pointed out, a proper object of criminological study and must be taken into account in framing theories of criminal behavior. Theories based on official crime statistics reflect, for the most part, the crimes of the lower classes, and cannot be generalized to the whole universe of criminal behavior. Furthermore, it is a matter of common knowledge, highlighted by systematic research, that such crimes flourish on a vast scale; their victims are competing business organizations or the consumer.

Very little has been done by way of developing theories to account for such behavior, but it is obvious that common-sense explanations of crime, in terms of poverty, broken homes, individual psychopathology, and the like, have little relevance. White-collar crimes are typically not conceived and executed by single individuals but are pursuant to policy decisions of large organizations. Their explanations are to be found in an analysis of organizational decision making within the setting of the American economy. On the face of it, white-collar crime is an aspect of the struggle for existence, stability, and growth among great and powerful organizations under conditions of competition. Many white-collar offenses, notably violations of the antitrust laws, are manifestly devices to reduce the insecurity and instability arising out of competition. However, a proper perspective on white-collar crime requires us to recognize that many of these crimes are forms of behavior that in many other advanced societies are equally prevalent or more so, but are not so closely regulated by criminal statutes or may even enjoy the status of fully legitimate business practices.

Therefore, to understand white-collar crime, especially in a comparative perspective, it is necessary to broaden our field of inquiry still further, to include the social factors that determine public attitudes, criminal legislation, and enforcement practices. Although this is manifestly true with respect to white-collar crime, it is probably equally true of most other offenses. The starting point for the sociological study of deviance in any society should be the ways in which deviance is conceived, the institutions and instruments for the control of deviance, including the criminal law, and the ways in which these are selectively used for different kinds of deviance. This is the direction in which sociology is slowly turning, but it still has very far to go along this road.

19 YOUTH IN MODERN SOCIETY

Charles E. Bidwell

What creates the "problem of generations"? Whenever discontinuities appear between the beliefs and actions of young people and the expectations of adults, the position of youth in society is raised as an urgent and troublesome question. This question may be voiced by parents vexed by their growing inability to talk with or control their offspring, by political or religious leaders decrying the advent of an "alien" generation, or by writers and social commentators who see exemplified by youth the distinctive tensions and strains of their time.

The disquieting characteristics attributed to youth have varied widely, but they generally express one of two contradictory themes: rebelliousness (in the guises of political or moral radicalism, delinquency, and bohemianism) or apathy (in such forms as irresponsible hedonism or blind conformity to adult standards of morality, religious devotion, or academic performance). The view of youth as rebellious typically is accompanied by a sense of moral outrage and a fear that the society will be destroyed by deviant behavior. The view of youth as apathetic carries a sense of disappointment and a conviction that society will decay from widespread indifference and disengagement.

The problem of generations is found almost entirely in modern societies and in societies on the path to modernization. An important issue for sociological analysis is to determine the factors in social modernity that determine the problem of generations, and to account for the differing forms in which this problem appears. A brief introduction to this issue will be attempted in this chapter. For the sake of simplicity the discussion centers on the middle classes and on males, but one must recognize that the diversity of modern societies creates very different problems for young women and at other class levels.

PROBLEMS OF SOCIAL AND BIOLOGICAL TIME

Societal modernization produces profound changes in the timing of lives. When a human being reaches adolescence, he is in his physical prime—strong, vigorous, and sexually mature. To the extent that physical prowess is demanded for adult status, adolescents are fully qualified for adulthood. But in no society can one participate as an adult without substantial preparation. Even in the least complex societies, the common language must be learned, traditions, myths, and the rules of social life acquired, and some skill in gathering or producing food developed. But in most traditional societies basic social learning is fairly continuous from one generation to the next, it occurs primarily within family or kinship circles, and it is completed by the time of full physical development. Consequently social and physical maturity are more or less coterminous. Moreover, the child's progress toward adulthood is quite well defined by his age position within his family; there is a strong tendency for movement toward both social and physical maturity to be specified and coordinated by a series of socially defined age-grades.

There is a sharp contrast with modern societies in which, because of a complex, highly refined division of labor, the attainment of adult status is determined by entry into an occupation. Few occupations, with the exception of unskilled work, depend in any direct or central way upon physical maturity; instead, they demand mastery of a distinctive technique and body of scientifically based knowledge necessary for rational work performance. Furthermore, the number of such occupations is increasing, while in many the skills and knowledge they require are growing more complex. The result, as Kingsley Davis pointed out some years ago, is for social maturity to lag behind physical maturity and for the gap to lengthen as social modernization

245

advances.[1] Under these circumstances one finds himself still a youth—someone preparing for adulthood—for some time after he is physically grown.

This gap is itself a source of strain, for the idea that physical maturity evidences adult status persists in weakened form in modern societies. But the centrality of occupations inexorably delays adulthood, even if (as in the case of the numerous married students in American graduate schools) one manages to gain the badge of adulthood that marriage conveys. Indeed the discrepancy between the adultness of marriage and occupational youth may itself create tension. Only in the lower reaches of the world of work, among the unskilled jobs that forecast dismal futures, is one able in a modern society to maintain the parity of physical and social maturation.

It is also important to note that one's status in his parental family is, in modern societies, no certain indicator of adulthood or of youth. As the young person moves through the more advanced stages of education—graduate or professional training, for example—he may move permanently away from his parents' household and even become financially independent of it, supporting himself or, more probably, depending on loans or scholarships. But he does not thereby gain adulthood.

Indeed, if he still is preparing for an occupation, he may reach a position within his parental family that, on other grounds, would carry adult obligations (as, e.g., the oldest son of parents no longer able to support themselves), without necessarily incurring these obligations. Here, too, are sources of strain for youth, for the rights and obligations attendant upon one's relation to his parental family are not voided by protracted youth, but are held in abeyance. One's inability to enjoy the pending fruits of adulthood may be frustrating, while failure to honor obligations is likely to be seen by oneself and others as improper.

The relation of youth to age also becomes a source of strain with modernization. Commonly in traditional societies, advancing age in itself is a sign of wisdom—a valued cumulation of experience. This occurs more or less independently of the distinctive qualities or past actions of individuals, and because such societies are relatively undifferentiated, older persons will have shared a large number of significant societal responsibilities. Thus the older persons become the society's statesmen.

But in modern societies advanced age in itself is of much less value. Rather than a common series of age-graded responsibilities and experiences, one finds careers that are specialized according to the occupations they involve and the sectors of the society in which they are pursued—for example, commerce, industry, government, the church. Thus advancing age in no way ensures a body of significant experiences in common with others of similar age.

Moreover, individuals move through their careers on the basis of merit rather than of seniority and thus at quite different rates, although careers differ importantly in this respect. In such professional careers as medicine or law, for example, some men end their careers in mediocrity. Others, with brilliant careers, attain the most respected posts at early ages; still others gain eminence in the fullness of their years. Moreover, eminence in careers is perishable, depending on continuing high-quality performance, not on the excellence of past contributions. Older persons who are no longer doing good work find themselves viewed as "deadwood," even though they may enjoy some residual deference. Rates and quality of career progress thus are viewed in modern societies as matters of individual responsibility. How well one does tells how good he is—in ability, motivation, and training.

For the youth who is preparing for a career, this continuing disjunction between age and occupational position poses problems. His age in itself is not a bar to the realization of his goals: occupational success, and the social status, income, and authority that success brings. Yet the fact that he will get older does not guarantee that he will gain any of these rewards. Moreover, the social definition of youth as preparation, coupled with prolonged aspiration and dependence, lends to the future vast importance. Past and present are of little intrinsic value; their personal significance is judged by what they may contribute to adult success.

These factors generate in many young people a keen impatience to get on with the career. Adults earn little respect because they are older; some may in fact be deadwood. Further, given the rapid scientific and technical change of modern societies, young persons in training may be better prepared for adult work, and more able, than their elders. Thus they may chafe under a system that seems to favor age more than merit—eager to display achievement rather than promise, to show what they can do and earn their just rewards.

THE INDETERMINACY OF ADULT DESTINATIONS

With the decline in modern societies of family and kinship as bases for distributing individuals among adult social positions, the range of choice facing the young person—in such matters as work, marriage, life style, religion, and politics—is relatively wide. The limits to occupational choice—to consider only the master role in modern societies—are not those of family rank, but rather such individual factors as capacity and desire for training and ability to afford both the direct and opportunity costs that training entails. One's family plays an important part by transmitting a genetic inheritance, forming motives and basic social competence, and providing financial and social support during the protracted period of youth, but the paternal occupation is not automatically inherited. The occupational tie between father and son is loosened even more by the continuous change that affects rationalized occupations. Moreover, the specific occupational break between fathers and sons is sharp and definite; the real teachers and competitors—old and young—are to be found outside one's family and group of kin.

The decline of occupational inheritance does not, however, free the son of responsibility to his parental family. Since occupational destinations are created anew with each generation, a family's class rank, income, and style of life cannot be ensured automatically as fathers are succeeded by their sons. Maintaining family status requires determined striving and is by no means assured of success. The task of youth, typically impressed upon them by their parents and often keenly felt, is to succeed in *some* occupation with a social ranking at least equivalent to that of the father's work.

Parental stress on success and mobility reinforces youthful impatience; it also preserves in an indirect way the domination of sons by their parents. During youth the son's adequacy, for himself, his family, and his peers, is measured very largely by his ability to survive occupational preparation and get well started in a career. The position of the young man, then, is ambivalent; he remains tied to the family as the bearer of its fortunes (and of his own fortunes, as well, for adult success is partly measured against family origins), while to meet the demands of career preparation requires him to cut loose from his parents and turn toward school and teachers, and competition with his peers.

In the lower ranges of modern societies, where the ideas of career and of occupational training have little meaning, social position is inherited willy-nilly, for sons cannot drop lower than their fathers, while few find a way to rise, though some may wish to do so. Yet, in a process of "rising aspirations," as careers and career mobility come to the fore, numbers of lower-class youth, like those of higher status, may look to the future. For these young persons, however, the prospect is grim, so that the activities of higher-status youth have little personal relevance.

THE CENTRALITY OF SCHOOLING

In modern societies universal compulsory education is a necessity, and children leave the family not to enter the adult world, but to enter school. Although in these societies the family may serve as a prime agency for forming the values and beliefs of new generations, societal complexity and rationalization demand an education in the more technical aspects of social life that few families can provide. This is most immediately apparent in training for work, but can be seen as well in such school subjects as citizenship and consumer education, in which the student learns how to participate in large-scale political and economic systems.

The pressure toward universal education is reinforced by the variable occupational destinations of young persons. Since these destinations cannot be forecast specifically from parental social position, a system of schools that can provide training of diverse

249

kinds is needed to mediate between families and the occupational destinations of their offspring.

From the viewpoint of the society, schooling is essential for two additional reasons. Because of the indeterminacy of adult destinations, which is accompanied by high levels of inter-generational mobility, all children and youth must receive a minimal, uniform education. Universal schooling cuts across disruptive variations in the ability of parents to educate their offspring. In addition, families tend to be parochial, reflecting the beliefs and ways of life characteristic of region, class, and religion and ethnicity. They tend to form children's loyalties in a similarly parochial fashion. Universal education, however, can strengthen loyalties to the society itself and foster commitment to its central values and sentiments.

Hence children in modern societies move out of the family into school, where, as they grow older, their lives increasingly center. Moreover, the complexity of training for occupations, and for other social roles as well, increases the volume of material to be taught, so that the school-leaving age tends to advance. Further higher education, as a necessary prerequisite to high-status occupations, holds large portions of young people (e.g., in 1961, 38 per cent, in 1939, 14 per cent of the eighteen-to-twenty-one age group in the United States).[2] These trends are reinforced by rising expectations among populations increasingly able to stand the costs of extended education and by the action of occupational groups—especially the professions—to control entry into their ranks by increasing the volume, complexity, and cost of the training that they require. In modern societies, in point of fact, it is the phenomenon of prolonged schooling that defines youth as a social category and lies at the root of the continued dependency of young people well past physical maturity.

Three aspects of prolonged education are especially important in the present context. First, schools and teachers have great power vis-à-vis their students, and their ability to dominate is not seriously lessened, for all but lower-class students, as education advances. In the secondary schools and colleges this power, in contrast to the diffuse moral authority of lower-grade teachers, is based on the ability of the teaching staff to control the occupational destinies of their students.

Teachers' grades and other assessments of students' capacities are central to their progress in the educational system and, later, in the world of work. But teacher authority, at the higher levels of education, is exercised intermittently. As students prepare more explicitly for autonomous adult performance and develop some competence, teachers supervise them less closely and exercise their authority by periodic examination.

Consequently youth in school are in an ambivalent position. Although they are in many ways independent, they are *permitted* this independence as part of their education. It is always hemmed about by teachers' expectations and judgments—from which there is no formal appeal. Moreover, the freedom of action that results as the youth move more clearly outside the family must be used in ways that will not hurt school work too seriously. Thus teachers and schools form for youth perhaps the most tangible barriers to adulthood, and young people will question their legitimacy to the degree that work in school seems unrelated to the adult future.

Second, despite the centrality of schooling to demanding adult roles, students even at the college level are not often exposed to excessive academic pressure. As David Matza notes, education in modern societies undoubtedly could proceed faster, with more rapid movement of youth into adulthood.[3] Yet the belief persists in modern societies that childhood and youth are carefree and happy times. This belief colors the timing of education, with its long vacations, and tempers the demands of teachers. As a result, youth is a time of unusual leisure, and young people have substantial reserves of time and energy to draw on as they wish. Students escape the consuming and determining impact of much adult work; youthful leisure persists into adulthood primarily among the lower occupations.

Third, schooling in modern societies contains contradictory tendencies toward the "impractical" and instrumental. On the one hand, resulting in part from the persistence of the aristocratic conception of liberal education and in part from the utility of personal flexibility in complex societies, many courses taken in secondary schools and colleges are offered as ends in themselves—as liberalizing—and have no direct part in occupational training.

On the other hand, schools present adult reality in an abstract and vicarious mode. The delay of adulthood means that adult roles must be experienced through talking and reading about the adult world or through simulated practice of adult activities. The complexity of modern societies forces abstractness, since children and youth must be prepared to master many diverse experiences by categorizing them and by learning quite generalized norms governing whole classes of situations. Florian Znaniecki argued that the abstract and vicarious quality of schooling destroys the immediacy of learning, and with it direct interest in the subject matter.[4] Instead, learning must always be for the sake of the future and appear artificial in the present. It becomes important and endurable only for the sake of more or less distant goals.

Consequently youth are likely to find school satisfying, to persist beyond the leaving age, and to do well to the extent that these distant goals have meaning and importance. These are the young people for whom parental expectations and teacher demands and sanctions seem sensible and legitimate; the vicarious quality of schooling, for these students, reinforces school authority. Others, for whom the link between present and future is more tenuous, find little that is sensible or legitimate in the expectations of parents or teachers, and the authority of these adults declines.

ALTERNATIVE CULTURAL PATTERNS OF YOUTH

Given the strains centered on the position of youth in modern societies, widespread youth protest might be expected—in the form of either rebellion or passive withdrawal. This protest would be directed at significant adult figures and organizations, particularly at the school and, in view of their persistent status expectations, at parents. The behavior of young people is often interpreted in this way, but there is little evidence that youthful protest against the adult world is in any way characteristic of modern societies.

Unfortunately, despite much talk about youth, the action and beliefs of young people have been studied but little; especially lacking are cross-national comparisons of youth. Nonetheless, it may not be amiss to suggest an alternative interpretation. If one looks closely, it is difficult to find a single pattern of belief or behavior among youth, just as there is no one adult pattern. The internal differentiation of modern societies, in fact, makes it possible for diverse cultural groupings to form, centered on alternative values and following quite varied styles of life. These differences in part reflect class-linked variations, but within these broad social ranks one finds marked diversity attributable to such factors as the specific variability of occupations, regional subcultures, ethnic and religious memberships, and differences of taste.

The fact that youth in modern societies is so much a matter of future aspiration suggests that young persons will tend to accept, not reject, adult values and standards. Here one must seek the sources of "youth culture."[5] This tendency toward adult culture should be reinforced by the dominant position of adults and adult agencies. Nonetheless, youth and adult cultures are not exact counterparts. The dependence and prolonged aspiration of youth will lead young persons to emphasize from among the range of adult values and behavioral styles those that best help them to cope with the strains of their ambivalent status. The fact that the adult culture itself is diverse increases the likelihood that it will provide a basis for reasonable accommodation to youth status by young persons of different backgrounds, opportunities, and interests.

Moreover, youth versions of adult values and styles tend to push these adult themes toward their limits, presenting them in variously idealized or romantically exaggerated forms. Young persons can act and think in the absence of the compromising constraints and responsibilities of adult life. The abstractness and vicarious quality of their schooling also tends toward an idealization of adult beliefs and of adult society. Further, the leisure of youth permits them to follow the adult patterns they adopt with some consistency and elaboration, even when they are not well integrated with academic work.

The adult observer may ignore the cultural diversity of his own peers and confuse the unusually high levels of achievement and commitment required in the more demanding occupations with the entire range of adult work. To him youth patterns then may indeed seem frightening and "anti-social." Indeed, most adults, including parents, can see very little of events within school walls, so that youth are visible to adults primarily in their leisured aspect. It then may be easy to confuse activities which to the participants are of secondary or partial importance with a whole round of life.

Little, however, is known about the distribution of types of youth culture or about the conditions that give rise to one or another of them. All that can be done here is to sketch briefly some of the chief patterns.

There can be little question that many young people adapt to their situation by strict observance of "official" adult norms. These are Matza's "studious" or "scrupulous" youth, who in the areas of academic achievement or religious-moral commitments accept readily the legitimacy of adult norms and largely turn aside from the alternative uses of leisure that other youth patterns present.[6] For some this may represent a neurotic over-conformity, especially among scrupulous youth, but surely there are many studious young people who accept the instrumental value of education and some, as well, who find satisfaction in liberal studies and devote themselves fully to the pursuit of these goals. Moreover, scrupulosity may in certain contexts reflect a straightforward acceptance of fundamentalist themes existing among adult religious and moral beliefs.

There is a second path—reflected in youthful hedonism or fun —that is most often taken as the youth culture and criticized for its lack of seriousness and strong commitment.[7] Once found in both the secondary schools and colleges, youthful play seems rarer now in higher education and may be declining in the high schools as well. This decline may result from the intensity of purpose generated by the instrumental linkage of studies and adulthood. Nonetheless, the hedonistic pattern is widespread and seems to mirror the escape from work commonly found among persons in all but the more demanding occupations and especially characteristic of the working and white-collar classes. It seems to be a particularly easy path for young persons from such backgrounds, for at these levels of the society, schooling, in neither its vocational nor liberal mode, is as closely linked to adult destinations as it is for the children of higher-status families.

Escape from school into hedonistic leisure may itself follow adult models and adult-created channels. Much of this activity occurs within school-controlled recreation and sports or in adult agencies outside the school (for example, the Y.M.C.A.). It is encouraged by adult support and enthusiasm for school athletics and other manifestations of "youthfulness." Parents themselves are likely, in less formal ways, to stimulate and channel youthful hedonism—encouraging sociability and fearing over-studiousness. There is some evidence that these forms of adult control are less characteristic of lower social classes,[8] but adult-dominated hedonism nonetheless seems widespread in modern societies as an important and "safe" expression of the strains of prolonged dependency and aspiration.

There are, of course, rebellious youth in significant numbers. Some, especially in the secondary schools, rebel because they cannot in fact see the relevance of school to their futures or tolerate the dependency inherent in adult-approved fun. These young people, most often from the lower social strata, may be continuing problems in the classroom and leave school for adulthood through undemanding, but perhaps presently satisfying, jobs. In its most severe form, this rebelliousness moves into delinquency, a special legal classification for youth that symbolizes the extremity of their behavior. But it is interesting that even delinquency may not represent a total rejection of adult sentiments or behavior. In a recent study of members of adolescent gangs in a Chicago slum, it was found that these young men spent a substantial portion of their time in adult-approved activities—especially athletics.[9] Moreover, gang leaders often can move with adult help into settled adult jobs.[10]

Youthful rebelliousness occurs also in the colleges and universities, as recently has been apparent in the United States. This rebellion, among students who are successful, well-motivated, able, and presumably firmly oriented to attractive futures, has reflected very clearly youthful impatience, but also substantial commitment to adult values and organizations. Here, in fact, in contrast to the general political indifference of youth, one finds an active political orientation and involvement.[11] In some cases rebellion has centered on the universities themselves, as a demand for a real voice in university affairs. One senses in these students a desire for adult authority, impatience to begin adulthood, and an attempt to remodel, rather than to overturn, their schools.

In other cases, students have moved beyond the universities and colleges, in the United States especially, as participants in movements for Negro civil rights. These students, too, have displayed impatience with adult structures and leaders, but it is coupled with a firm moral sense and with a devotion to certain central values that they see violated. It is significant that this student activity, with few exceptions, has not been initiated in the colleges. Rather, these American students have turned to a movement led by important adult spokesmen of the moral order —drawn especially from the clergy. It is a movement supported chiefly by religious groups and a number of other respectable adult agencies. These rebellious students have found a system of adult values and adult agencies through which to express their own moral imperatives and impatience with prolonged youth.

NOTES

1. Kingsley Davis, "Adolescence and the Social Structure," *Annals of the American Academy of Political and Social Science,* CCXXXVI (November 1944), 8–16.
2. Martin Trow, "The Democratization of Higher Education in America," *European Journal of Sociology,* III (1962), 231–262.
3. David Matza, "Position and Behavior Patterns of Youth," in R. E. L. Faris, ed., *Handbook of Modern Sociology* (Chicago: Rand McNally, 1964), p. 197.
4. Florian Znaniecki, "Educational Guidance," *Social Actions* (New York: Farrar and Rinehart, 1936), pp. 189–231.
5. Talcott Parsons, "Age and Sex in the Social Structure of the United States," *Essays in Sociological Theory* (2nd ed., Glencoe, Ill.: The Free Press, 1954), pp. 91–94.

6. Matza, *op. cit.*, pp. 200–214.

7. Cf. Paul Goodman, *Growing Up Absurd* (New York: Random House, 1960).

8. Muzafer and Carolyn Sherif, *Reference Groups* (New York: Harper and Row, 1964), pp. 238–239.

9. Roberta Ash, "An Educational Experiment in the Inner City," Working Paper No. 56, Center for Organizational Studies, University of Chicago, 1966.

10. James Short, "Street Corner Groups and Patterns of Delinquency," mimeographed, 1961.

11. Cf. Robert Lane, *Political Life* (Glencoe, Ill.: The Free Press, 1959), pp. 216–217.

20 RACE RELATIONS IN THE UNITED STATES: A SOCIOLOGICAL PERSPECTIVE

Thomas F. Pettigrew

American race relations appear to most of us as largely a series of violent newspaper headlines. Recall, for instance, the widely publicized disturbances in Little Rock, Arkansas, in 1957 and at the University of Mississippi in 1962, the bombings and violence in Birmingham, Alabama, in 1963, and the Watts riots in Los Angeles in 1965.

These heralded events are important indicators of the process of racial change in the United States. They expose the bitter resistance of some white Americans and the desperate insistence of some Negro Americans. Yet sensational episodes highlighted by the bright glare of mass-media attention cannot in themselves provide the broad sociological perspective necessary for a full understanding of the sweeping changes currently under way on the American racial scene. This chapter, then, endeavors to go behind the headlines and to outline a broader perspective on this vital issue.

FOUR KEY FACTORS

All relations between groups are conditioned by four inter-related classes of factors: *historical, socio-cultural, individual,* and *situational.*[1] The first set relates to the unique history of the groups—especially the history of the contact between the groups. Thus, no one can fully appreciate the highly patterned group relations of the Republic of South Africa without a thorough grounding in the peculiar and complex history of the contact between Africans, Afrikaners, Coloreds, English, and Indians who inhabit that troubled land.

The second general class of variables relates to the *socio-cultural setting* of the intergroup contact. Here a myriad of cultural, economic, political, demographic, and ecological factors come into play. Often these variables can predict at a gross level the rate of change in group relations. For example, in the southern United States a variety of indices of Negro-white conflict and harmony—from violence to the rapid desegregation of public facilities—can be reliably predicted for different geographical areas by the use of such demographic variables as the percentages of Negro and urban residents in a locality.[2]

Individual factors comprise a third broad category. Deep-seated personality dispositions toward out-group prejudice are important and well-studied considerations—for example, the authoritarian personality. But important, too, are less deeply rooted personality needs to conform and gain social approval, needs which also lead to out-group rejection when it is the in-group sanctioned "thing to do." Likewise, individual phenomenology must be considered, for intergroup behavior is often determined more by the perception of realities than by the objective realities themselves. Such perceptions can be shaped by political ideologies and "racial" myths, or merely by the individual's need to perceive the situation selectively.

The final category—the face-to-face intergroup *situation*—provides the vital structure connecting these various levels. It is here that the historical, socio-cultural, and individual factors come to a pointed focus and, conditioned by the particular characteristics of the situation, produce intergroup *relations* as such. In India, for instance, it is the actual situation in which members of diverse castes encounter each other that ultimately determines whether the resulting relations will reflect the ancient traditions of the caste system or the dictates of the modern Indian government, which wishes to abolish caste distinctions.

Let's look more closely, then, at the operation of these four sets of factors in Negro-white relations in the United States.

HISTORICAL CONSIDERATIONS

First, consider the historical setting. Ever since their arrival in Virginia in 1619, Negro Americans have been an integral part of the society. It is erroneous to think of Negroes as merely transplanted Africans or as a separate group with a separate culture totally divorced from American society at large, for this view misses a vital historical point. After fourteen generations as part of the scene, Negro Americans truly belong in the United States; not even white racists question their belongingness. Negroes are Americans in every conceivable sense—and this fact ironically poses the problem: although an integral tenth of their nation, Negroes have been denied their full rights as citizens. Their current protest for change is a protest to gain these rights and to participate fully in American society with the dollars and dignity of other Americans. In short, Negro Americans *want in,* not out. And it is in this fundamental desire for inclusion that their protest differs from today's dominant cry for independence heard from Quebec to Angola.

The roots of the problem trace back to slavery. Legalized in Virginia during the late seventeenth century, slavery placed upon the Negro American a stigma of assumed inferiority which is only now being erased. And this fact presents us with an important question: Why did slavery in the United States leave such a deep and lasting scar while other areas of the world, such as Brazil, have had the institution longer and yet have more successfully thrown off its effects? The answer to this query lies in the peculiar nature of slavery under English law. The historian Frank Tannenbaum points out that the Iberian countries of Spain and Portugal, unlike England, had centuries of experience with slavery prior to the founding of the New World.[3] Hence, under Iberian law there evolved a special category for the slave as a human being. But English law, unfamiliar with the institution, had no such special category and treated the slave as merely dehumanized property—no different legally from a house, a barn, or an animal. Consequently, Latin America, emulating Iberian law, never developed the totally dehumanizing stigma surrounding slavery that the American colonies did, following

English law. This is not to say that slavery was not also cruel in Latin America or that there are no race problems there at present; but it is to say that their different legal definition of slavery left them with less of a dehumanizing legacy of racial stigma. Incidentally, Professor Tannenbaum's thesis receives comparative support from the history of South Africa, for slavery began in South Africa under Dutch law, which, like English law, placed the slave in the same category as property.

President Abraham Lincoln's Emancipation Proclamation in 1863 formally ended slavery, but it could not eradicate the institution's profound effects upon Negro and white Americans alike. The freed Negroes of the late nineteenth century were overwhelmingly a rural southern peasant group, dependent in many ways upon the very whites who had subjugated them prior to the Civil War. Following a brief period of promise after the war when three critical Amendments for the protection of the Negro's rights—the Thirteenth, Fourteenth, and Fifteenth—were added to the United States Constitution, race relations steadily deteriorated in the South. Finally, at the turn of the century, the nation allowed the South to disfranchise the Negro and to construct the vast system of racial segregation of public facilities which only now is being dismantled. Thus, the historical burden borne by American race relations includes not only two centuries of dehumanizing slavery, but an additional century of degrading segregation.

SOCIO-CULTURAL CONSIDERATIONS

We turn to the importance of socio-cultural factors when we trace the last fifty years of the Negro's existence in the United States. In particular, 1914 marks a watershed year. World War I burst forth across Europe, causing war orders to hit American industry while at the same time abruptly cutting off the flow of immigrants into the nation. Northern companies responded to the resulting labor shortage by sending recruiters into the South with a railroad ticket and the promise of a job for those who would come north.

These conditions triggered a massive migration of Negroes

out of the rural South and into the urban North, a migration pattern that still continues. The significance of the phenomenon is suggested by a few figures:[4] almost half of all young Negro males, age fifteen to thirty-four, in Georgia left home during the 1920's; and when World War II opened employment opportunities for Negroes, almost half of Mississippi's young Negroes similarly left their state during the 1940's. As recently as the 1950's, over one and a half million more Negroes left the South and came to the urban North and West. Consequently, while in 1910, 89 per cent of America's Negroes lived in the South, most of them on farms, today over 40 per cent of all Negroes live outside of the South and three out of four reside in cities. Indeed, Negro Americans now concentrate in the nation's largest cities and are proportionately more urban than white Americans. At the extremes, more than half of all Negro Americans currently reside in metropolitan areas of over half a million people; and less than a fourth are left in the rural South. In short, the last fifty years have witnessed the transformation of the Negro from a rural Southerner into an urban dweller located throughout the United States.

This vast shift of the Negro population restructures American race relations in many fundamental ways. Obviously it converts the treatment of Negro Americans from a regional concern into a nation-wide issue. It also means that Negroes have been leaving the Deep South areas most resistant to racial change and going to cities where—even in the South—racial change is more readily accepted. Urbanization leads directly to a more sophisticated people, cognizant of what discrimination over the years has denied them and capable of more effective protest. It also produces large concentrations of Negroes, facilitating communication and organization that simply could not be achieved in scattered rural districts.

Urbanization also generates political power. Combined with important Supreme Court decisions and recent federal civil-rights legislation, the move to the city has meant a rapid rise in Negro voting even in the South. Over two million Negroes are registered to vote in the South today—*eight* times more than in 1940. Glaring cases of the denial of the franchise are limited to rustic parts of the Deep South, and even here federal registrars are now available to enroll new voters.

In addition, the massive migration out of the rural South has resulted in large concentrations of Negro voters in key electoral states such as New York, Pennsylvania, Ohio, Michigan, Illinois, and California. Their new numbers give Negroes the balance of power in many of these states' elections. Indeed, both the late President John F. Kennedy and President Lyndon Johnson won a number of states even in the South by the margin of the critical Negro vote. And in local and state-wide elections during the 1960's, Negroes were elected for the first time in this century to the Georgia legislature, to state-wide offices in Connecticut and Massachusetts, and to hundreds of lesser offices throughout the country.

Not so dramatic as these political advances but equally fundamental are the gains in education, employment, and income that have accrued to the Negro from his migration out of the poor rural South and into the more prosperous cities.[5] Thus, from 1940 to 1960, the percentage of Negroes who had attended college more than doubled, and the median years of schooling for Negroes in the crucial twenty-five-to-twenty-nine-year-old age group increased from seven to eleven years. Likewise, employment opportunities have gradually expanded for Negro youth in the professional and clerical categories as well as in the more traditional service fields. These trends in turn have generated income increments. From 1947 to 1962, the median family income of Negro Americans more than doubled, from $1,600 to $3,300. As a consequence of these greater opportunities, social class differentiation has resulted and an expanding Negro middle class has emerged throughout the nation. In fact, roughly one out of every three Negro Americans today can be sociologically classified in terms of education, occupation, and income as middle class.

We have been describing the Negro's progress in recent years, progress in politics, education, and economics. But one might well ask: Why, with these steady improvements, do Negro Americans call so strongly for racial change at this point in history? Conventional wisdom dictates that Negroes should be more content today, following a generation of progress, than ever before. Yet conventional wisdom neglects a basic tenet of social motivation. An important principle of human behavior is that after the primary physiological needs such as hunger and thirst are satisfied, the vital element becomes the difference between what you have and what you aspire to have. In other words, it is not so much the absolute level of attainment that is important as the *relative* discrepancy between what one anticipates and what one attains. The current demand of Negro Americans for change during a time of prosperity and progress is not the exception but the rule in world history; for restlessness and revolution generally follow periods of initial improvement, periods in which aspirations of what life could be rise faster than actual advancement.

The fact is that Negro American frustration has greatly increased—not lessened—during two decades of sweeping change. Though they have made important absolute gains in the political, educational, and employment realms, their hopes for a better life as truly equal citizens have risen even more rapidly. In a phrase, they are relatively more deprived than they were in the 1940's. This is true in large part because the absolute gains of Negro Americans in many areas have not been gains relative to the attainments of white Americans. For example, the annual median Negro family income remains just slightly more than half that of the median white family; though the Negro income in absolute terms doubled in the fifteen years 1950–1965, so did the white income.

Lacking an appreciation of the importance of this *relative deprivation*, some white American spokesmen for the status quo have boasted of the present position of the Negro in glowing international comparisons. Negroes in the United States, goes one boast, have a consumer buying power comparable to that of similarly populated Canada. And the percentage of Negroes attending college is larger than it is among residents of the British Isles. But such glittering statements must not blind us to the fact of greatest sociological importance. Negro American standards have their meaning relative to the standards of other Americans, not of the Canadians or the British. The Negro American judges his living standards, his opportunities—indeed, even judges himself—in the only cultural terms he knows, those of the United States. Dr. Martin Luther King, Jr., the Nobel Peace Prize winner and Negro protest leader, makes the point bluntly: "The Negro lives on a lonely island of poverty in the midst of a vast ocean of material prosperity . . . and finds himself an exile in his own land."

INDIVIDUAL CONSIDERATIONS

But the Negro demands more than mere material equality; he also demands the same dignity accorded other Americans. And this leads us from purely socio-cultural considerations to those of our third category involving the individual. The dignity demand is an effort to throw off forever the slave stigma which still confronts the Negro in much of American society. Once again, comparisons of American race relations with group relations in other nations prove enlightening.

A psychoanalytic distinction can be made between two out-group stereotypes which recur throughout the world. One type of rejected-group image focuses upon super-ego concerns; it ascribes to an entire group such personal traits as being overly ambitious, crafty, clannish, shrewd, intelligent, sly, and dishonest. By contrast, the other type of image focuses upon id concerns; it ascribes to an entire group such personal traits as being unambitious, lazy, happy-go-lucky, loud, irresponsible, stupid, dirty, odoriferous, uninhibited, and hypersexed.

The psychoanalytic interpretation of these strangely reciprocal stereotypes is straightforward. These two types of contrasting out-groups serve in part as alter-egos for the bigot. Intergroup animosity in these terms is interpreted as a projection of the bigot's own unacceptable inner impulses onto an out-group. The prejudiced individual thus personifies his own super-ego sins of ambition, deceit, and egotism in his image of the first type of out-group and his own id sins of the flesh in his image of the second type.[6]

The selection of which stereotype as applied to various groups is determined by the full range of historical, socio-cultural, individual, and situational factors. The super-ego stereotype is typically applied throughout the world to middleman minorities, groups consisting largely of merchants who are structurally squeezed between the landed and the laboring classes. The id stereotype, however, is typically invoked throughout the world for groups found at the bottom of the social structure.

The classical middleman situation was that of the European Jews in the Middle Ages. Barred from owning land and encouraged to handle financial matters, they assumed their intermediate status because of the special historical circumstances of the period. This story has been repeated throughout recorded history, partly because the out-group member may actually perform better than the in-group member in market situations requiring objectivity and impersonality. To use the familiar sociological concepts, *gemeinschaft* bonds may often hinder *gesellschaft* relations.

Cultural and racial minorities generally occupy this middleman role, probably because they serve as ideal scapegoats, as shock absorbers who protect the elite from the masses. The history of the European Jew bears tragic witness to this buffer function. During episodic crises—from depressions to revolutions and epidemics—the Jew has served as a unifying target of temporary coalitions between landed and laboring classes. Even in relatively peaceful times the Jew has often been the representative of the elite, the tax collector, or the object of minor frustrations and competitiveness in market dealings. Hence, the super-ego stereotype of the Jew as ambitious, sly, and dishonest took root. Significant, too, is the fact that this stereotype has also been applied to other groups caught in the same middleman position. Consequently, the Chinese merchants of Malaysia and Indonesia are often called the "Jews of Asia" and the Muslim Indian merchants of East and South Africa the "Jews of Africa."

Out-groups assigned an impulsive id stereotype occur in a wider range of intergroup situations, though these groups are almost invariably at the bottom of the social structure and are generally far less technologically skilled than their detractors. With a history of slavery, segregation, and poverty, Negro Americans have long labored under the image of a lazy, happy-go-lucky, stupid, dirty, hypersexed people. So have the Gypsies of Central Europe, for centuries an outcast group. So, too, have the poor of southern Italy and the Algerians in southern France. Research reveals that the views held by many northern Italians of their fellow countrymen in the south and by many Frenchmen of migrant Algerians are strikingly similar to the views held in the United States of Negro Americans.[7]

A further example to illustrate that the id stereotype is not unique to Negro Americans comes from modern Israel. Social research shows that higher-status Israelis of European origin often look down on the lower-status Oriental Israelis from North Africa and Asia. The prevailing stereotype of the less technologically advanced Orientals is the familiar id image, described by one social scientist as "instability, emotionalism, impulsiveness, unreliability, and incompetence . . . habitual lying and cheating, laziness, boastfulness, inclination to violence, and lack of culture"—virtually identical to the American anti-Negro stereotype.[8]

SITUATIONAL CONSIDERATIONS

The world-wide character of these two contrasting stereotypes has led some observers to assume that conflict, discrimination, and prejudice between racial and religious groups will always be with us. Intergroup hate, they conclude in despair, is part of the human condition. But such a view overlooks many outstanding instances throughout the globe where intergroup hostility has in fact been alleviated—if not eradicated. Moreover, such a cynical analysis leads to the acceptance of correctable situations and the neglect of possible remedies.

Consequently, social scientists have explored other possibilities. What are the structural ways societies might be changed so as to increase intergroup acceptance? In considering this question, social scientists have systematically investigated the effects of contact between two previously hostile groups. Obviously, intergroup contact *per se* will not necessarily have beneficial results. Considerable research demonstrates that increased interaction, whether of individuals or groups, intensifies and magnifies the processes already under way. Hence, more intergroup contact can result in either greater prejudice and rejection or greater respect and acceptance, depending upon the situation in which it occurs. The basic task, then, is to specify the situational conditions under which contact leads to distrust and those under which it leads to trust.

The eminent social psychologist, Gordon Allport, has reviewed the relevant research and concluded that four characteristics of the contact situation are of the utmost importance. Prejudice and conflict are lessened when the two groups (1) possess equal status in the situation, (2) seek common goals, (3) are cooperatively dependent upon each other rather than in competition, and (4) interact with the positive support of authorities, law, or custom.[9] Instances throughout the world of intergroup conflict where these situational conditions are not met come readily to mind: caste conflict in India, Greek-Turkish contact on Cyprus, racial contact in South Africa. But more solid evidence comes from controlled research. And opportunities for this research abound in a nation such as the United States, where intergroup patterns are undergoing extensive alterations.

Thus, Allport's four contact principles can be seen in operation in a series of racial situations which have been desegregated in the past generation. For example, in the late 1940's President Harry Truman ordered all American merchant ships to end racial segregation and discrimination. Soon after, one study showed that white American seamen tended to hold racial attitudes in direct relation to how many voyages they had taken with equal-status Negro American seamen—the more desegregated voyages, the more positive their attitudes.[10] Similarly, a study of the police force of the city of Philadelphia found that those white policemen who had personally worked with Negro policemen were far more favorable toward the further desegregation of the force than other white policemen.[11]

Such interracial bonds built through optimal contact situations can even withstand severe crises. For instance, while Negro and white mobs raged in the streets of Detroit during that city's race riot of 1943, desegregated co-workers, university students, and neighbors of long standing carried on their interracial lives side by side.[12]

268

Mention of neighborhood desegregation introduces the most solid research evidence available. Repeated investigations have found that racially desegregated living in public housing developments which meet all four of Allport's contact criteria sharply reduces intergroup prejudice among both Negro and white neighbors.[13] Likewise, these same investigations demonstrate that living in segregated, but otherwise identical, housing developments structures interracial contact in such a manner that, if anything, intergroup bitterness is enhanced.

An important qualification, however, must be made concerning attitude and behavior change through intergroup contact: at least in the early stages, the change is frequently limited to the specific situation involved. Thus, another research study found that white steelworkers in the northern United States generally approve of the racial desegregation of their union to the point of sharing all union facilities with Negroes and electing Negroes to high office, yet they also sternly oppose the desegregation of their all-white neighborhoods.[14] In this case, as in many others, institutional structures limited the contact effects. Interracial attitudes and behavior have changed in the work situation with the support of the union organization; but these changes have not generalized to the neighborhood situation where a community organization resisted desegregation.

Policy implications follow directly from these research findings on interracial contact. The United States must continue and intensify its present efforts to abolish all of the barriers which have impeded equal-status, cooperative contact between Negro and white Americans. Clearly, as a first step the practice of racial segregation must be ended, for segregation severely restricts contact which meets Allport's four criteria. The Supreme Court of the United States formally opened this campaign in 1954 with its famous decision ending legal segregation of public schools. Another landmark came in 1964 with a sweeping Civil Rights Act designed to increase Negro voting and to eliminate discrimination in public accommodations and employment. More recent efforts center upon problems of housing segregation and the *de facto* racial separation in urban public schools created by segregated housing patterns.

269

Progress will not always be rapid. As the first-priority problems are solved, the succeeding steps become increasingly difficult. For example, as employment discrimination is completely eradicated, the problem becomes how to prepare enough qualified Negroes for better and more skilled jobs when they are often handicapped by poverty and an inferior education. Massive social change always creates its own new problems, always has its own lags and inconsistencies, and racial change in the United States is no exception. But the direction is unmistakable. And one ultimate outcome is clear: increased contact between Negro and white Americans under conditions of equal status, common goals, cooperation, and social approval.

A FINAL WORD

Gunnar Myrdal, the great Swedish sociologist and economist, keenly observed over twenty years ago that the United States found itself enmeshed in a painful dilemma. He noted the dilemma was posed by the contrast between the nation's highest principles of equal rights and opportunities for all its citizens and its lowly treatment of the Negro. Today this American dilemma is working itself out. To be sure, more violent flare-ups will occur—some initiated by whites, others by Negroes. Indeed, the next two decades or so will mark an uneasy transitional era in race relations in the United States. But the sporadic violence and the general uneasiness are reflections of the rapid racial progress taking place. The form of the solution to America's dilemma is already clear, even if its final attainment is still in the future.

NOTES

1. Adapted from the model proposed in G. W. Allport, *The Nature of Prejudice* (Cambridge, Mass.: Addison-Wesley, 1954), Chapter 13.
2. T. F. Pettigrew and M. R. Cramer, "The Demography of Desegregation," *Journal of Social Issues*, XV, No. 4 (1959), 61–71.

3. F. Tannenbaum, *Slave and Citizen: The Negro in the Americas* (New York: Knopf, 1947).

4. Karl E. Taeuber and Alma F. Taeuber, "The Negro Population in the United States," in J. P. Davis, ed., *The American Negro Reference Book* (Englewood Cliffs, N.J.: Prentice-Hall, 1966), Chapter 2.

5. T. F. Pettigrew, *A Profile of the Negro American* (Princeton, N.J.: Van Nostrand, 1964), Chapter 8.

6. Bruno Bettelneim and Morris Janowitz, *Social Change and Prejudice* (New York: The Free Press of Glencoe, 1964).

7. M. W. Battacchi, *Neridionali e Settentrionali Nella Struttura del Pregiudizio Ethnico in Italia* ("Southerners and Northerners in the Structure of Ethnic Prejudice in Italy") Bologna, Italy, Societa Editrice II Mulino, 1959).

8. R. Patai, *Israel between East and West* (Philadelphia: Jewish Publication Society of America, 1953).

9. Allport, *op. cit.*, Chapter 16.

10. I. N. Brophy, "The Luxury of Anti-Negro Prejudice," *Public Opinion Quarterly*, II (1946), 456–466.

11. W. M. Kephart, *Racial Factors and Urban Law Enforcement* (Philadelphia: University of Pennsylvania Press, 1957).

12. A. M. Lee and N. D. Humphrey, *Race Riot* (New York: Dryden, 1943).

13. Morton Deutsch and Mary Collins, *Interracial Housing: A Psychological Evaluation of a Social Experiment* (Minneapolis: University of Minnesota Press, 1951); D. M. Wilner, Rosabelle Walkley, and S. W. Cook, *Human Relations in Interracial Housing: A Study of the Contact Hypothesis* (Minneapolis: University of Minnesota Press, 1955); and E. Works, "The Prejudice-Interaction Hypothesis from the Point of View of the Negro Minority Group," *American Journal of Sociology*, LXVII (1961), 47–52.

14. J. D. Lohman and D. C. Reitzes, "Note on Race Relations in Mass Society," *American Journal of Sociology*, LVIII (1952), 340–346.

PART VI

Total Societies
and Their Change

21 MODERN SOCIETY

Reinhard Bendix

The phrase "modern society" is taken from common speech. It refers to the social conditions of the present, or of recent times including the present, as contrasted with those of an earlier period. The sociologist often begins his work with such a common-sense expression, but he usually tries to make his own meaning more precise. For example, he may note that the meaning of the term "modern society" depends upon an implicit comparison with an earlier society. As we alter this reference to an earlier society, we also alter the meaning we associate with "modernity."

Take the field of technology. Our first impulse may be to think of "the modern" entirely in terms of jet travel, space exploration, and nuclear power. But this reference to the latest technical developments rather restricts our meaning of the term. It would oblige us, for example, to include earlier types of air travel or other sources of energy, such as electricity, among the characteristics of an earlier, older technology. There is a point in doing this. The extraordinary technical developments of the last generation have prompted some scholars to speak of a "second industrial revolution" as distinguished from the first, which dates from the late eighteenth century and was marked initially by the development of the steam engine and its employment in industrial production. But to use the word "modern" only with regard to recent technical developments confuses a general term with one of its more restricted meanings; i.e., it confuses "modern" with "the most modern." Clearly, a broader interpretation is more useful. It allows us to speak of a technology as "modern" which depends on inanimate sources of energy and the application of scientific research. This accords well with common usage. It makes good sense to say that the term "modern society" encompasses the whole era since the eighteenth century when the technical basis was laid for the industrialization of societies. Indeed, the terms "industrial society" and "modern society" are often used interchangeably.

Such definitions always have a somewhat arbitrary quality. One could argue, for example, that the meaning of "modern society" should be extended back to the age of exploration, which for us starts with Columbus' discovery of America in 1492. That discovery was part of the world-encircling expansion of Europe. If one thinks of such early scientists as Copernicus and Galileo in the sixteenth century, one realizes that without the scientific foundations laid in the Renaissance European expansion around the world would probably not have had such lasting effects. But today several non-European countries have developed their own independent scientific establishment, which is utilized not only in their industry, but also in the development of nuclear power. If one dates modern society from the age of European expansion based on the superiority of cannons and guns, perhaps the end of this age will come to be dated from this proliferation of scientific capability in the field of nuclear power. This possibility suggests that an expression such as "modern society" is in some sense limited to a historical period, with an end as well as a beginning, however arbitrary such dating is bound to remain. It is not surprising, therefore, that some scholars are already using phrases like "post-industrial" or "post-modern" society in order to express their sense of the temporary or transitional quality of what we mean by "modern society." Every social structure, and so also "modern society," can be looked at as a transition from what went before to what is to come. These long-run considerations have their own interest, but they do not invalidate our inquiry into the characteristics which distinguish modern society.

This interest is in fact as old as modern society itself, if we roughly date its beginning from the late eighteenth century. At that time several writers used the phrase "civil society" to refer to the manners and customs of the people at large, in contrast to the earlier practice of restricting the meaning of "society" to what we would now call "high society"—i.e., to the minority of the wealthy and powerful. This more inclusive use of the word "society" implied a new awareness that the lives of the common people mattered a great deal, even if they had no voice in political affairs. This extension of the concept "society" to include more and more people has been a gradual process which is continuing today. To get a picture of the "modern society" which has resulted from such developments, it is actually easiest to contrast what we find today with what was true of society some two or three hundred years ago.

At the end of the seventeenth century, England and Wales had a population of 5.2 million people; today the corresponding figure is about 45 million, a ninefold increase. With regard to births and deaths, the contrast between the early and the recent figures indicates one reason for the rapid growth of population. In 1750 there were 35 births and 30 deaths per 1,000 population in England and Wales, whereas by 1950 these figures had declined to 16 births and 12 deaths per 1,000. Due to modern medicine, sanitation, and improvement in nutrition, deaths have declined sharply: three centuries ago average life expectancy at birth was a bit over 30 years; today it is over 70. Along with these demographic changes have gone changes of attitude, though here we depend on circumstantial evidence. When life was on the average very short, deaths in the family were obviously frequent, especially deaths of children during infancy and of mothers during childbirth. Under the circumstances parents wanted many children so that at least some would survive, while remarriages were frequent. One may surmise that attitudes toward children were quite different in those days; a recent study by Philippe Ariès suggests that during infancy children were not considered of much account, but once weaned they were treated as little adults. The very idea of childhood emerged rather slowly from the sixteenth century on. Eventually this led to a feeling of solicitude for each child which fits in well with the practice of birth control and the expectation that the

277

nuclear family of parents and children will survive as a unit. One may consider this changed attitude toward the child an index of the importance we attach to each person as an individual, and this individualism has many ramifications in modern society.

Take the political realm, for example. Sociologists and political scientists are in the habit of distinguishing between rulers and ruled, but in "modern society" these words do not have a clear meaning. Those in high office are temporary incumbents, while the people at large, although ruled, also exercise a control through periodic elections. At an earlier time in our history that distinction was quite unequivocal, however. Let us take seventeenth-century England again. Most adults and all women were economically dependent upon the head of the household to which they belonged. Until well into the nineteenth century such economic dependence prevented persons from being considered full members of the community. Deference to their superiors was the attitude expected of them, and even ordinary heads of households, who were entitled to cast a vote in local elections, probably shared this respect for rank and wealth. This complete subordination reduced a majority of the people to a kind of second-class status. Though adult, they did not count in the sense that public affairs were the exclusive concern of "their betters," as the phrase went. Under these conditions no importance was attached to the ordinary person as an individual; that kind of attention was reserved for those who "counted" in society, who belonged to the ruling minority of the country by virtue of their birth and wealth.

All this has changed; perhaps the simplest indication of that change is the extension of the franchise. During the nineteenth century the conditions of citizenship were redefined quite gradually, so that universal suffrage—the right to vote on the part of all adults over twenty-one years of age—was instituted only after World War I. (Some European countries still exclude women from the right to vote, and many countries retain some minimum residence requirements.) Obviously there was much resistance to this extension of the right to vote or it would have been instituted more quickly—incidentally a good illustration of the fact that it took quite a time for Western societies to modernize. Still, the fact that every adult has the vote is a token of the regard in which he is held as an individual and a citizen. At the same time, those whose rights are still abridged by a second-class status will make their claim by appealing to the principle of equality. As the great French scholar, Alexis de Tocqueville, wrote in 1835: "The nations of our time cannot prevent the conditions of men from becoming equal." He would have felt confirmed in his judgment had he had an opportunity to observe the many countries which achieved independence after World War II and directly introduced a universal franchise.

The great changes brought about in the family and in the political sphere are paralleled by changes in economic life. Reference was made to changes of technology, and here again one can best appreciate what is true of "modern society" by means of contrast with an earlier society. The typical unit of production three centuries ago was the household enterprise, consisting of the lord, his family, servants, estate agents, and various ranks of peasant families with their children, or of the master craftsman, his wife, children, and unmarried apprentices, journeymen, and servants. Under those conditions there were only a few categories of persons who worked away from their own homes, such as miners and sailors. Also, paupers depending on charity were forced to live in workhouses. In modern society this situation has been reversed. There are only a very few left—mostly small independent farmers, writers, artists, and a few professors —who can remain at home when they work. Everyone else makes his living at a place of work away from his home. The reason is obviously that modern conditions of production require a work force concentrated in an enterprise employing complex machinery, such as assembly lines, open-hearth furnaces, business machines, and so on. Even scientists depend on the libraries and laboratories assembled in research institutes and universities.

One reason for this whole development was understood quite early. Such writers as Adam Ferguson, John Millar, and Adam Smith pointed out in the late eighteenth century that productivity depends on an increasing division of labor. At the time this meant for the most part that production was subdivided so that each worker could specialize and become more proficient. In this way work operations became increasingly simple until it was possible in many instances to replace manual labor by machinery. The over-all result has been an increase in productivity for which there is no precedent in history.

In the United States, in 1800, 73 per cent of the gainfully occupied population was employed in agriculture; by 1960 that proportion had declined to 6.3 per cent. During the same period agriculture's share in the national income declined from 39 to 8 per cent. Taking more recent figures and projecting them into the near future, we find that the population of the United States has increased from 30 million in 1857 to 180 million in 1958 and is expected to reach 210 million by 1970. From 1910 to 1959 the Gross National Product increased from $118 billion to $480 billion and is expected to reach $750 billion by 1970. During the same period output per man-hour increased from 42 in 1912 to 146 in 1959 and is expected to reach 199 in 1970, a development made possible by many factors including the increased use of technical equipment in the process of production and the increasing skills of the population.

The resulting signs of affluence are all about us; there is no need here to cite examples of the feats of production which a highly industrialized society can accomplish. But I noted earlier that the workplace away from home and the increasing division of labor were important features of modern society. Hence it aids our understanding of that society to see how the gainfully employed population is distributed among the several occupations. Mention has been made of the declining proportion of persons engaged in agriculture; there has also been a decline in the proportion of unskilled workers and domestic servants. All other occupations have increased proportionately, most notably white-collar workers, professionals, craftsmen and foremen, managers—roughly in that order. The whole development reflects a relative shift in the distribution of the gainfully employed not only away from agriculture, but into the so-called tertiary sector of the economy, namely occupations having to do with transport, communications, merchandising, services, professions, and others. The increasing importance of education in modern society is very much part of this picture, since that society depends not only on an increasingly complex technology, but by the same token upon an increased level of skill in the population. In 1920, 91 per cent of the children between seven and thirteen years of age were enrolled in school, and by 1960 this high proportion had risen to 98 per cent; even more significant, however, is the fact that in the same period the proportion of young people of eighteen or nineteen years of age attending school had increased from 18 to 42 per cent.

So far this chapter has been concerned with some broad characteristics of "modern society." The remainder of the chapter could easily be devoted to a further elaboration of this theme, but the effect would be to leave the reader with a somewhat bloodless picture. To avoid this, we need to ask which countries should be called "modern" in terms of this discussion, and whether this identification is entirely satisfactory.

We might answer the first question by listing all countries with less than 50 per cent of their active population engaged in agriculture. This would comprise most countries of Europe, with Spain, Greece, Poland, Yugoslavia on or near the borderline; in the Americas it would include Canada, the United States, and Argentina; in Africa only South Africa; and in Asia only Japan. Straddling Asia and Europe, Russia also belongs on this list. Such a grouping of countries covers a considerable variation, however, even in terms of this single index. The proportion of persons engaged in agriculture ranges from a low of 5 per cent in Great Britain and 6 per cent in the United States to a high of 45 per cent for the Soviet Union and 49 per cent for Japan. This example may serve as an illustration of what we could expect to find were we to examine, say, changes in population or occupational structure, to mention just two factors referred to earlier. That is, we could expect a gross similarity but also much variation among the countries with less than 50 per cent of their active population in agriculture.

Some observers incline to the view that these remaining variations will decrease as the countries, roughly classified as modern societies, industrialize further. However, we do not know this. No one can say beforehand how far a country will industrialize or what will befall it in the interim. To be sure, we can speak with confidence of some linkages in the course of change. We know of no society deserving to be called "modern" that has reached this condition without increasing specialization of occupations or without the separation of the workplace from the family household. There are other features to be found in all modern societies, such as long-life expectancy, the concentration of population in urban areas, and other by-products of a technology based on applied science. It is more difficult to be sure of the less tangible effects of modernization.

One reason is that societies enter upon the process of modernization with their own specific natural resources, historical experiences, and cultural ways. Two such obviously related societies as England and the United States, which by most standards are equally "modern," still differ from one another in striking ways. Take the field of education. In England and Wales about 4 per cent of those in the ages from twenty to twenty-four attended institutions of higher learning in 1956, contrasted with 27 per cent for the United States. Great efforts are now being made in England to expand educational facilities, but it is as much a question of differences in quality as of numbers.

A colleague of mine, Professor Ralph Turner of the University of California at Los Angeles, has pointed out that in American schools students compete with one another as in a sporting event. They are engaged in a contest among equals, and the qualities most admired are the enterprise and perseverance of those who must overcome handicaps in order to win. Because of the underlying equalitarianism their victory counts for more than, say, the success of the most intelligent and best-educated students who have no personal handicaps to overcome. While the phrase "may the best man win" is common enough, the glorification of the self-made man puts the accent on the special merit of having come up from behind. In the American creed, that merit counts for more than excellence as such, though in practice the distinction is blurred. One can see in this pattern a legacy of American history. Immigrants were greatly handicapped when they made their start in this country. The ideal of the man who succeeds in overcoming the obstacles facing him probably appealed to them as much as it did, for very different reasons, to the success-ful businessman.

These patterns have no exact parallel in English culture. The idea of a "contest among equals" is absent from the process by which students are selected. Instead, they are judged in terms of whether and to what degree they possess the appropriate qualities of mind and character. Rather than winning or seizing the high positions to which educational success would give him access, the student is selected for them by an elite of judges who find that he possesses the requisite qualifications. In Profes-sor Turner's phrase such "sponsored" mobility differs strikingly from the "contest" mobility in the American case. Excellence as such is prized, the quality of a performance irrespective of how it is achieved; indeed achievement without manifest effort is considered especially praiseworthy. One sees this reflected in the style of English writing, in the thrust and parry of debate, and in much else. England has become a middle-class society, but her culture retains a sense of priorities that is essentially aristocratic.

The comparison of England and the United States serves to remind us of still other ways in which "modern societies" differ. Take again our simple index of the proportion of people en-gaged in agriculture. In 1850 that proportion was 65 per cent in the United States, but had already fallen to 22 per cent in Great Britain. By 1900 the proportion had declined to 38 per cent in the United States and to 9 per cent in Great Britain. England had made an earlier start in the process of industrializa-tion and hence was further along in the shift of her gainfully employed population out of agriculture. But having started earliest also implies that other countries, entering the "race" later, could take advantage of technical developments already achieved abroad. England, which had pioneered many of these developments, found it gradually more disruptive and costly to scrap old equipment and take advantage, through heavy in-vestments, of the most modern techniques. One experience dur-ing World War II graphically illustrates the point. According to Donald Nelson, then head of War Production, it was a matter of mass-producing the new model of a tank in the United States, away from the danger of German bombing attacks. The model had been developed in England and the blueprints were sent over. Then it was discovered that these blueprints were unsuitable for American production methods, having been developed in the context of a greater reliance on skilled labor in England. Accordingly, the new model which had actually been built was sent over, taken apart, and blueprinted anew by Detroit production engineers; then the production of the tank could move forward, American style.

With this example, we return to the point I made at the beginning. There I suggested that usually we use the phrase "modern society" to refer to the whole period since the first industrial revolution in eighteenth-century England. Now I have added the idea that the time at which a country begins the process of modernization, and the speed and the methods with which it proceeds, have important consequences for the distinguishing character of its modernity. This is the second reason for the marked differences which persist among societies which must be classified as modern by many criteria.

The point deserves some elaboration with regard to the most obvious contrast, which I have left to the end. Both Soviet Russia and the United States are modern societies. In such matters as occupational specialization, increased life expectancy, urban concentration of population, advanced technology, a highly developed educational system, modern means of communication, a high regard for science and material values, a strong national patriotism, and others the two countries have many things in common, though this is not to deny that notable differences remain. There are other similarities rather unrelated to our topic: for example, both countries are continental in scope and encompass a diversity of ethnic groups, but one group (Great Russians and white Protestant Americans) tends to dominate the others. The differences are equally noteworthy—in the economic achievements to date and above all in the political sphere. These obvious differences are directly related to the speed and the methods with which modernization has been achieved in the two countries. Whether one looks at Russia at the time of Peter the Great, during the industrialization drive in the 1880's, or again under the Soviet regime since the late 1920's, the impression is always of a nation on a forced march, under conditions of simulated combat, with every citizen a recruit in a collective undertaking. By contrast, as one looks at the United States at the time of the Revolution, during the long period of westward expansion, at the period of the great business tycoons from the late nineteenth century to the 1920's, or at the welfare state since 1933, the impression is one of a diversity of individuals and groups pursuing a variety of ends, and only national emergencies can achieve a temporary coalescence of wills. It is certainly not a black and white contrast; high idealism and inhuman abuses are found in both societies.

But one need only glance at the apparently similar problem of youth in both societies to see that the divergence remains enormous. On the surface, Soviet Russia and the United States are experiencing similar difficulties with the younger generation, who go in for a good bit of wayward behavior ranging from poetry, eccentric hairdos, and sex to drugs, petty theft, jazz, and arcane preoccupations like Zen Buddhism. No doubt Russian and American youths react along these lines in many different ways, but these differences are minor compared with the main point, or so it seems to me. Russian youths are bucking an all-powerful state which would coordinate every individual's effort so that each must find what satisfaction he can from the progress of the whole. Under these conditions, deviance means the expression of one's personality; opposition means being somebody who sees value in finding himself. For American youths the situation is quite different. They are not opposing a state or a society that seeks to coordinate all their efforts in a collective undertaking. Rather, they are disillusioned with, and hence oppose, the conventional opportunism of individual careers; they find too little collective purpose in their society, not too much. I have the strong suspicion that a well-meaning American observer would find the wayward behavior of Russian youth far more appealing to him than the wayward behavior of American youth, simply because by expressing themselves the former seek individual freedom, while the latter seek a purpose in life.

I have wandered a bit from my subject, modern society, but

not too much. I began by noting some problems of defining the term. Then I examined certain distinguishing characteristics of modern society in the social, political, and economic spheres. Having established my meaning for the term, I turned next to the persistent differences between England and the United States, and the United States and Soviet Russia. These three societies are modern but still different due to their divergent cultural backgrounds and their divergent processes of modernization. In my concluding example, I suggested that even such similar behavior as that of Russian and American youth does not appear very similar on closer inspection. This paradox may serve as a reminder that a term such as "modern society" is an abstraction which is useful for certain purposes but must always be related again to the actual experience of people in society.

22 SOCIETY AND SOCIETIES: THE MACRO-SOCIOLOGICAL VIEW

Edward Shils

I

When we speak of American society or British society or Arab or African societies, we certainly do not have in mind anything like a voluntary association such as a cooperative society or a debating society or a society for the protection of ancient monuments. Nor do we have in mind the "society" of the wealthy, the beautiful, the powerful, and the well dressed whom we used to see in *The Tatler* and whom we still see in the newspapers and magazines in many parts of the world. We think of something "deeper," more permanent, more rooted in the constitutive properties of man's being; we think of something less particular in its ends, less contrived in its genesis, less calculating in its conduct, or less trivial and less frivolous. But depth, fundamentality, persistence, and seriousness are found among families, neighborhoods, villages—in all those modes of the organization of life which sociologists call "primordial communities." These would, however, be recognized by us as societies only under special circumstances. The most special circumstance is self-sufficiency: self-regulation, self-reproduction, self-generation.

In other words, a social system is a society if it is predominantly not *part* of a larger society. A kinship group or a tribe is not part of a larger society if its marriages take place within it, if it has a territory which it regards as its own, if its new members are recruited primarily from those born to those persons already acknowledged to be members, if it has its own system of government, if it has a name of its own, and if it has a history of its own—that is, a history which many or most of its adult members think is a historical account of their links with "their own past"—and finally if it has a culture of its own.

Now, a cooperative society has some of these characteristics. It has a name of its own; to some extent it has a system of government of its own, and it might even have a history of its own; but it lacks certain other very important features. It has no territory which is exclusively its own, its members are not recruited by birth from among those who are already members, and its system of government must act within laws promulgated by a more powerful government which prevails over the territory within which the cooperative society is located. What is singular to the phenomenon which we wish to distinguish is that it is a kind of social system which has a genetic history and territory of its own and which has parts but is itself not a part of a more embracing system of authority exercised over that territory but located and resident outside it. The definition of a society when applied to a modern society presupposes the existence of families, neighborhoods and cities, churches and sects, states and provinces, schools and universities, firms, farms, industrial plants, and cooperative societies, all interpenetrating each other and performing and exchanging services with each other within a common, bounded territory and possessing a common, all-inclusive system of authority which makes and enforces rules and suppresses or adjudicates conflicts. But it is just as applicable to non-modern, primarily agricultural societies with less differentiated institutional systems. In such societies the concept of society also presupposes the existence of kinship and territorial units, religious beliefs and organization, economic organization, and so forth. The main point is that these are all units or subsystems of a larger whole. They themselves are not self-contained, but the larger whole is self-contained.

But what is contained within them? We have already said that the more differentiated among them contain not only families and lineages but also associations, unions, firms and farms, schools and universities, armies, churches and sects, parties, and numerous other corporate bodies or organizations, and these too have boundaries which define the membership over which their respective corporate authorities—parents, managers, presidents, and the like—exercise some measure of control. There are also systems organized formally and informally around a territorial focus—neighborhoods, villages, districts, cities, regions—and these too have some of the features of societies. Then there are those unorganized aggregates of human beings within societies—social classes or strata, occupations and professions, religions, and linguistic groups—which have a culture more common to those who possess certain status or occupy certain positions than it is to those who do not. Why are all or any of these not societies? We have already answered that question, but we will now formulate the answer somewhat differently. Each of them exercises such authority as it does exercise within the framework of or in subordination to a *common* authority which is outside themselves and which is the authority of the whole society.

Of course, self-containedness or self-sufficiency is a relative matter. No social system that we call a society is wholly self-contained or self-sufficient. Few societies which we recognize to be societies recruit their populations solely by natural increase. Most larger societies have no single history but rather an amalgam of histories of the various peoples who have been incorporated into the society through conquest or immigration. Some societies do not have clearly delineated boundaries of their territories, and in the past the proportion of those with clearly delineated boundaries was smaller than it is nowadays. No society today has a culture which is exclusively its own. Even the best and most firmly established societies of North America or of Western Europe do not have cultures which are exclusively theirs. The United States shares its language and literature with Great Britain, Mexico with Spain. France shares its language with parts of Belgium and Switzerland and with Francophone Africa, and it shares its culture with much of the world. No society which conducts anything approximating a modern scientific enterprise is scientifically self-sufficient: even the countries which are most advanced scientifically have drawn many of the basic ideas of their science from other countries, not only in the past but in the present as well.

On the economic side, too, there is no society which is economically completely self-maintaining and self-sufficient. They all import goods from other countries and export to other countries. They are involved in complex relationships, in contracts which they usually observe and which they breach to their disadvantage (but not always).

Sovereignty with respect to other sovereign states is one of the properties of a society nowadays, and something like sovereignty has always been a feature of societies even in ages and in cultures in which the concept of sovereignty had not become as clear-cut as it is today. And today, when the concept of sovereignty is relatively clearly defined, the United Nations constitutes an infringement on it. It is not, it is true, a very powerful infringement, but it is an infringement nonetheless, not so much because of any really coercively enforceable authority possessed by the United Nations as through the opinions which its organs enunciate and echo.

Thus we see that *complete* self-sufficiency is not an absolute prerequisite for a social system to be defined as a society. To be a society, a social system must have its "center of gravity" within itself, i.e., it must have its own system of authority within its own *boundaries*. It must also have its own *culture*. Part of its culture it will necessarily share with other societies from which it derives and with which it has intercourse, but part of this culture will be peculiar to itself. It will consist of beliefs about the history and nature of the society, its relationship to certain ideal or transcendent values, its origin and destiny. It will include beliefs about the rightfulness of its existence as a society and about what qualifies its members to belong to the society. It will, of course, include works of art, literature, and thought—many of which will reflect on the just-mentioned beliefs. There is a tendency for societies to be "national" societies.

Modern "national" societies—societies which claim that they embody a quality of nationality, with their own national cultures, their own more self-contained than "unself-contained" economic systems, their own systems of government, with their own genetic self-reproduction and their own sovereignty over a bounded territory—these national societies are the most self-contained of all the social systems that we know through the course of human history, and in their respective epochs.

II

Thus we see that a society is not just a collection of corporate individuals and of primordial and cultural collectivities inter-acting and exchanging with each other. All of these collectivities form a society by virtue of their existence under a *common authority* which exercises its authority over a *bounded territory*, which maintains and imposes a more or less *common culture*. These are the things which constitute the composite of relatively specialized primordial, corporate, and cultural collectivities as a society.

Every component part bears the impress of the fact that it is a *part* of a *society*, of that society and no other. It is one of the numerous tasks of sociology, and of that particular branch of sociology which has come to be called macro-sociology, to eluci-date the mechanisms or processes by which this collection or aggregate of primordial, corporate, and cultural groups function as a society.

The main factors which establish and maintain a society are a central authority, consensus, and territorial identity. Central authority forms a society not just through the actual authority which it exercises over any particular actions in any particular circumstances, although such acts of authority are important as such. Particular acts of authority also leave behind a residue among those over whom they are performed. The residue is: (1) a central focus of attention; (2) a sense of identity with others who share the experience of being under this authority—all those who share the territory over which the authority is exercised; and (3) the belief of the legitimacy of that authority to act as it does. These three residual effects of subordination to a com-mon authority make those so subordinated into members of their society by affecting their imagery and beliefs. Ecological interdependence and coercive power do not constitute, but they do help to engender, the culture which is essential to society.

These three residual effects enter into the culture—that is, into the beliefs and symbols of the members of the society. Membership in a society does not as such generate the culture of the society. The culture of a society is the product of the creative and imaginative powers of creative individuals—religious prophets and saints, scientists, great writers and lesser ones, artists, journalists, philosophers, elders and sages—whose vision of the world recommends itself to their contemporaries and to their descendants. The culture is the product of the need of ordinary, less creative persons to have an image of their world which gives meaning to the major events of existence and which explains why things happen and why some things are better than others. The main culture and the variant cultures of a society are in a certain measure self-generating. They are never wholly and seldom even largely creations of the existing central authorities of any society.

Yet the three residual effects which I have mentioned above become assimilated into the culture of the various cultural groups. They do so because the creators often refer directly, in their religious promulgations or in their philosophic discourses or in their literary and artistic creations, to the facts and emblems of the central authority. The central authority is on their minds and they cannot avert their minds from it. They do so because the might and majesty of central authority have overtones which enter constitutively into the preoccupations of creative persons. Furthermore, the three residual effects of central authority are matters of belief, and as such they are themselves parts of culture. They are therewith bound to enter and to fuse in various ways with the products or contents of the self-generating religious, literary, artistic, and reflective or philosophical culture.

In consequence of these processes, therefore, every society acquires, alongside the central system of authority—which is, as we shall see, by no means exclusively governmental or political or military—a central cultural system. The central cultural system consists of those beliefs and expressive symbols which are concerned with the central institutional system and with "things" which transcend the central institutional system and which reflect on it. The central cultural system has its own institutional system—churches, sects, schools, universities, libraries, museums, and the like. The elites or those who rule these cultural institutions enter into various and frequent relations with the central institutional system and become parts of it. The educational system is that part of the central power-institutional and cultural-institutional complex which inculcates considerable parts of the central cultural system on other sectors of the society. It contributes thereby to the formation and diffusion of the common culture.

The central cultural system in most societies for much of their duration includes many cultural productions which have an affirmative attitude toward the central institutional system. Where the central cultural system becomes predominantly alienated from or has never been unitary with the central institutional system, the latter loses or fails to acquire some of its legitimacy and therewith its capacity to exercise its authority peacefully and effectively. Severe conflict results and pronounced changes are in store.

III

Every society, seen macro-sociologically, may be interpreted as a center and a periphery. The center consists of those institutions (and roles) which exercise authority, whether it be economic, governmental, political, military, or cultural (religious, literary, educational, and so on). The periphery consists of those strata or sectors of the society which are the recipients of commands and of beliefs which they do not themselves create or cause to be diffused. The periphery is very segmented; it may be said to cover a large area around the center. Some sectors of the society are more peripheral than others—the more peripheral, the less powerful, the less creative, the less possessed of the culture which emanates from the center, the less continuously reached by the power of the central institutional system.

The center commands attention as well as demanding obedience. It has an attractive power which enters into imaginations and often preoccupies them. It both seeks to do so—although in varying degrees in different kinds of regimes—and it does so simply by its existence.

It should be added in passing that all territorially extensive societies tend to have a spatial center as well, which is, or is thought to be, the seat of the central institutional and cultural systems. Much of the population looks to the center or centers for guidance, instruction, and command, concerning conduct, style, and belief. The center of a given society might also be in some respects the center of other societies (so, for example, Paris has been for several centuries the cultural and artistic center not only of France but of much of Europe and of French-speaking Africa).

Thus far we have been speaking of society in general—almost as if all societies were the same. But societies are not the same. Just as families and family systems differ from each other from epoch to epoch and from society or region to society or region, or as universities and university systems differ, so do societies differ. From the point of view of our macro-sociological interest, they differ with respect to the relationship between center and periphery.

In some societies there is a more intense relationship between center and periphery than in others. Whereas in some societies, where there is a major center there are also minor centers the existence of which diminishes the centrality of the major center, in the societies of the type of which we wish to take note at this point there is a center which excludes all other centers and seeks to pre-empt their functions. To put it somewhat differently, the periphery in the type of society under consideration is under more intense, more continuous impingement from the center. In such societies, there is also a great distance between center and periphery—the two may seldom come close to each other, but there is a constant outward flow from a center the incumbents of which seek to saturate the periphery by their commands and their beliefs. This is the pattern which has been aspired to by the totalitarian societies of the twentieth century. There the elites have tried to make the mass of the population, down to the smallest and most outlying rural areas, believe what they themselves believe on every subject; they have also tried to make the conduct of the mass conform completely with models and prescriptions emanating from the center. The center dominates and saturates the periphery—at least it aspires to do so, and to some extent it succeeds. The society becomes more integrated—from the center outward—in belief and in action.

This is one type of a pattern of unilateral relations between a center and a distant periphery. Another is one which has been much more frequent in world history. It, too, is characterized by a great distance between center and periphery; but in this second type of society much of the periphery, for most of the time and in most spheres of action and belief, lies outside the radius of effectiveness of the center. The outermost fringes of the periphery remain very remote and, except for the occasional ill-administered collection of taxes and tribute and the occasional imposition of certain services, the periphery is left alone. These remote zones of the periphery, which might include most of the population of the society, have their own relatively autonomous centers. Indeed, in many significant respects this pattern stands at the margin of our conception of what a society is. There is a minimum of common culture and the issue of legitimacy arises only intermittently because of the very discontinuous actions of government. Such societies usually have had little public political life; such as there was of public life and all that there was of secret political life were carried on within the center itself or very close to its outer circles.

This was the pattern of the great bureaucratic-imperial societies which, despite the fluctuating aspirations of their rulers for a higher degree of integration, were on the whole very minimally integrated societies. The pattern of the bureaucratic-imperial societies, which resembled the totalitarian societies of the present century as regards the difference in dignity between center and periphery, stands at the opposite pole from the totalitarian societies with respect to amount of domination and saturation of the periphery aspired to and attained by the center.

There is an intermediate pattern of great distance between center and periphery. In this, the distance is filled by a series of graded levels of authority, each of which possesses a certain measure of self-sufficiency while acknowledging the pre-eminence of the great center. Feudal systems (and federal systems to a lesser extent) are instances of this pattern of a major center and a plurality of subcenters. A manor was a small quasi-society. Its partial character arose from the derivation of the power of the lord of the manor from his superior in the hierarchy of nobility and from the dependence of his culture and the culture he sought to impose upon his subjects on the culture of the kingdom and the religious institution which was associated with it.

Then there are societies in which center and periphery do not stand far apart. Certain of the so-called traditional or tribal African societies in some respects resembled the Greek *polis* in the sense that nearly everyone was known to nearly everyone else. In such societies, to the extent that the rulers and the ruled were not the same persons, the two strata were characterized by the strong sense of affinity which bound them together. They were "closer" to each other.

This proximity of rulers and ruled, of elites and masses, is found in modern "mass societies." These are far more complex and differentiated than the other societies which show a similar proximity. The proximity which the modern "mass societies" exhibit is therefore not manifested in situations of face-to-face contact between those resident in the center and those resident in the periphery. The sense of approximate equality works rather through representative institutions and ultimately through attitudes of affinity, beliefs in the common existence of certain crucial properties in all or most of the members of the society which are thought to be approximately equally distributed. The most important of these are the simple and indefinable fact of humanity and the plain and obvious fact of membership in the civil community which is manifest in long residence there.

IV

This is one of the major differences between modern advanced societies and those which are found in earlier epochs and in the Orient. Whereas in practically all large societies prior to modern mass society and in most small societies which have outgrown their basis in lineage, charisma has been thought to inhere in the center, in modern mass society charisma is thought to be dispersed more widely. The common culture in modern "mass" society includes the belief that human beings as such, by virtue of their membership in the national community and their residence on the shared and bounded territory, possess a charismatic quality which was previously thought to be the possession of the elites of the central institutional and cultural systems.

What is this charismatic quality? It is a quality which an individual or a class or a lineage or a cluster of roles possesses. It is a quality possessed by virtue of being "connected" or being "infused" with a "metaphysical essence." This metaphysical essence is a construction of the human mind, which senses that some things in life are of fundamental importance, so important indeed that they call forth reverence or respect or deference. Their fundamental importance is constituted by their "ultimate" character—ultimate in the sense of being irreducibly right, good, and powerful.

Throughout most of human history the "ultimate" has been symbolized as "divinity"; and even now, in an age when at least the educated classes are less religious in any traditional sense than they have ever been before, this conception of the ultimate is still most frequently defined in terms which bear marks of a religious imagery. But regardless of whether this metaphysical essence is formulated in traditional religious terms or in terms of modern political theory regarding the "rights of man" or of the "sovereignty of the people," the fact remains that the population of the periphery has changed its status vis-à-vis the center. It has acquired some of the fundamental qualities which were once thought to be a monopoly of the center and which were thought to be accessible only through the mediation of the center, as in the performance of religious rites by priests or in the granting of titles, ranks, and privileges by earthly rulers.

It would take us too far afield to attempt an explanation of this change. It must suffice to say that economic advancement through the greater productivity of the economy, changes in political institutions and ideas that have given more power and dignity to those in the periphery, a more widespread diffusion of education, and changes in religious beliefs in a more equalitarian direction have all contributed greatly.

V

One major consequence of this change in the culture of modern societies which began in the West has been decolonization —the growth of nationalist movements in colonial territories and the establishment of many new states in Asia and Africa. Before the imposition of European imperial rule, Asia consisted of societies which were of the type which we have characterized by a great distance between center and periphery. Where they were feudal or bureaucratic-imperial regimes, there was only intermittent contact and a very feeble sense of affinity of rulers and ruled in these countries. The periphery was not saturated by the center.

In such a condition of loose integration, the intrusion of a new foreign ruling class, although resented bitterly by the former rulers, at first made little difference in the periphery. Foreign rule and the gradual and partial incorporation of the colonial societies into the economy, polity, and culture of the Western society brought about very important changes in the colonially dominated societies. The creation of a small educated class, urbanization, a somewhat increased rationalization of agriculture, and some small measure of industrialization set loose some of the same tendencies which had been in operation earlier and on a larger scale in Western Europe and America. Here and there in the colonial territories, scattered individuals and organizations began to desire a society more like that which had developed in the West. It is true that to some extent this desire was shaped by the content of Western education and Western political thought. This cultural influence was, however, only part of the larger story.

Fundamental attitudes began to change. A society in which there was a closer affinity between the center and the periphery began to be desired. For those who wanted such a closing of the distance between center and periphery, between elite and mass, the fact that the elite was ethnically alien stood as an obstacle. The fact that the center was only a center of political and economic authority, and that it was not also a center of cultural values, made the sense of insuperable alienation of the periphery from the center all the more acute.

The growth of national sentiment was the growth of a belief that a society should be constituted by those who share the common experience of long residence in a definite territory. Had the British or the Dutch settled in India or Indonesia, as conquerors had done in the past, rather than serving as the transient agents of remote, territorially disjunctive areas of the earth's surface, the nationalist movements would have gathered only a smaller momentum. But the foreign elites never became parts of the societies in which they ruled; they remained parts of other societies. They could not therefore be included in the incipient emergent demand for a self-contained civil society.

Simultaneously with these developments, the changes in the structure of the metropolitan societies rendered more intelligible and more acceptable the idea that societies should be self-contained, that center and periphery should be in closer affinity, and that the culture of the center should saturate the periphery. It was evident that the culture of the center in the colonial countries could not saturate the periphery. (Indeed, the colonial political authorities by and large had studiously avoided efforts at such saturation.) These two concurrent movements, both in the same direction, created a public opinion in the metropolitan countries which was favorable to colonial independence. (It was, of course, stronger in the United Kingdom than it was in France and the Netherlands—proportionately to the greater advancement of the former to the condition of a modern "mass" society. Portugal, which belongs in its domestic structure to a hybrid of bureaucratic oligarchy and totalitarianism, is the least sympathetic with the strivings of colonial populations to form self-sufficient, that is, self-governing, societies.)

Since independence, none of the formerly colonial societies has succeeded in forming itself into a modern mass society, civil in its politics. India has come closest because it was the society in colonial times which was the most modernized in the sense of possessing a substantial indigenous political elite, a large intellectual class, a considerable middle class, and the beginnings of an urban proletariat. In sectors of Indian society the stirring for a self-sufficient society in which membership and rights were defined by long residence on Indian territory began. It was at bottom a changed conception of who is a member of society that was at work; on top of this was the further belief that the boundaries of the territory to be ruled defined the qualifications of those who were to rule it. If a population was to form a society, its rulers were to be evidence of its self-sufficiency.

For the present at least, the properties which made India susceptible to the acceptance of foreign rule are hindering its progress toward the condition of a modern society. The belief that charisma resides in hereditary rulers, in landowners, in ethnic groups and lineages and castes, blocks India's path toward the civility of a modern mass society. Poverty is one of the principal causes of this, together with a deeply rooted central cultural system which for centuries has existed in separation from its central institutional system.

The same applies, *mutatis mutandis*, to many other new states of Asia and Africa. They have not yet become societies in a modern sense, and that is why the valiant efforts of some of their politicians and many of their civil servants to bring them forward economically have thus far not been very successful.

VI

I should like now to make a few concluding observations.

All human collectivities have a tendency toward closure into self-containment. They seek through their authorities to establish and maintain a certain identity, to define their boundaries, and to protect their integrity. They try to maintain their numbers and to prevent the slipping away of members. In very many of these collectivities this tendency is weak because their members join them for restricted and special purposes and they do not

allow the claims of the collectivity to become too strong. Furthermore, in large-scale societies of an openly pluralistic sort, individuals are members of many collectivities and there are competing
and conflicting claims for time, loyalty, and obedience which
cannot all be gratified simultaneously. Yielding to the claims of
one practically always involves refusing the claims of others.

There are certain types of collectivities, however, in which the
tendencies toward closure are stronger than in others. Primordial
collectivities such as families, tribes, and villages are of this sort.
Where human beings define their membership and perceive other
members with respect to certain primordial properties or characteristics, such as common biological characteristics (for example,
origin from a common parentage or ancestry) or a common territorial location (for example, a household or a village), there
will be a greater responsiveness to the demands of closure. Even
these, however, cannot become completely closed: ecological exigencies, the pressure of external power, and the force of individual affections and wants break through the boundaries which the
process of closure would establish.

One of the major features of historical development or evolution has been the erosion of some of the primordial grounds of
closure. Kinship and tribe have diminished in their relative significance. Locality has likewise diminished. These diminutions
have not, however, yielded entirely. In the case of locality, which
is a specific variant of territoriality, the category has remained
but its reference has changed. Territoriality has shifted from
locality to a larger territory, larger than what any average individual could know immediately and from his own experience.
This shift to a larger territoriality has been fostered by ecological
changes caused by the growth of larger markets and improvements in the technology of transportation and communication.
Education has helped to reveal the existence of a larger territory.
The increased activity and the greater efficiency of governments
have made men more aware of the larger territory in which
they live.

This increased awareness of the larger territory has gone hand
in hand with the diminution of the purely biological criterion

of affinity among human beings. It has in part been replaced by the territorial criterion of affinity—which, as locality, had hitherto been associated with the biological criterion.

As long as governments were weak and inefficient and as long as they could not imagine complete dominion over their subjects —even when they were thought to be absolute rulers—societies were bound to have numerous minor centers around which some measure of closure occurred. The major center in societies such as the bureaucratic empires and feudal systems was too unimposing. It could not gain the ascendancy over the imaginations of its subjects because it could not exercise its authority permeatively or effectively.

When, however, the sense of affinity changed its reference and when governments became more active and powerful, the major center of society began to win over the lesser centers. It has never been able completely to abolish the lesser centers—even in societies in which the rulers have been totalitarian in their aspirations; nonetheless, a shift has occurred toward the predominance of the major center. This shift has inevitably changed the range of what was enclosed by the tendency toward closure. Now the enclosed became that which transpired among those who lived in the larger territory. Citizenship began to replace kinship and membership in the village and tribe. The biological-primordial criteria have not been obliterated. Not only does the family survive but ethnicity has come forward, replacing wider kinship and lineage.

Ethnicity is a construction of the imagination, and when a wider territoriality became the major criterion for discerning one's fellow man, ethnicity was sublimated and transformed into nationality. Even where nationality has divested itself of ethnicity (or race), there is still much that is mythological in the conception of nationality, since it is a construction of the imagination.

Mythological or not, nationality now forms an essential component—the cultural component—in modern societies. In some of these societies—for example, those in Asia and Africa which have not yet become societies in the modern sense and which are still confronted by weakness at the center and considerable strength among lineage, ethnic, and local subcenters—nationality has not yet become well established throughout much of the population. For this reason, the center remains weak. If, however, the administrative machinery and the machinery of order are strengthened or remain strong, and if the economies become national or market economies, the major center will impose itself on the periphery and will come to dominate the minds of those who dwell there. The center will, in doing so, begin to become the center not only of the institutional system but of the cultural system as well. In this way, the new states might succeed in becoming the modern—that is, integrated—societies which some members of their elites at present wish them to be.

Integrated societies in which the authoritative institutional and cultural systems are well established can become civil societies with a wide diffusion of the virtues required for the effective practice of citizenship. They can become so where closure around the center is accompanied by the approximation of center and periphery. This is the path which has been followed over the past century and a half in Western Europe, the United States, and Australia, and to a lesser extent in Japan and Canada. In these countries, the mutual interchange between center and periphery, and the heightened sense of affinity which attends this interchange, have brought larger proportions of the population into the center and obliterated to some extent the boundary which has in the past separated center from periphery.

This alternative is not, however, the only possibility; but this cannot be entered into in a short exposition which has already covered so many complex problems.

23 IDEOLOGY AND SOCIAL CHANGE

S. N. Eisenstadt

I

The study of the relations between a society and the various types of ideas and beliefs embodied in some of its central institutions and held—even if in different degrees of intensity— by its members has been among the most central concerns of sociological analysis since the very beginning of modern sociology. It has encompassed many fields, such as the study of religious beliefs and institutions, the study of the development of scientific thought in its social setting, and the study of the sociology of art and literature. Within this broad context there developed in sociological thought a rather specific place or focus for the study of ideology.

This study of ideology, as it developed in modern social thought in general and in sociology in particular, was closely related to two of its major intellectual roots or predispositions. The first was the strongly a-religious or anti-religious thrust of much of the thought of the Enlightenment, of rationalism— a thrust which tended to belittle the significance of non-rational or non-"scientific" ideas and which in its evolutionary garb tended to depict the trend of development of human society as moving from primitive stages bound in the shackles of religion and tradition to the great liberating phases of rationalism and science. Comte's description of the three main stages of development of human society is perhaps the best known, even if certainly not the only, illustration of this trend.

The second root of the specific attitude to ideology which greatly influenced the way it was studied in modern sociology, although closely related to the first, was of a somewhat different order. It was grounded in the strong emphasis on the perception of concrete "real" interests as the main motives and mainsprings of human activity and tended to look on ideas or symbols either as reflections or camouflages of such interests, manipulated by various groups or individuals—especially by the ruling groups —to further their own "material" or "real" interests, or as sort of hallucinations best suited for deranged or upset people.

The fullest and best-known exposition of this attitude was the Marxist one, fully developed in the long struggle against the various "idealist" conceptions of history and society, which envisaged the march of history as the incarnation of preordained ideas, and popularly known in the phrase which defined religion as the opium of the people. But the thrust of this analysis was not limited to religion; it was very quickly transferred to the analysis of other systems of ideas, and especially to secular social and political ideologies—all of which were depicted in rather similar broad terms.

Truly enough, within most of these analyses, however much they stressed the predominance of "real" interests and belittled the autonomy of ideas, there always remained a strong residuum of belief in some "real," "pure" reason or ideas which even if bound to some interests (in the Marxian phrase to the interests of the proletariat) would yet ultimately become liberated from the limitations of such ties and would blossom fully in the realm of human freedom.

Thus in Marxism itself the ideal of a society in which people are no longer alienated from their society and from the products of their work was also depicted as the stage in which human reason would no longer be bound by the shackles of oppressive and limiting interests.

II

These starting points of sociological concern with ideology have necessarily greatly influenced the development of the ways in which ideology was dealt with in sociological, anthropological, and political inquiry. This influence was twofold—in the formulation of the central problems for such inquiry and in the more or less hidden assumption which guided the consideration and analysis of these problems. It is only lately that sociological analysis has been freeing itself from this pseudo-rationalistic, anti-religious bias on the one hand, and from viewing ideology as a mere derivative of interests or psychological predispositions on the other, and has consequently been able also to reformulate the basic problem of its inquiry.

Four such basic problems could be discerned in the development of this branch of sociological inquiry. First was the attempt to specify the distinctive nature of the different spheres of systems of symbols and of their internal characteristics and dynamics—for instance, to explain what differentiates religion from science, science from ideology, and so on.

The second major problem, to which we have already alluded, was that of the interrelations between these varied symbolic fields in any given society and in the broad trend of development of human society: How are religion, science, ideology, philosophy, and art organized in different types of societies, be they primitive, historical, and modern societies or various types thereof? What are their concrete interrelations? How are they organized institutionally? What spheres of life and of human activity are most strongly influenced by them? And can we discern any trend in their development, and in their relative importance? Does there indeed exist some general trend in the direction of growing rationality, or growing secularism?

The third was the problem of the ways in which social reality influences the nature of different systems of ideas—by their contents, general orientations, or organizations. Around this problem a special discipline—the "sociology of knowledge"—has developed.

The fourth was the problem of the "social role" of ideologies:

306

Are they only forces of conservatism or are they forces of change; are they only cloaks for existing vested interests or do they constitute an independent focus of cultural creativity and social change; whatever their concrete alignment with any given social group or stratum, do they contain within themselves the seeds of autonomous development; are they able to influence the behavior of men and the shape of society?

These are the most general problems that have developed in the realm of the sociological study of symbolic or cultural systems in general and of ideologies in particular. The very force of accumulated research on the one hand and the progressive liberation from the initial assumptions on the other have not only provided some answers to them but have also given rise to a reformulation and specification of the problems themselves. We shall present first some very general considerations of these answers and of the changes in the formulations of these problems, and then proceed to the analysis of one specific problem, that of the relation of ideologies to social change. Because of shortage of space we shall leave out entirely the whole area of the sociology of knowledge and deal only—albeit also in a general way—with the three other problem areas.

III

The first problem—the delineation of the specific characteristics of different symbolic spheres—has constituted a center of interest in various social sciences, and especially in anthropology and sociology. Not only were the great evolutionists like Morgan or Tylor concerned with these problems but some of the major figures of modern anthropology such as Malinowski devoted a very large part of their work to the explanation of the nature of the different symbolic realms—especially of religion, magic, and pragmatic science, and of their effects on social structure and behavior—attempting to destroy the assumption about the existence of a special, distinct, primitive mentality and to show instead the universality of these varied types of mental and ideational attitudes in all societies.

Thus we see that although the delineation of the different

symbolic spheres and their characteristics may seem the least problematic of all the problem areas of the sociological study of ideologies, it has also been plagued continually by the varied evaluative assumptions which greatly influenced the initial sociological or anthropological approach to these problems. Only lately a more balanced and systematic approach—seen, for instance, in the works of Parsons and Geertz—can be discerned.

One upshot of all these developments is that definitions of the different symbolic systems are tentative—for several reasons. First, within each symbolic sphere many distinctive subspheres may develop, and claim symbolic and organizational autonomy of their own. Thus in the field of ideology proper, the definition of either Parsons or Geertz may be too broad to take full cognizance of the internal dynamics of such specific and distinct types of ideologies as a militant secular ideology—for example, modern communism or nationalism—that attempts to provide a whole, coherent, close world view which encompasses all the other spheres.

Moreover, the emergence of such specific symbolic subsystems may also point up the fact that the assumption of natural "boundaries" between the different symbolic spheres has to be continuously re-examined. It indicates that under certain conditions such varied differentiated systems may become fused or reorganized together in a new way—and that this may well happen not only in "primitive" or prehistoric societies but also under various modern conditions.

But the significance of any classificatory schema is determined mainly by the nature of the problems to which the classification is addressed; hence even the designation of the specific characteristics of the different symbolic spheres has been greatly influenced by the more substantive problems to which social scientists address themselves.

IV

Thus we come to the second problem—namely, that of the interrelation between the different symbolic systems and of the possible trend of their development in the history of human society. The implicit evolutionary schemes of old which assumed a continuous progressive trend of development toward rationalization and secularization have by now, in their simplest form, been abandoned.

Sociological and anthropological research alike have clearly shown that all types of symbolic realms exist—even if in different degrees of articulation and autonomy—in all societies. There is no society in which there does not exist what we would call scientific—empirical, religious, philosophical, or ideological—orientation and symbols as basic ingredients of their symbolic templates and world view in which they are not organized in specific activities, roles, and organizations on the one hand, and permeate wider realms of social life and human discourse on the other.

But societies differ here greatly in two respects. First, they differ with regard to the extent of what may be called structural and symbolic differentiation of these different realms. Thus in many primitive societies these various realms are not fully differentiated from one another, both symbolically, that is, in terms of the problems posed and the nature of the answers given, and institutionally, that is, in terms of the roles the incumbents of which specialize in the creation and transmission of symbols. Both types of differentiation—symbolic and organizational—tend to increase, although certainly not always in the same degree, as we pass from primitive to archaic, historical, and modern societies.

But the extent of differentiation of the various symbolic spheres is not the only important criterion according to which societies can be compared. The second such criterion is the relative predominance of the different spheres within the over-all symbolic structure or cultural tradition of a society, and this relative predominance may vary independently of the degree of structural differentiation of the major symbolic systems. Thus, for instance, great historical empires with relatively similar degrees of structural differentiation—like the Byzantine, Arab, and Chinese empires—may greatly differ in that in the Chinese empire the semi-secular Confucian ideology was predominant as against the greater predominance of religious-philosophical orientations in the Islamic or the Byzantine empire.

Similarly in some modern industrial societies, like the Soviet, a militant secular ideology is predominant, while in others—the Western—a more pluralistic system of open ideologies and scientific orientations seems to predominate.

It is this fact that belies any simple evolutionist conception of a unilinear trend of development, or evolution of symbolic spheres in the history of human societies. To some extent it is true, of course, that in one sense we can easily discern a general trend toward what may be called secularization of the cultural realm as concomitant with the development of modernity. This is true in the sense that religious symbols tend to lose their centrality and semi-monopolistic predominance in the cultural realm and that autonomous developments of science, ideology, and philosophy take place.

It is also true that within each symbolic sphere—religion, philosophy, and ideology—a general trend of rationalization in terms of growing abstraction in the formulation of their problems, growing logical coherence, and general phrasing appears. But even here there exists a great variety in the relative predominance of these various spheres and of the scope of the autonomy of the different cultural institutions.

Moreover, the very emergence of such autonomous scientific or ideological orientations and groups does not necessarily entail a total abandonment of religious orientation. Very often they are greatly influenced by specific types of transformation of religious symbols and beliefs, and find within them the motivational mainspring of their activities.

The very recognition of this complexity poses new problems and brings us also closer to the third major problem—namely, that of the social functions of ideology.

V

As we have seen, this problem was first posed in the broad terms of the extent of derivation of ideologies, from material interest and/or of its serving the vested interests of various groups as against its potential autonomous and innovative tendencies. This attitude to ideologies has been further developed in many psychological or social-psychological studies, which stressed that ideology serves as a rather illusory means of expressing psychic stress or emotional instability.

But here, with regard to other problems and with the development of research, such general and often totally dichotomical posing of problems gave way to a more differentiated one which recognized that ideologies may fulfill both functions and that in every society, within its basic symbolic structure, both types of social or psychological orientation of ideas—conservative and innovative, derivative and autonomous—can be found.

One of the best-known attempts to distinguish analytically between these two aspects of thought or symbolizations was made by Karl Manheim in his famous book *Ideology and Utopia,* published in German in the early thirties, whose very title stresses this distinction. According to him, ideologies are those thought systems which legitimize, in symbolic terms, the status quo, while utopias want to go beyond it and change it in some new direction.

VI

These varied developments have not, indeed, diminished the importance of the various broad problems in the sociological analyses of ideologies outlined above. They did, however, give rise to an important shift in the formulation of these problems.

They gave rise to a much more differentiated approach—an approach which distinguished in a much more subtle way among the various aspects of ideologies, recognized the great variety of possible ideological orientation within any society, and, above all, instead of asking in very general terms about the global nature of ideas or of the over-all trends of their development, stressed more and more the investigation of the conditions in which different types of systems of ideas tend to arise, can become institutionalized, maintained, and changed.

Thus, instead of discussing in general the "nature" of the trend of the universal development of ideas from religion to science, more and more emphasis has been put on investigating the conditions under which, for instance, growing differentiation among the various symbolic systems takes place, under which many specific structures and organizations occur, and under which different types of ideas tend to develop.

Thus we find many investigations of the conditions of emergence of different types of cultural organizations—sects, denominations, and churches, or in the more secular realm of scientific orientations and organizations, of scientific autonomy on the one hand and of militant, secular ideologies and of so-called "alienated" intellectuals, who very often are the bearers of such ideologies, on the other.

VII

In the space at our disposal, I shall limit myself to a detailed analysis of one specific problem from within the broader area of the so-called social functions of ideologies. Mannheim's distinction between ideology and utopia pointed to some new ways of formulating the problem, and especially to the importance of the study of the social conditions under which each of these types of ideological symbols tends to develop, of the types of social organizations and structures which may facilitate the development of these symbols, and of the conditions under which they may become influential in shaping the behavior of groups, strata, and individuals.

This last point—the importance of studying the conditions under which systems of ideas are influential in shaping the concrete behavior of people and the contours of institutions whether in a "conservative" or an innovational direction—entails a very interesting and important reformulation of the whole problem of the social function of ideologies. Hitherto most of the approaches assumed that within the "objective" limits of their basic nature, ideologies were indeed very forceful in shaping the behavior of individuals, groups, or strata.

But the results of research and of broader experience alike have indicated that this cannot be taken for granted, that this in itself constitutes a problem. Or, in other words, it was found that different systems of thought or ideas may, under different social conditions, in different social settings, vary in the effectiveness of their influence on human behavior and that therefore the study of the conditions of these different outcomes should constitute one of the central problems of sociological inquiry.

We shall illustrate this problem by an examination of one of sociology's most classical theses, namely, Max Weber's thesis about the influence of Protestantism on the development of capitalism—i.e., the thesis which allegedly imputed the rise of modern capitalism in the West to the "spirit" of Protestantism. Although the simplistic interpretation of this thesis has not been accepted, it has been recognized as a very important contribution to the analysis of the emergence of modernity. Hence, whatever the correctness of the details of this thesis, it poses, from the point of view of our discussion, several very important questions. One such question is: What are the characteristics of a symbolic—in this case, a religious-ideological system which is capable of greatly influencing, changing, or transforming the behavior of people? Second, What are the characteristics of the social groups and settings in which such influence can become most effective? Third, What are the mechanisms through which this influence is operative?

Let us start, then, with the first two questions and ask ourselves what is it in the Protestant symbolic system and in the social setting of its bearers that facilitated the development of new social institutions and individual motivations.

It seems that the aspects of the Protestant value orientation which are most important from the point of view of our discussion are its combination of "this-worldliness" and transcendentalism—a combination which orients individual behavior to activities within this world, but at the same time does not ritually sanctify any of them, either through a mystic union or any ritual act, as the final point of religious consummation or worthiness. Second is the strong emphasis on individual activism and responsibility. Third is the unmediated, direct relation of the individual to the sacred and to the sacred tradition—an attitude which, while strongly emphasizing the importance and direct relevance of the sacred and of tradition, minimizes the extent to which this relation can be mediated by any institutions, organization, or textual exegesis. Hence it opens up the possibility of continuous re-definition and re-formulation of the nature and scope of such tradition, a possibility which is further enhanced by the strong transcendental attitude which minimizes the sacredness of any "here and now."

These religious orientations of Protestantism and of Protestants (and especially Calvinists) were not, however, confined only to the realm of the sacred. They were closely related to and manifested in two major orientations in most Protestant groups' conception of the social reality and of their own place in it, i.e., in what may be called their status images and orientations.

Most of the Protestant groups developed a combination of two types of such orientations. First was their "openness" toward the wider social structure, rooted in their "this-worldly" orientation which was not limited only to the economic sphere but which also, as we shall see later, could encompass other social fields. Second, they were characterized by a certain autonomy and self-sufficiency from the point of view of their status orientation. They evinced but little dependence—from the point of view of the crystallization of their own status symbols and identity—on the existing political and religious centers. All of these aspects of the Protestant ethic were conducive to its great transformative capacities and its ability to influence and change the behavior of people and the shape of institutions.

But the extent to which these beliefs could indeed become influential depended, to no small degree, on the social organization of their bearers and of the broader social setting within which they were operative. Here, in general, it seems that such transformative tendencies of religious and ideological systems and movements tend to be greater the more they are borne and promoted by relatively cohesive elites with a strong sense of self-identity, and especially by secondary elites which, while somewhat distant from the central ruling one, yet maintain positive solidary orientations to the center and are not entirely alienated from the pre-existing elites and from some of the broader groups of the society.

Similarly, the effects of such transformative potentials of the religious and ideological movements will be greater—as we have indicated above—insofar as the existing social structure is characterized, in its totality or in those of its parts within which these religious and ideological developments are intensive, by some extent of autonomy of the social, cultural, and political orders, and by relatively strong cohesiveness of the more active broader strata. Also, the existence, within broader social strata and family groups of relatively strong internal cohesion, of some status-autonomy and flexibility together with openness toward the center, may greatly facilitate the internal transformation of these groups, the development within them of positive orientations to the new centers, and of willingness to provide these centers with the support and resources needed by them.

Conversely, insofar as such autonomy is small and the self-closeness of wider social groups great, it can easily, through withdrawal of resources and through the development of intensive unregulated demands on and from the center, undermine the very conditions of the functioning of these new institutional centers.

It was by virtue of the combination of these value orientation and social characteristics that within the Protestant ethic there emerged some psycho-social mechanisms through which the influence of ideas on behavior became operative. The most important of these seems to have been a new type of personal identity, which has reference, but not a too rigid one, to a given collective identity. Such identity was not entirely bound up with any one political system, with any one state or community, but had some flexible openings to a variety of collectivities and communities. Yet it also generated a very strong, even flexible, emphasis on the personal commitment to do something both in and for a community. In addition, it also entailed a very strong connection between personal commitment, personal identity, and several types of institutional exchange activities—economic, political, administrative. It opened up the connections between this personal and collective identity to a great variety of concrete "this-worldly" activities.

Thus, if we look closely at Weber's thesis, we see that whatever the correctness of its details, we have here an attempt to explain a whole social cultural transformation through a change in the type of relations between personal, collective identities on the one hand, and between them and various concrete institutional activities on the other hand. And it was this symbolic transformation which has at least facilitated some new institutional developments—though it did not "cause" them.

VIII

Weber's analysis was focused on the effects of a religious system of ideas—albeit on its effects in transforming a religious civilization in the direction of growing secularism. But in a way the same problem—that of the transformative capacity of systems of ideas, of ideologies—exists with regard to various secular ideologies, the importance of which becomes especially great in the modern and contemporary sciences, where there have emerged many new secular ideologies—socialist, nationalist, and the like—which aimed at the transformation of the behavior of men and the contours of society. It seems that the broad implication derived from our analysis of Weber's thesis can indeed be applied to such secular ideologies, and that the same broad considerations apply to the transformative capacity of secular ideologies.

It may perhaps be useful to distinguish between growth-stimulating and stagnating social elites. A stagnating social elite is one which while creating new symbols and political frameworks is not able to effect within its society any structural transformation facilitating continuous growth. Examples of growth-stimulating elites are the elites of Mexico, Turkey, Soviet Russia, Japan, and Israel and the first modernizing elites of Western Europe which have been relatively successful in effecting growth.

The elites which were to some extent successful in effecting such transformation aimed in the ideological and value spheres at the development of a new, more flexible set of symbols and a collective identity which, while not negating the traditions, could incorporate them into these new symbolic frameworks. They aimed at the transformation of the internal values of wider social groups and strata and at the development, among these groups, of new, more flexible orientations.

They developed simultaneous orientations to collective ideological transformation and to concrete tasks and problems in different "practical" fields. They perceived their own legitimation in terms of such wider changes and not only in terms of providing various immediate benefits to different social groups—although they hoped that ultimately the new political system would also bring marked improvements in the standard of living of the broader groups and strata of the population.

An illustration from the basic modern ideology of my own country, Israel, is the image of the pioneer which combines a strong orientation to personal responsibility and broader transcendental orientations that go beyond any given here-and-now social reality. The image has proved to be a very dynamic force with great transformative capacities.

In both these cases—of Protestantism and of the dynamic secular ideologies—we find also that those very ideologies which at certain stages of development might have been mainsprings of change, may become at later stages of development foci of social conservatism. But what is significant is that they do retain some of the qualities of commitment, of being able strongly to influence and shape the behavior of individuals, groups, and strata whether in an innovative or in a conservative direction.

As against these orientations we find among the elites of the other countries a certain "closeness," a ritual emphasis on certain specific and very limited types of status. These usually have not contained any "transcendental" or broadly universalistic orientations, their internal ideological and value transformation was relatively small and they have tended to view the national collectivity in terms of exclusive, limited values and symbols of status, often derived from the preceding social structure and hence also to limit their own field of perception and the scope of their own activities.

Or, in other words, they did not develop that combination of value orientations which would facilitate the development of new collective and personal identities which could also influence various concrete institutional activities.

Moreover, the social setting of these ideological groups did not facilitate the development of such orientations. These ideologies were borne mostly by elites which were relatively non-cohesive and were alienated from other elites and from the broader groups and strata of the society, and which were either very distant from the existing center or succeeded in totally monopolizing it, to the exclusion of other groups and elites.

In most of these countries the elites were composed mostly of intellectuals, and in many cases intellectuals constituted the only initially available modern elite. They had but very few even ambivalent internal social and ideological contacts or identifications with either the bearers of pre-existing traditions or with the wider groups of the society. The modernizing orientations of these elites were focused mostly on the political, much less on the economic sphere. Surprisingly enough, they were also very often less focused on the cultural sphere, in the sense of redefinition and reformation of their own basic internal value orientation. Consequently they were not able to establish a strong internal cohesiveness and strong ideological and value identifications and connections with other, potentially modernized groups and strata.

On the other hand, the elites in Turkey, Israel, Japan, and Mexico, or some of the more cohesive elites in countries in the later stages of modernization, however great the differences between them, still had some contrary characteristics in common. They were not usually composed only of intellectual groups entirely alienated from the pre-existing elites and from some of the broader groups of the society, but were to some extent placed in secondary elite positions in the preceding structure, and had somewhat closer relations with many active, broader groups.

In the ideological and value spheres they aimed at the development of a new and more flexible set of symbols and collective identity which, while not negating tradition, would also provide some new meaning for the new processes of change. Hence they tended on the one hand to be more cohesive, while at the same time to effect some internal value transformation within the broader groups and strata.

This chapter is necessarily only a very brief preliminary and inadequate examination of this problem, which should constitute a focus of continuing comparative research. It may, however, serve as an illustration—taken from one problem area—of the ways in which such problems are being dealt with in sociological research.

24 AN OVERVIEW

Talcott Parsons

This book deals with sociology as an intellectual discipline, with special reference to its position and practice in the United States. Sociologists classify themselves predominantly as practicing one of the "pure" intellectual disciplines, as distinguished from such applied fields as social work and education. Thus their closest relations in the social field are to economics, political science, psychology, and anthropology.

As an intellectual discipline, the main organizational location of professional sociologists is in the academic world, in the universities and colleges of the country, and within them mainly in arts and sciences faculties—only about one in seven academic sociologists is appointed in a "professional school" faculty. The wide scope of the American system of higher education has provided exceptional opportunity for the various disciplines to expand and develop. Sociology is now taught as a distinctive subject in all the leading American universities and all but a very small number of the better kind of liberal arts colleges, though it is interesting that resistance to its acceptance has been strongest in the latter type of institution.

In common with virtually all its sister disciplines, but especially in the sciences both natural and social, sociology has been the framework of a rapidly increasing volume of research activity and publication of results. Qualification to do research together with accomplished research output has become perhaps the most important single criterion of professional standing generally, and all of the higher standing members, with few exceptions, are productive in research after their training period. There has been in recent years a rapid increase in the number of journals which serve as a channel for the publication of sociological materials, and the volume of book publications has rapidly increased.

The group which can be called professional sociologists has also rapidly increased. The total membership of the American Sociological Association in 1966 was about 10,000. Of these about 40 per cent are regularly qualified professional sociologists or, in a few cases, representatives of neighboring disciplines with a "major commitment to sociology"; the others are student and associate members. The number of professionals more than doubled in fifteen years. In 1966 it was larger than the number of anthropologists, about the same as that of political scientists, considerably smaller than that of economists, and much smaller than that of psychologists; many of the last, however, are "practitioners" of clinical psychology rather than representatives of a predominantly pure academic discipline.

Recruitment to the sociological profession in the United States is of course primarily through the programs of graduate training of the universities. In 1947–1948, only 66 doctoral degrees in sociology were granted; in 1961–1962 the number had grown to 173. This occurred because of the expansion of already established programs and the inauguration of new programs in universities not previously offering them.

In numbers and in various other respects—for example, financial support of research—American sociology has grown faster and gone further than sociology in any other country. Nevertheless its growth is part of a world-wide movement which has gained in momentum in almost all areas. Registered attendance at the, until recently, triennial meetings of the International Sociological Association has, since 1953 at least, followed a geometric progression, with no increase in the proportion of Americans attending. This record of course underestimates the numbers involved in places very distant from the location of meetings, such as Japan and India. A further highly significant development has been the rapid recent growth of sociology in a number of communist countries, notably the Soviet Union, Poland, Czechoslovakia, and Yugoslavia.

None of the disciplines in the area of social and behavioral science has grown up on the basis of pure focus on theoretical problem areas alone; in the whole development there has been a great deal of what, in that context, has been "historical accident." Nevertheless there is a rather impressive approximation to a meaningful intellectual division of labor among them, which will give the reader a guide to the primary focus and character of sociology.

As distinguished from the two most generally oriented of its neighboring disciplines, sociology is concerned with the analysis of social systems, with special but by no means exclusive reference to the type of social system we call a society. A society is a relatively self-sufficient social system, as judged by criteria of the balance among territorially oriented political organization, access to economic resources, the recruitment and socialization of its population, and its cultural legitimation as an independent entity.

Psychology, at the human level, is concerned with the personality of the individual, including, in social psychology, his interaction with and interpenetration of social systems, whereas the focus of sociology is on the social system as such, that is, the system of processes and relations constituted by the interaction of a plurality—often a very large number—of human individuals.

The specific position of anthropology is more difficult to characterize, because in certain respects it has tended to pre-empt a field broader than that of sociology itself, while in others it has concentrated on nonliterate cultures and societies. Insofar as an analytically defined focus can, however, be formulated, it seems to lie in the analytical study of phenomena of culture, of the patterned symbolic-meaning systems in and by which social systems and personalities are oriented and guided. In this relationship anthropology stands in a particularly close relationship, on the one hand to the humanistic disciplines which deal with cultural content at the higher civilizational levels, especially where documentary sources are involved, and on the other hand to linguistics which studies the most generally fundamental vehicle of cultural communication and expression. Social psychology is paralleled by the interstitial discipline of social anthropology, which essentially deals with social structures and processes with special reference to their cultural settings and involvements, and traditionally, especially for the "simpler" societies.

From the above discussion it should be clear that we are treating social systems, including societies, not as the concrete aggregate of interacting and otherwise behaving human beings, but as an analytically defined subsystem of the totality of human social action, abstracted with reference to the interaction processes and the structures assumed by the relationships among actors. Otherwise the social system would not be distinguishable, on the one hand, from the personalities of individual participants—which also must be analytically defined with respect to their individual as distinct from interactive reference. On the other hand, it would not be distinguished from the pattern references of the cultural system, which focuses on symbolic-meaning components and their relations, including the codes in terms of which these meanings are symbolized.

Contrary to many current views, I do not treat sociology as the discipline dealing with the total social system, even in this analytically abstracted sense. This would either deny to economics and political science the title of being *social* science disciplines in the strictest sense or would make them subsidiary branches of sociology. Neither alternative would be acceptable. I therefore conceive sociology as concerned with one primary functional aspect of social systems, namely the understanding of the structures and processes especially concerned with the *integration* of social systems, which of course includes the failures of integration and understanding of the forces impeding as well as favoring integration. By integration in this context I mean the structures and processes by which the relations among the parts of a social system—persons in roles, collectivities, and normative pattern components—either become so ordered as to promote harmonious functioning in their respective involvements with each other in the system, or in specific and understandable ways fail to do so. Integration has both a negative and a positive aspect. The negative concerns the prevention or minimization of action which would disrupt the integration of the system, by mutual destructiveness or by blockage. It is important to realize that consequences of actions in the axis of integration are to an important degree independent of the intentions of the participant units. The traffic jam is a classic example. It is safe to say that very seldom does any group of drivers intend to create a jam, but the consequence of too many of them trying to use the same road system at the same time, in the absence of adequate traffic control, often is to create such a jam. Positive integration, on the other hand, is the phenomenon of mutual support and facilitation among the units of a social system, seen in the perspective of the "functioning" of the system as a whole. The typical phenomenon of cooperation in the accomplishment of a group task is a case in point.

By contrast with this focus of sociology on integration we conceive that of economics, in a correspondingly analytical sense, to lie in concern for the structures and processes of social systems which have primarily adaptive functions. These concern the production and mobilization of relatively generalized facilities, accessible to the various units and subsystems of society or of an intersocietal order. In relatively modern societies these involve above all markets and the mechanism of money in its various forms, and the ways in which innumerable actions are oriented toward and in terms of monetary and market phenomena.

Political science, then, I conceive to be concerned especially with the organization of social systems in the context of attainment of collective goals. At the societal level and that of its segmental territorial subsystems the focus is on the phenomena of government. The same basic theory, however, is relevant to the functioning of any goal-oriented collectivity, the larger and more complex the more so. Thus the large modern business firm, or indeed university or church, has an exceedingly important political aspect. Power, as a generalized medium of mobilization of obligations to contribute to collective functioning—including refraining from destructive or obstructive action—has a place in the analysis of political systems in some ways parallel to that of money in economic systems.

The main substantive focus of sociological analysis, seen in the above context, may be said to lie in the *institutional* aspect of social action. In the most general terms, this is the area in which the *normative expectations* operating in social systems,

323

which are grounded in the culture and which define what people in various statuses and roles in *one* or more of various senses, *ought* to do under various circumstances, are articulated. These expectations are integrated with the *motives* of actors, i.e., the kinds of things the actors are, in the relevant positions and circumstances, "driven" to do, or "want" to do. Since, however, the system reference of sociology is to social systems rather than to the personality of the individual, it is *collectivities* composed of individuals rather than individuals even in roles as such in which the most important sociological interest lies. Where motivation is concerned, therefore, it is the types and rates of motives and the resultant behavior, rather than the individual case, which are the primary focus.

Let us review a few of the general conditions of societal integration. On the normative side there are imperatives of sufficient degrees of consistency, definiteness, and generality of the norms which define expectations. Consistency has a double reference. Since norms must guide the action of individual persons in roles, and of collectivities, the norms defining expectations in different contexts of the action of *the same individual* or collective unit must be relatively consistent with each other. On the other hand, such a system of norms must be relatively consistent for the societal system as a whole, since they apply to different situations.

At one level definiteness and generality may seem to be incompatible, and indeed many normative systems in fact attain definiteness at the sacrifice of generality, such as some systems of "religious law." The two criteria may, however, become compatible on high levels if general principles can be used to define clearly the limits of freedom and discretion in action, and the ways in which several different principles converge in defining expectations for particular classes of roles or acts. Thus the principle of "equal protection of the law" prevents Congress from assessing certain types of discriminatory tax, but the tax liability of a given citizen may still be quite precisely defined. Levels of generality of the normative system are of the very first importance to the combination of high levels of social integration with high adaptiveness in the economic sense and high effectiveness in the political. Definiteness, on the other hand, is of the first importance to the motivation of participants. Ambiguity in the expectation system is the principal source of the widespread type of disturbance Durkheim first identified by the concept of *anomie*.

The content of normative expectations is significantly independent of their mode of sanctioning. In all highly developed societies a major portion of the normative system has *legal* status in that rights and obligations have authoritative definitions laid down by governmental agencies; specific penalties are attached to noncompliance with them; and specific governmental agencies are charged with responsibility for their interpretation and enforcement. The legal system, however, is never exhaustive of normative content, and many other than legal sanctions in the form of authoritative interpretation and governmental enforcement are always important. Moreover, these two ranges of variation are independent of each other: norms with legal status are sanctioned in other ways as well as the legal, and sometimes nonlegal norms are coercively enforced. The second most important basis of normative obligation, along with the legal, is what we ordinarily call the moral. The actual effectiveness of legal systems is heavily dependent on the moral backing they receive as being—from the point of view of most of those subject to them—"intrinsically" right.

There are, however, two other major types of sanction and therefore bases of "appeal" for conformity with normative expectations. On the one hand, there are not only "interests" in practical efficiency and effectiveness but also *obligations* to act "rationally" in what we have called economic and political contexts; sometimes these are enforced, but often not. Thus there is strong condemnation of waste in many different connections, and bungling inefficiency in getting practical tasks done is not looked upon with favor. Another type of sanction more specific to social integration, however, is the obligation of loyalty, which is the counterpart for the participating unit of the solidarity of the collectivity in which the individual participates. Relatively independently then of legal obligation, and of strictly moral considerations, membership in collectivities tends to carry obligations of loyalty, of supporting the collectivity and the other members in their membership capacities. Sometimes this reaches extremes, as in the case of the maxim "my country right or wrong."

Insofar as a system of norms has become integrated with a presumptively effective set of supporting sanctions we speak of it as *institutionalized*. Generally this implies that there will be a clustering of the types of sanctions just outlined and any given component of the normative system will have two or more types of sanction back of the desirability of conformity with the expectations it defines.

In the sanction system, however, a special place is occupied by the category we have called "moral." It is the moral obligatoriness of a pattern of action—an obligatoriness which includes not only performing specific acts and refraining from others, but respecting certain areas of freedom for others and taking the responsibility for proper use of freedom within such a range oneself—which is the manifestation in action of commitment to values, and, hence, the main point of articulation of a societal community with the normative aspect of the cultural system. Values, as constituent components of a social system, I would define as commonly held conceptions of the *desirable type of social system*—in the most important case, society as held by its own members. Such social values are to be differentiated from values concerning desirable types of object other than social systems, e.g., personalities, organisms, or physical objects.

The articulation of a system of norms and the expectations associated with the values which "govern" them is what we may call the *legitimation* of the normative system. This is the most important single point of articulation of a social with a cultural system. In the "last analysis" legitimation leads back to religious considerations, but in complex societies there are many levels of legitimation short of that Values, like norms, may be said to be institutionalized insofar as, first, the main outline of normative expectations institutionalized in the society is consistent with these value premises, and the latter are habitually invoked when problems of their legitimation arise. Second, they are institutionalized insofar as invoking the value premise will normally settle a problem of legitimation in the sense that "seeing" the connection will activate effectively operative value commitments on the part of those concerned. The value premises of American society, for example, are above all formulated in such historic documents as the Declaration of Independence, the Preamble to the Constitution, and the Bill of Rights.

We may now turn to the other side of the basic problem of sociological integration, the one which above was called "motivational." This "ultimately" concerns the motivation of the individual at the personality level. So far, however, as the individual is treated as a participant in a more or less institutionalized system of social interaction, we speak of him as acting in a *role*. The role is conceived not only as a "sector" of the concrete action system of the individual of reference, but, in accord with our general analytical conception of the social system, as such a sector insofar as it is at once subject to a specific set of normative expectations relevant to the social system and as it involves a set of interactive relations with others of the type we conceive as constituting a *collectivity*.

A collectivity is, then, a unit in a social system—including from certain points of view the definition of the system as a whole—constituted by the social interaction of a plurality of human individuals in roles, and governed by a specifically relevant set of normative expectations. The primary focus of sociological analysis is the articulation between normative systems and collectivities, with roles as the more "outlying" components in the direction of personality systems, values more "outlying" in the direction of cultural systems.

Complementary to the institutionalization of the normative system, we speak of the *internalization* of the expectation system in the personality of the individual. This presumes that the overall result is a set of expectations which is rewarding to the participant individuals, in a sense complementary to that in which a normative system must be culturally legitimized. This rewardingness, however, can be broken down analytically into three components which correspond to the definiteness, generality, and consistency of the normative structure.

The first of these is the internalized goal structure of the individual in his role participation. In the most general sense it is

327

the aspect of internalization which is psychologically grounded in the internalization of achievement motives, specified into the avenues of achievement which are appropriate to the particular role-set in the society of reference. However, back of commitment to levels and type of role achievement must lie motivational concern with relevant performance capacities, which, of course, to be effectively implemented and hence rewarding, must be matched with the opportunity structure of the society. Finally, since the individual must act within a system of collectivities, a basic condition of their solidarity—which in turn is one primary aspect of the integration of the social system—is the internalization of motivation to the requisite levels of loyalty to collective interests and demands.

The process of internalization of these motivationally relevant structures is what sociologists call *socialization*. The process grounds in the genetically given plasticity of the human organism and its capacity to learn. Its earlier phases are everywhere centered in the kinship system, with special reference to the nuclear family. Though socialization goes on in all social groups, beyond the family it is of course especially concentrated in collectivities devoted to formal education, which become progressively more important with the advancement of social evolution.

A critically important feature of social systems with which sociology is especially concerned is the pluralistic character of their structures. The main point of reference for this problem is the fact that in no society is an individual, if he lives beyond early infancy, ever a member of only one collectivity. Thus the incest taboo ensures that if he marries he will be a member of two independent nuclear families—of which he is the only common member—and he will also belong to numerous other collectivities organized on bases of residence, occupational function, collective decision making, religious observance, and various others.

The differentiatedness of the society therefore must be articulated with the capacities of its individual members to manage these plural role participations, which, with greater differentiatedness, inherently involve potentialities of role conflict as well as indefiniteness of normative expectation.

328

There is a basic complementarity to this on the normative side. A highly differentiated society is necessarily normatively as well as collectively pluralistic. This is to say that the same value premises must serve to legitimate a wide variety of different norms, differentiated according to the functions of the component acting units to which they apply and the situations in which they have to act.

Given the fact that there are strongly entrenched tendencies to the stabilization of rather specific patterns on both the cultural and the personality sides of this relationship, the essence of the sociological problem is highlighted in the form of what may be called a "Kantian" formulation, namely that from the normative side situational pressures continually operate in a centrifugal direction to "dilute" the commitments which root in cultural factors. Correspondingly, on the motivational side, the diversification of the whole situational system presents the individual and subcollectivities not only with opportunities but with strong pressures to choose lines of achievement which are in some kind of conflict with the system of normative expectations. This possibility of course is enhanced by the fact that the normative system is itself never fully adequate; there are always elements of inconsistency, over- or under-definiteness, ambiguity, and over- or under-generalization in it. People are both motivated to nonconformity, or as sociologists often say, deviance, and also are often with the best will simply *unable* to comply fully with societal expectations because of the difficulty of knowing what they ought to do. The general process by which such discrepancies between the expectation system and actual behavior are minimized is what is called by sociologists the process of social control.

The first line of social control is clearly the interplay of the normal sanctions of the social interaction process. Approved achievements are encouraged by the prospect of various sorts of reward, and disapproved behavior discouraged by prospective punishments or withholding of reward. The importance, however, of the internalization of societal norms and values in personality systems means that it is not sufficient to rely on the more obviously rational concerns with self-interest, because internalized ambivalences, conflicts, and the like may make it impossible for people to behave rationally on many occasions. Complex societies therefore tend to develop specialized mechanisms of social control which in certain respects are complementary to the mechanisms of socialization which have been mentioned. Durkheim was one of the first to understand that certain religious rituals have this significance, in strengthening motivation to maintain social solidarity and with it to fulfill normative expectations more fully. A type case here is the functions of funeral rituals in counteracting the motivational disturbances occasioned by bereavement and promoting maintenance of the continuity of the social units which have lost a valued member. One particularly important class of institutions with a special significance for social control is that organized around "therapeutic" processes. Their roots lie deep in the history of religion and magic, but they have also become associated with some aspects of science in the various health fields, particularly that of mental health.

Just as all types of sanctions are involved in processes of social interaction, they all have some kinds of significance in the processes of social control. There is, however, one type of generalized sanction which is particularly crucial at the sociological level of interaction processes, corresponding to some degree to the role of money in economic systems and power in political systems. This is what some sociologists have called *influence* in a technical sense. It is the rewarding of approved action and the discouragement of nonapproved action by a concurrent appeal to loyalty to the relevant collectivities in which both the influencer and the object of influence share membership and to the fulfillment of the normative expectations which are institutionalized in the relevant roles in these collectivities. The magnitude of the influence possessed by a unit—individual or collective—may be called its level of *prestige* in the system. As such it is a form of generalized capacity to persuade. Where persuasion is oriented to overt collective action, especially in political contexts, we may speak of leadership as a position of high influence.

Institutional complexes in the sense of this discussion come to be differentiated along the lines of types of overt action, roles, and collectivities, though not in one-to-one correspondence with these; thus the institutional complexes primarily concerned with economic functions in a society are what we call contract and property, centering on the regulation of the processes of exchange, and of rights relative to the commodities exchanged, the latter including money in all its ramifications. Employment of human services presents special problems which should not be too closely identified with either contract or property where only money and commodities are involved. In a sufficiently differentiated situation, employment of services tends to be institutionalized in terms of the occupational role, which involves a special link with the political complex. Whether or not employing organizations be primarily economic in function, as is the case with the business firm, their authority systems should be classed as political rather than economic.

Indeed if property is the central economic institution, its political counterpart is authority, which is the generalized right to invoke binding obligations in the interest of collective goals. The generalized medium for the exercise of authority is what we call power in our technical sense. Authority, then, is linked to sets of regulatory institutions with reference to impinging economic resources and interests, including the contractual and property interests of the collectivities of reference. On the other side it is linked to the institutionalization of leadership as capacity to determine goal-oriented collective processes by persuasion and influence rather than authority and power. Elective office in government or private associations is a particularly important type of link between the two, since persuasion is the paramount means of getting elected, whereas once in office certain defined access to power is provided.

A third institutional complex is concerned with the articulation of a social system with the deeper layers of the personality structures of its members and with the cultural system which legitimizes and otherwise orients its members' action. The two foci of these complexes are, with special reference to personalities, the kinship system, and, with special reference to cultural legitimation, religion. Religion here is interpreted as a functional universal of societies, so I should not hesitate to call Marxism-Leninism, as it is institutionalized in communist societies, a "secular-political religion." The most important third complex in this category, then, is that which links cultural content with personality through education, and the very closely related set of functions concerned with cultural innovation as such, which in modern societies is most conspicuously found in the activities we call research.

In accord with the general dual reference to normative and motivational components, the institution as most directly involved with the core societal community may be classified in two primary categories. The first may be called adjudicative, a term borrowed from the law. This includes the legal process of adjudication which concerns not only the settlement of particular cases at issue but also the all-important function of judicial interpretation. However, I should like to conceive the complex more broadly than in the legal reference alone to include any normatively authoritative process of determination of the normative structure, especially, besides the legal, in the moral context. The focus here is on the institutionalization of procedures by which normative uncertainties can be resolved in relatively specific ways. A particularly important range of adjudication concerns the allocation of resources, rewards, and burdens.

The second main complex of integrative institutions is constituted by the patterns of social stratification. This concerns the normatively legitimized ordering of units of the society in terms of criteria of relative prestige, which in turn is the primary basis of influence. A "vertical" dimension is of course inherent in stratification systems, but it must be kept in mind that the more highly differentiated the society, the more pluralistic the stratification system. Influence is not a linear medium which varies only in quantity, but it also has reference to the kind of subject matter to which the particular source of influence is relevant; thus one does not in general consult his physician on questions of the justification of casting his vote for a particular candidate in an election. Influence hence varies both in level, with respect to a particular basis of prestige, and in scope, with reference to the comprehensiveness or relevance of the considerations involved to the functioning of the relevant social system.

Stratification is one major, though by no means the only, focus of structured conflict in social systems. Stratification in turn, however, is strongly affected by a whole variety of distributions of valued objects, positions, opportunities, and the like, and conflicts can become highly generalized when they involve the generalized media of money and power, and also influence and prestige. Regional, ethnic, and religious differences may of course also be bases of conflict, to say nothing of the interests and commitments of independent politically organized societies.

Because of its special concern with the problems of the integration of social systems, sociology naturally tends to emphasize the importance of the conditions of stability. However, the processes of change are equally important and are subject to the same basic order of theoretical analysis as are the processes by which order and stability are maintained. The ubiquity of deviant behavior is one source of change, as is the prevalence of various sorts of conflict—indeed most conflict involves considerable ingredients of what can properly be called deviant behavior. There is, however, also a variety of other sources of change which are partly indigenous to the social system itself, partly affect the state and modes of interdependence of various of its components.

Though rates of population growth are by no means independent of social systems, they can, as is evident in much of the world today, be an extremely important relatively independent factor, as can climatic changes, exhaustion of natural resources, and a variety of others on similar levels. At the other end, perhaps the most important of all factors of change are found in cultural systems. More than any other sociologist, Max Weber showed the importance of great religious movements, both in differentiating broad types of society and in providing, through the institutionalization of values deriving from them, a major impetus to certain types of change, notably in the case of ascetic Protestantism, a major contribution to the development of the modern industrial type of society. Another particularly important cultural source of change in our own time is the development of science, which of course, like that of religion, is in part a social process.

Generally speaking, sociologists have abandoned the old arguments about the priorities of different factors in the processes of social change. Thus the problem of whether the theory of economic determinism is acceptable is no longer a realistically significant problem. In principle all factors impinging on human behavior from the physical environment and the biological composition of the population, through psychological, economic, political, legal, and other intrasocietal factors, to those of the cultural system, are worthy of detailed consideration as factors of social change. Very much depends, not only on the specific case, but on the nature of the problem of change which is under consideration.

In the earlier beginnings of sociology, evolutionary ideas were very prominent—for instance, in the very different versions of Auguste Comte and Herbert Spencer. Then, for approximately the first half of the present century, with the major exception of Max Weber, such ideas went into an eclipse—which in sociology was closely related to the climate of opinion in anthropology. The most recent period has seen a marked revival of interest along such lines, an interest which is strongly shared by the present author. This revival has been importantly influenced by developments in the relations between the biological and the social sciences, which make it increasingly clear that the continuity between them under the general category of "life sciences" is fundamental. If this is the case, such a fundamental conception as that of evolution could hardly fail to be common to both categories. This new evolutionary interest is closely related to the rapid recent development of comparative studies.

In this chapter I have chosen to discuss mainly the substantive theoretical content of sociology, in terms which I hope are not too seriously idiosyncratic to a particular author. Though the phenomenon of "schools" has by no means disappeared from our discipline, it is clearly much less prominent than it was even one generation ago. We are undoubtedly still in an early phase of development as a scientific discipline, but have been making considerable progress in attaining such a status. The outline I have presented here is meant to give the reader a certain rationale for the organization of the book as a whole in terms of what seems to me to be the main outline of the intellectual content of sociology as well as of its present phase.

In conclusion, I should like to mention two aspects of the

discipline of sociology that are not strictly scientific. Any such discipline of course has—the more so, the more "social" it is— two main ways in which it relates beyond itself. The first is the field of application, the most familiar examples of which are the engineering applications of physics and chemistry and the medical applications of the biological sciences. The applications of sociology so far are modest, though I think that they can claim to be quite significant in a variety of fields such as deviant behavior, mental health, community organization, and political processes. The prospect is certainly for major progress along these lines in the future.

The second field of "extension" concerns the place of the discipline in the more general intellectual culture. Here a notable development has taken place for sociology in the last generation. It is scarcely too much to say that from the days of Ricardo through the great vogue of Marx, economics was held to be the key discipline for the understanding of what was happening in the social world, having on the whole replaced the primarily political preoccupations which had preceded it. For a brief period, there were a number of psychological foci, especially associated with psychoanalysis. In our day, however, sociology has begun to emerge as a focal area of concern.

It is in the field of ideology that this is most conspicuous, or, in the version adopted by some, sociology has begun to replace what has been called ideology, especially of the Marxist variety. In any case the contributions of sociologists are coming increasingly to be referred to as central to the interpretation of the social scene, whether they are identified with the "establishment" or are counted among the principal opponents of modern establishments. This situation clearly poses serious dangers for a discipline which, on the whole, is dedicated to the scientific values of objectivity. It is, however, an important index of our current cultural situation, and presents an opportunity for sociologists to have an important impact, both on the culture and on the development of the society.

Index

academic ability, 136
achievement, social class and, 137
Achieving Society, The (McClellan), 105
administration, bureaucracy and, 57–62
adolescent, problems of, 44, 245
Adolescent Society, The (Coleman), 29
Adorno, T. W., 105
adulthood, problems of, 248–252
advertising, 21–22, 150
affinity, territory and, 302
affluent society, United States as, 280
Africa, 37, 87, 162
aggression, suicide as, 5
agriculture: employment in, 280–281; scientific, 84; society and, 288; urbanization and, 75
alcoholism, 6, 234
Alexander, Norman C., 30
Algeria, 82
alien generation, 244
Allport, F. H., 47
Allport, Gordon, 20, 268–269
American Bar Association, 177
American Medical Association, 55
American Sociological Association, 105, 131, 204, 320
American Soldier, The (Stouffer et al.), 105
ancien régime, legitimacy and, 160
anthropology: ideology and, 307–308; sociology and, 321; symbolic realms in, 309
Arab states, 162
Arensberg, Conrad M., 147
Aries, Philippe, 277
attitudes, sociology of, 19–31
authoritarianism, 12

Authoritarian Personality, The, (Adorno et al.), 105
authority: central, 292; charismatic, 158; civil, 163; in community, 68–69; defined, 185; institutional, 331; leadership and, 161; legitimacy and, 158–159; and Protestant ethic, 314–315; rational-legal, 158, 161; in self-contained society, 288–289; stratification and, 185
autonomy, 314–315; *see also* self-sufficiency
Axiom of Cumulative Inertia, 114

Bach, J. M., 49
Bales, Robert F., 49–50, 105
Barber, Bernard, 184–195
Barnard, Chester I., 61
Barton, Allen H., 106
Bavelas, A., 49
Becker, Howard S., 105
behavior, probability theory and, 111
behaviorism, Watsonian, 21
Bellah, Robert N., 154, 214–228
Bendix, Reinhard, 154, 275–286
Berndt, Ronald, 218
Bidwell, Charles E., 244–254
Bill of Rights, 327
Bion, W. R., 50
birth rate, 277
Blau, Peter H., 29, 54–65
Bloom, B. S., 12
Bogardus, E. S., 39
Booth, Charles, 32
Boulding, Kenneth, 36
bourgeoisie, 185
Bourguiba, Habib ben Ali, 160
Bronze Age, 219, 221, 224
Buddhism, 215–216, 220–221
bureaucracy: careers in, 58–59; eco-

bureaucracy (cont'd)
nomic life and, 153; hierarchic levels of, 58; informal organization in, 60–62; legal procedures in, 177; professionalization in, 64; seniority and merit in, 60; size and, 63; Weber's theory of, 57–60
Bureau of Internal Revenue, 55
Burgess, Ernest, 148
Burrow, T., 50

California, University of, 282
Calvinism, 151, 222, 314
Campbell, Ernest, 30
Cantril, Hadley, 9, 22–23
capitalism: Calvinism and, 151, 314; and Protestant ethic, 7, 158, 313–318; traditionalism and, 167
Carr-Saunders, A. M., 40
Cartwright, Dorwin, 27
Castro, Fidel, 161, 167
central cultural system, 292–293
charismatic leadership, 124, 158, 161; defined, 297
Chicago, University of, 12, 20, 29, 148, 208
child rearing, parent role in, 15
children: changed attitude toward, 277–278; educational system and, 141
China, 80, 162; family in, 126; religion in, 225
Chinoy, Ely, 154
Churchill, Winston S., 211
city: versus country, 85; national patterns in, 78–80; pre-industrial form, 84, 148; social organization in, 80; see also urbanization
civil authority, 163
Civil Rights Act of 1964, 269
civil service, 126–127
Class in American Society (Reissman), 104 n.
class structure, 16, 55–56, 66; bureaucracy and, 58–59
cliques, 27
Cohen, Albert K., 231–234
Coleman, James, 28–29, 111
collective bargaining, 70
collectivities: defined, 327; loyalty to, 325; organization of, 56, self-con-

tainment in, 300–301; social systems and, 324
college attendance, 132–133
colleges, task of, 142
colonialism, 83, 299–300
Columbia University, 21, 25, 29, 127, 200, 211
communication, mass media and, 21–25, 240
Communist China, 162
community: autonomy of, 67–68, 71–72; defined, 66; sociological issues about, 66–74; violence in, 6, 73
Community Conflict (Coleman), 28
computer: as calculator and logic machine, 115–117; in group studies, 50–52; in industrial psychology, 39; measurement and, 101–102
Comte, Auguste, 304, 334
concept specification, 96
conformity, sanctions and, 325
Confucianism, ideology of, 223, 309
Constitution, United States, 327
consumption: conspicuous, 191; family life cycle and, production and, 36–37
contextual relationship, 29–30
Cooley, Charles H., 47, 53
Cornell University, 113–114
Cravan, Ida, 42
creativity, 205, 292
crime: white-collar, 241–242; see also deviant behavior
cultural lag, science and, 201
culture: economic life and, 152–153; education and, 141–142
culture conflicts, 166
culture system, central, 292–293
cumulative inertia, axiom of, 114

Davis, James A., 19–31
Davis, Kingsley, 147, 245
decision-making: in community, 71–72; control of, 67; and democracy, 164; judicial, 173; legitimacy and, 158; and political sociology, 157
de Gaulle, Charles, 162
delinquency, 3–6; see also deviant behavior
Delinquency Areas (Shaw), 5
democracy, 159, 164

demographic research, 16, 77
desegregation, 268–269; *see also* Negro determinism, versus probability, 110
Deutsch, K., 49
deviant behavior, 231–243; democracy and, 232–233; as "goods and services," 233; sources of, 3–6; 236–237; in Soviet Union, 285
Dickson, William J., 61
dictatorship, oligarchy and, 165
differentiatedness, of society, 328–329
division of labor, *see* labor
dominance, theory of, 110
drug addiction, 237
Durkheim, Emile, 4–6, 47, 53, 131, 215, 218, 325, 330

economic life, 143–155; political and cultural variables in, 150–155; primary groups in, 146–150; self-sufficiency and, 287–289, 295–296, 299
education: centrality of, 249–252; as "contest," 282; contradictions in, 251; in developing nations, 138; mass, 134; in modern society, 280–282; of Negro, 263; reforms in, 138–139; schools of, 134; secondary, 134, 138–139; social stratification and, 136, 187; sociology of, 131–142; universal, 249
Education of Sociologists in the United States, The (Sibley), 109
Eisenstadt, S. N., 304–318
elite: in decision-making, 72; growth-stimulating, 316
Epstein, Scarlett T., 148
Erikson, Erik H., 9
Erlich, Eugen, 178
Escape from Freedom (Fromm), 7–8
ethnic groups: nationality and, 302; stratification and, 188–189; *see also* race relations
evolution, social change and, 334
exchange relations, 55–56
expectation: normative, 323–327; rising, 162

Fads and Foibles in Modern Sociology and Related Sciences (Sorokin), 106
family: bourgeois, 125; Chinese, 147; cities and, 148; consumption and, 149; industrialization and, 128–129; kinship and, 121–130; in Middle East, 148–149; Negro, 130; nuclear, 124, 128; as "organization," 55; role structure in, 52; in Soviet Union, 125; status in, 246
Ferguson, Adam, 279
Festinger, Leon, 49
First New Nation, The (Lipset), 161
formal organization, 56–65; Weber on, 57–60
Formal Theories of Mass Behavior (McPhee), 112
freedom, personality and, 7
French, J. R. P., Jr., 28
French Revolution, 85
friends and friendship, 27–29
Fromm, Erich, 7–9
F scale, 12

gambling, 233
Gandhi, Mohandas K., 225
Geertz, Clifford, 308
George Washington University, 211
Gilbert, D., 11
Glaser, Barney G., 207
Glueck, S. and E., 6
goal escalation, deviance and, 239
goal structure, internalized, 327
Goode, William J., 127, 129, 148
goods and services: consumption of, 36–37; and deviant behavior, 233; distribution of, 143
Gordon, Gerald, 208
Gouldner, Alvin W., 61
Great Britain, agriculture in, 281
Gross National Product, 280
group: individual and, 47, 52–53; industrial output and, 48; primary, 150; scientific study of, 46; self as, 51; self-analytic, 50, 53; small, 45–53; therapeutic, 47–50
group loyalty, 163, 325
group processes, 45–53, 258–259
group therapy, 47, 50

Harary, Frank, 27
Harvard University, 51, 212
Hawthorne experiments, 146–147
Heider, Fritz, 24, 26–28

Henry, A. F., 5
Hinduism, 223
Homans, George, 27
Hsün Tzu, 214
Hughes, Everett C., 32–44
Human Group, The (Homans), 27
Hunter, Floyd, 153
Hurst, J. W., 181–182
husband, family role of, 122–123

ideology: secular, 310; social change
    and, 304–318; social function of,
    306–307, 312–314; sociology and,
    335; symbolic spheres in, 307–308;
    value orientations and, 317
Ideology and Utopia (Mannheim),
    311
id stereotype, 265–267
incest taboo, 123, 163
income: leisure and, 35; prestige and,
    94–95; stratification and, 186
India, 149, 299–300
individual: collectivities and, 324;
    and group, 47, 52–53
industrialization: versus agriculture,
    280–283; ideology of, 309–310; lei-
    sure and, 32–33; and nuclear fam-
    ily, 128; urbanization and, 76, 81,
    85, 88; value system of, 129
industrial output, group and, 48
industrial psychology, 39
inertia, cumulative, 114
influence, 330
informal organization, 60–62
Inkeles, Alex, 3–17, 185
institutional complexes, 330–331
institutionalization, 326
interactional process analysis, 111
intergroup relations, 259–260, 267–268
International Sociological Associa-
    tion, 320
interpersonal relationships, 27–29
*Introduction to Mathematical Sociol-
    ogy* (Coleman), 111
Invasion from Mars, The (Cantril),
    22
Islam, 81–82, 220, 223

James, William, 97
Japan, religion in, 221, 224–227; ur-
    ban history of, 80–81

Jews, 164, 266
jurisprudence, conceptual and func-
    tional, 172, 174, 177
juvenile delinquency, 3–6, 235; *see
    also* deviant behavior

Kaplan, Norman, 211
Kardiner, Abram, 9
Katz, Elihu, 25, 150
Kemeny, John, 112
Kennedy, John F., 263
Kenyatta, Jomo, 160
Kimball, Solon T., 147
King, Martin Luther, Jr., 265
kinship: Chinese, 147; family and,
    121–130; government and, 127; and
    poverty, 240; stratification and, 188
knowledge, sociology of, 306
Kulturkampf, 166

labor: division of, 245, 279–280, 321;
    intellectual, 321; racial and ethnic
    discrimination in, 37–39
Landecker, Werner S., 105
Landes, David, 147
language, urbanism and, 86–87
Language of Social Research, The
    (Landecker), 105
Latin America, education in, 138
law: enforcement of, 179–181; "equal
    protection" of, 324; race relations
    and, 175; sociology of, 171–183
Lazarsfeld, Paul F., 25, 29, 93–106,
    150, 190
leadership, 49, 124, 152, 330; *see also*
    charismatic leadership
least action, principle of, 28
legislation, by community, 73
legitimacy: civil authority and, 163;
    crisis in, 158–159; in political soci-
    ology, 158–165; sources of, 158–160
legitimation, of normative system, 326
leisure: and consumption of goods,
    35–36; redistribution of, 35; unem-
    ployment and, 43–44; work and,
    32–44
Lenski, Gerhard E., 105
Le Play, Pierre G., 47, 53
Lerner, Max, 124
Levinson, D. J., 11
Lévi-Strauss, Claude, 77

Levy, Marion, Jr., 147
Levy-Bruhl, Lucien, 217
Lewin, Kurt, 48–49
life style, 190–191
Lindeman, F. A., 211
linear graphs, 27
Lipset, Seymour Martin, 156–169
Litwak, Eugene, 149
local autonomy, community and, 69
localism, ideology of, 68, 71

McClellan, David C., 105
McGinnis, Robert, 107–117
McPhee, William, 112
macro-sociological view, 287–303
magic, religion and, 307
Mahayana Buddhism, 215–216
Malinowski, Bronislaw, 123, 307
management, scientific, 146
Mannheim, Karl, 311–312
marijuana, 233
Markov chain, 113–114
Marx, Karl, 151–154, 335
Marxism, 305, 331–332
mass culture, 70, 112
mass media, 21, 23, 101, 240
mass production, 39
mass societies, 296–299
Mathematical Models in the Social Sciences (Kemeny and Snell), 112
mathematics, in sociology, 109–117
Matza, David, 251, 254
Mayhew, Leon, 171–183
Mayo, Elton, 48
Mead, G. H., 20–21, 23, 25, 31
Meaning of Truth, The (James), 97
measurement, 93–105; computer in, 101–102; concept specification in, 97; imagery in, 96–97; scales and indices in, 98; variables in, 100
Merton, Robert K., 11, 71, 200–205, 207, 239
Michigan, University of, 27, 208
migration: labor market and, 38; urbanization and, 87
Millar, John, 279
Miller, Delbert, 15, 153
Mills, C. Wright, 153
Mills, Theodore M., 45–53
Mississippi, University of, 258
mobility, *see* social mobility

modern society, 275–286; affluence in, 280; cultural change in, 298; education and, 280–282; Great Britain compared with United States, 283; historical span of, 284
Moede, W., 47
monarchy, democracy and, 159
morals, law and, 172
Moreno, J. L., 48
Morgan, C. L., 307
Mosca, Gaetano, 156
mother, family role of, 122
Myrdal, Gunnar, 270
mythical world, religion and, 217–218

narcotics, 233–234, 237
Nasser, Gamal Abdel, 160
National Association for the Advancement of Colored People, 175
nationalism: ethnicity and, 302; religion and, 226; youth and, 299
need achievement, 12
Negro: civil rights and, 256, 269; demands of, 265; family problems of, 130; frustrations of, 264–265; history of in United States, 260–261; poverty among, 239; progress of, 263–264; relative status of, 264–265; socio-cultural considerations and, 261–265; in Southern agriculture, 38; stereotype of, 265; violence of, 259, 270; voting of, 262–263, 269; in World Wars I and II, 262
Nelson, Donald, 283
networks: kinship, 27–29; sentimental, 30
New York City: delinquency in, 235; population density, 78
Nkrumah, Kwame, 161
Nobel Prize, 204, 208, 265
normative expectations, 323–325; influence and, 330
normative system: inconsistency in, 329; institutionalized, 326; legitimation of, 326
nuclear family, 124, 278; economic activity and, 146; industrialization and, 128–129

obedience, legitimacy and, 163

occupational inheritance, 194, 248–249
occupational prestige, 41, 95–96; stratification and, 184–185
Ogburn, William Fielding, 148, 201–202
oligarchy, dictatorship and, 165
opinion leadership, 25
organization, 54–56; formal and informal, 56–65; legal rules and, 180–181
Organizational Measurement (Barton et al.), 106
out-groups, race relations and, 265–267

parent-child relationships, 15, 248–249
Pareto, Vilfredo, 156
Park, Robert E., 32
Parsons, Talcott, 49, 123, 148, 308, 319–335
Pelz, Donald, 208–209
People's Choice, The (Lazarsfeld et al.), 105
Personal Influence (Katz and Lazarsfeld), 25
personality: general theory of, 3–10; modal patterns in, 10–15; social change and, 10; social movements and, 6–10; and social organization, 7–8, 13–15
personality types, race and, 14
Pettigrew, Thomas F., 258–271
physical sciences, 109
Polish Peasant in Europe and America, The (Thomas and Znaniecki), 20
political parties, 165–167
political science, 323
political sociology, 156–169; defined, 156–157; legitimacy and, 156–165
popularity, hierarchy of, 28
population, 83, 277; personality and, 6–7; rank-ordered movements of, 79; registration and, 76–77; and social structure, 10, 333; variability in, 67; world, 45–46
poverty: deviance and, 239; kinship and, 240; religion and, 226
power: political systems and, 160;

stratification and, 186
P-O-X triangle, 24
Pratt, J. H., 47
prejudice, 14, 268; *see also* race relations
prestige: income and, 94–95; occupational, 41, 95–96, 184–185; relative, 332; *see also* status
prestige suggestion, 23–24
Price, Derek, 209
Price, Don K., 212
primary group, 146–150
Principles of Sociology, The (Ross), 28
probability theory, 110, 113–114
Problems of Inference and Proof in Participant Observation (Becker), 105
problem-solving, religion as, 216
process analysis, 111
production: versus consumption, 36; economic activity and, 146; economic sociology and, 143–144; machinery and, 280; and social structure, 151
professionalization, 64
professional occupations, 40–41
Prohibition era, 33–34, 101, 172
projective techniques, 99–100
propaganda, 21–22
prostitution, 233, 237
Protestantism, 221; autonomy and, 314–315; capitalism and, 7, 151, 313–318; Reformation and, 221
psychic states, religion and, 215
psychological tests, 14
Psychologie Économique (Tarde), 34
psychology, sociology and, 321
public schools, desegregation in, 269; *see also* education

race relations, 14, 258–271; law and, 175; out-groups in, 265–267; stereotypes in, 265; super-egos and alter-egos in, 265–266
radio studies, 21–22
reality, religion and, 216
recreation, leisure and, 43
Reiss, Albert J., Jr., 66–74
Reissman, Leonard, 104 *n.*
religion: archaic, 219; early-modern,

222–223; as functional universal, 331–332; historic, 220–221; legitimation through, 221; magic and, 307, 330; in modern era, 226–228; mythical world and, 217–218; politics and, 167–168; primitive, 217–220; salvation and, 220; science and, 214–215, 311; secularization of, 222, 331–332; as social control, 330; sociology of, 214–228; stages in, 217–220; stratification and, 188; as symbolic sphere, 215–217, 224, 310; well-being and, 225–226; Western versus Eastern, 223

Religious Influences (Booth), 32

research: new developments in, 107–117; "style" of, 208

revolution: family loyalty and, 122; and social class, 167

revolution of rising expectations, 162

Rhee, Syngman, 161

Ricardo, David, 335

rioting, community and, 73

ritual, 219, 330

Roethlisberger, Fritz J., 61

role behavior, 11, 327–328

role recruitment, 13

role-set, 328

Roman Catholic Church, 222, 225

Roosevelt, Franklin D., 22

Rosen, B. C., 12

Ross, E. A., 28

Rossi, P. H., 185

rugged individualism, 21

Russia, *see* Soviet Union

salvation, religion and, 220

sanctions: conformity and, 325; institutionalizing and, 326; in social control, 329

Schachter, S., 49

school dropouts, 44, 244–245

Schulze, Robert, 153

Schumpeter, Joseph, 164

science: as creative act, 205; and cultural lag, 201; current activities and, 203–213; ethos of, 203; ideology of, 310; industry and, 210; innovative, 209; literature of, 205; as profession, 206; recognition in, 207; religion and, 214–215, 311; research

in, 107–108, 208, 212; as social change, 201–202; society and, 210–213; sociology of, 199–213; structure and dynamics of, 203–206; value system in, 207–208

Science and Democratic Social Structure (Merton), 202

Science and Society (Kaplan), 211

Science and the Social Order (Merton), 202

scientific management, 146

scientists: freedom of, 206; morale and productivity of, 206–210

second industrial revolution, 275

segregation, 261; *see also* Negro

self, group as, 51

self-discipline, 140–141, 241

self-sufficiency, 287–289, 299; in bureaucratic society, 295–296; in collectivities, 300–301; Protestantism and, 314

Selznick, Philip, 60

Semrad, Elvin V., 50–51

sex, culture conflicts and, 166

sex drive, 163

Shaw, C. R., 6

Sherif, Muzafer, 47

Shils, Edward A., 49, 71, 287–303

Short, J. F., 5

Sibley, Elbridge, 109

Siegfried, André, 156

Simmel, Georg, 47

Sjoberg, Gideon, 148

skepticism, science and, 203

slavery, Negro and, 260

small groups, defined, 45; social pressure from, 46; sociology of, 45–53

Smelser, Neil J., 143–155

Smith, Adam, 279

Snell, Laurie, 112

social anthropology, 39, 321

social change, 333–334; ideology of, 304–318; legitimacy and, 160; personality and, 10

social class: educational achievement and, 137; revolution and, 167; *see also* social mobility; social stratification

social conflict, 332–333

social control: community and, 68; deviant behavior and, 236; sanc-

social control (*cont'd*)
tions and, 329–330
Social Effects of Aviation, The (Ogburn), 202
socialization, defined, 328
social mobility: defined, 192; mathematical theory of, 112–113; and occupational prestige, 184–185; opportunity and, 16; sponsored, 283; time and, 111; urbanization and, 85–86; wealth and, 186; *see also* social stratification
social norms: egalitarian, 193; law and, 171–172; power of, 176
social psychology, 19–31, 321
social sciences, 111
social stratification: conflict and, 332–333; education and, 136, 187; law and, 175; politics and, 167–168; and religion, 188; and social mobility, 184–195
social structure: organization and, 55; population of, 10; religion and, 218; science and, 202
social symbols, 20–21, 215–217, 292, 307–309
social system: center of gravity in, 290; desirable type of, 326; integration of, 322; micro-systems and, 46; normative expectations of, 323–324; personality and, 13–15; pluralistic structure of, 328
social time, problem of, 245–248
society: age and, 247; agricultural, 288; beliefs and symbols of, 292, 307–309; bureaucratic-imperial, 295; central system in, 290–295; colonial, 299–300; component parts of, 291; cooperative, 288; creative individuals and, 292; defined, 291; development of, 308–309; differentiatedness of, 328–329; as games and rules, 240–241; integrated, 303; macro-sociological view of, 287–303; mass, 296–299; modern, 275–286 (*see also* modern society); periphery of, 294, 299; post-modern, 276; primitive, 308; psychological theories of, 9; self-sufficiency in, 287–289, 299;

sovereignty and, 290; youth in, 244–254
sociologist: as fact-gatherer, 107; professional, 320; as theorist, 107–108
sociology: anthropology and, 321–322; attitudes and, 19–31; in communist countries, 320; computer as aid to, 115–117; concern of, 322; economic, 143–145; extension of, 335; ideology and, 304–318, 335; integration of social systems in, 322–323; as intellectual discipline, 319–320; mathematics in, 109–115; modernization and, 155; political, *see* political sociology; as profession, 320; "psychologistic" school of, 9; psychology and, 321; recruitment in, 320; scales and indices in, 98–100; "schools" of, 9, 334; of science, 199–213; teaching and, 319
Sociology of Education, 131
Sorokin, Pitirim A., 9, 106, 201
source credibility, 23–24
South Africa, 258, 261
Soviet Union, agriculture in, 281; deviance in, 285; family in, 123, 125, 129; industrialization in, 284–285; sociology in, 320
Spencer, Herbert, 20, 131, 334
Stanleyville, enclaves in, 87
status and status systems, 12, 95, 123
Status Crystallization (Lenski), 105
Stein, M. I., 12
stereotypes, race, 265–267
Stern, G. G., 12
Stevens, S. S., 105
Storer, Norman W., 199–213
Stouffer, S. A., 103, 105
structural balance, theory of, 24
style of life, 190–191
success, parental stress on, 248–249
suffrage, universal, 278–289
suicide: as aggression, 5; delinquency rates and, 4; group ties and, 47
Suicide, Le (Durkheim), 5
Suicide and Homicide (Henry and Short), 5
Sumner, William Graham, 56
Supreme Court, United States, 174,

262, 269
Sutherland, Edwin H., 241–242
Sutton, Francis, 154
Swanson, G. E., 15
symbols and symbolism, 20–21, 215–217, 227–228, 307–309

Talmon-Garber, Y., 122
Tannenbaum, Frank, 260–261
Tarde, Gabriel, 34
Taylor, Frederick W., 146
teacher, role and status of, 135
technological change, 133, 279
television, mass culture and, 71
temperance movements, 33–34
Thematic Apperception Test (TAT), 14
Theory of Dominance, 110–111
therapeutic processes, 330
Thernstrom, Stephen, 70
this-worldliness, 313
Thomas, W. I., 26, 47
Thrasher, F. M., 47
Tilly, Charles, 75–89
time: as central factor, 111; social and biological, 245–248
Touré, Sekou, 160
Toward a General Theory of Action (Bales), 49
Trow, Martin, 131–142
Truman, Harry S., 268
Turner, Ralph, 282–283
Tylor, E. B., 307

unemployment, leisure and, 43–44
United Nations, 23, 77, 138, 290
United States: affluence of, 280; city growth in, 79; class structure in, 66; compared with Great Britain, 283; deistic symbolism in, 227–228; deviant behavior in, 231–243; Gross National Product, 280; industrialization in, 285 (see also industrialization); law development in, 182–183; race relations in, 133, 258–271; settling of, 37–38; urban problems and, 69 (see also urbanization)
universalism, 203
universal suffrage, 278–279

universities, task of, 142
Unraveling Juvenile Delinquency (Glueck and Glueck), 6
urbanization, 16, 69, 82–83; forms of, 75–89; industrialization and, 76, 85, 88; migration and, 87; Negro and, 262; as way of life, 86; see also city

value orientations, ideology and, 317–318
variables, in measurement, 100
Veblen, Thorstein, 191
violence, community and, 73
Voegelin, W. L., 220
Vogel, Ezra F., 121–130
voting, Negro and, 262–263; research in, 25–26, 165–167

Wallace, Walter, 29
Waller, Willard, 28
War of the Worlds, The (Wells), 22
wealth: deviance and, 238; stratification and, 186
Webb, Eugene J., 105
Weber, Max, 7, 39, 57, 59–64, 151–154, 156, 158, 164, 201, 222, 313, 315–316, 333–334
Wells, H. G., 22
white-collar: crime, 241–242; worker, 280
wife, family role of, 122–123
Wirth, Louis, 86
women: voting rights of, 278–279; work and leisure for, 35
work: leisure and, 32–44; mass production and, 39; morale and, 152; organization in, 61
World Revolution and Family Patterns (Goode), 127
World War I: army organization in, 54; monarchy in, 159–160; Negro and, 261–262; political democracy since, 159; recreation and, 33; suffrage after, 278
World War II: classroom teacher after, 135; education following, 133, 187; group loyalty in, 48; group therapy and, 50; mass production in, 283; Negro and, 262; psycholog-

World War II (*cont'd*)
ical studies during, 103–104; science and, 202; and sociology of education, 131–132; universal suffrage and, 279

Wright, Christopher, 211

Yale University, 209
Y.M.C.A., 255
Young, Michael, 187
youth: anti-social, 254; cross-national comparisons of, 253; cultural patterns of, 252–256; leisure and, 251; in modern society, 244–254; rebellious, 255–256; school dropouts among, 254–255; teachers' grades and, 251

"youth culture," 253

Zelditch, Morris, 123
Zen Buddhism, 227, 285
Znaniecki, Florian, 26, 252

Soc
HM
51
P34

DATE DUE

JUN 30 1975	
SEP - 8 1975	DEC 0 1993
'JUN - 7 1976	MAY 0 9 1999
AUG 23 1976	JAN 0 3 2000
FEB 14 1977	MAR 2 5 2005
FEB 28 1977	2004
MAR 2 7 1978	
OCT 30 1978	
DEC 25 1978	2004
1984	
NOV 1988	